Young Babe Ruth

Young Babe Ruth

His Early Life and Baseball Career, from the Memoirs of a Xaverian Brother

by BROTHER GILBERT, C.F.X.

Edited by HARRY ROTHGERBER

WITH A FOREWORD BY *Brother John Joseph Sterne, C.F.X.*

McFarland & Company, Inc., Publishers
Jefferson, North Carolina, and London

Frontispiece: Brother Gilbert (Phillip F. Cairnes) was born in Somerville, Massachusetts, in 1884 and died in Lowell, Massachusetts, in 1947. This is the photograph that is displayed at Malden (Mass.) Catholic High School where he was the founding principal in 1932. "Brother Gilbert's was the great heart; anybody in or out of the community could enlist his assistance." (Courtesy of Xaverian Brothers Heritage Collection, with special thanks to Malden Catholic High School.)

Library of Congress Cataloguing-in-Publication Data

Gilbert, Brother, C.F.X., b. 1884.
    Young Babe Ruth : his early life and baseball career, from the memoirs of a Xaverian Brother / by Brother Gilbert; edited by Harry Rothgerber; with a foreword by Brother John Joseph Sterne.
        p.   cm.
    Includes bibliographical references (p.   ) and index.
    ISBN 0-7864-0652-6 (sewn softcover : 50# alkaline paper) ∞
    1. Ruth, Babe, 1895–1948 — Childhood and youth.   2. Baseball players — United States — Biography.   3. Gilbert, Brother, C.F.X., b. 1884.   4. St. Mary's Industrial School (Baltimore, Md.)
    I. Rothgerber, Harry, 1947–   . II. Title.
    GV865.R8G55   1999
    796.357'092–dc21
    [B]
                                                    99-34439
                                                       CIP

British Library Cataloguing-in-Publication data are available

Manufactured in the United States of America

McFarland & Company, Inc., Publishers
    Box 611, Jefferson, North Carolina 28640
        www.mcfarlandpub.com

Contents

Foreword

by Brother John Joseph Sterne, C.F.X.

My name is Brother John Joseph Sterne, and I am a member of the Congregation of the Brothers of St. Francis Xavier (C.F.X.). My early adolescent years were spent at St. Mary's Industrial School, a few short years after its most famous resident departed.

With God's grace and help from my mother, I entered this world near the U.S. Capitol in Washington, D.C., as Howard Arthur Sterne. Eventually I began my studies to become a Xaverian Brother in 1923. I have been a fan of George Herman "Babe" Ruth for almost eighty years, and in a moment I'll tell you why.

Born on October 27, 1909, I had come to St. Mary's in the summer of 1919 when the boys were temporarily living in barracks at Camp Holabird near Baltimore. Camp Holabird was one of the many army camps which would soon be closed after World War I ended on November 11, 1918. My family had problems which caused my parents to send their children to boarding schools. For reasons best known to themselves my parents' marriage was heading for the rocks. I must say that I never heard them argue over their differences. However, around 1916, when I was seven, my brother nine, and my sister eleven, our home broke up. Though neither parent was a churchgoer at that stage, when it came to the practicality of finding boarding schools for their children, they found them in places operated by Catholic nuns. This fact made all the difference in the world in my life.

My brother Louis, or "Buck" as we always called him, was getting a little too old for the age group that the nuns cared for. So he was taken to Baltimore to St. Mary's Industrial School. This was not long after the time that its famous alumnus, George Herman Ruth, left the school to start his outstanding baseball career as one of Jack Dunn's Baltimore Orioles.

In 1919, at age 10, I too was taken to St. Mary's, and Buck and I were together again. Here I met and learned to love the Brothers of St. Francis Xavier, known as the Xaverians. And it is precisely for this reason that, in God's

St. Mary's Industrial School, Wilkens and Caton avenues, Baltimore, Maryland, was located conveniently on the streetcar line (courtesy of Xaverian Brothers Heritage Collection).

Providence, the unwelcome breakup in our family proved eventually to be a blessing in disguise, though not appreciated as such at the time.

Let me tell you something about St. Mary's Industrial School, and of the Babe's strong connection with the school and the Xaverian Brothers who had built the school and who cared for the boys. Back in 1866, shortly after the Civil War, the Catholic Archbishop of Baltimore, Martin John Spalding (recently elevated to that position from that of Bishop of Louisville in his native Kentucky), had become aware of the dire need for a nurturing and protective home for the many young boys in the area. The loss of so many fathers from the recent horrific conflict is easy to imagine. It was this same Bishop who, in 1854, had arranged for some members of the newly founded Congregation of the Brothers of St. Francis Xavier to come from Belgium to teach the boys of Louisville, many of whom were immigrants or children of immigrants from Ireland and Germany. Bishop Spalding had been so impressed by these Brothers that he applied to Europe for a colony of Brothers to start his home for boys in Baltimore. Come they did, and St. Mary's prospered, so that by the time little George Ruth arrived there in 1902, the large facility in the western part of the city had already educated and cared for thousands of boys. It would continue to provide nurturing supervision for boys until it closed in 1950.

George Ruth was born in Baltimore in 1895 and was brought by his father to the care of the Brothers in 1902 when only seven years old. This lively youngster needed more care than his parents, busy operating a neighborhood saloon, could give him, and so they took this difficult action for the lad's good. He lived primarily at St. Mary's until 1914, thus passing most of his formative years with the Brothers.

Having spent four years there myself from 1919 to 1923, I can recall the daily routine that Babe and the rest of the boys followed. We were divided into groups called "Dormitories," since we were also in the same groups at bedtime. The dormitories were wide-open spaces with beds all in rows. At the side were lavatories with plenty of facilities. The Brothers had private rooms as part of the floor plan with glass windows in the doors. Their presence tended to encourage the boys to be quiet and sleep.

We were aroused in the morning at six o'clock. Soon we were on our way to the school chapel, large as a cathedral, for daily Mass. Religion was stressed as part of happy living, and it was taught as a special subject in the classroom. Breakfast followed Mass, and almost immediately we were in school until noon. We rarely used paper but instead had a slate, something like a miniature blackboard, that we could hold on our lap. With our special slate pencil, we could do our arithmetic and other assignments. When we finished with one set of materials, we could erase the slate writings. The palm of the hand was often used, as was the sleeve of a lad's jacket. My recollection is that we were a busy and happy lot and there was much stress on the importance of saying prayers and being good boys. After lunch and a short recess, classes resumed. Meanwhile the older boys, who were being trained in such trades as carpentry, tailoring, shoemaking or business subjects, were busy in their departments. Boys in the band were required to practice hours every day in addition to the general rehearsals.

Usually, by mid-afternoon, we had several hours for recreation and just plain exercise. Each dormitory had its own "yard." While there was a gymnasium and a large swimming pool in my day, over the years the Brothers found many varied ways to keep the boys busy. However, the most popular game was always baseball. And, as in the days of Babe, we had many leagues and we learned to love the national pastime by our daily play.

The food was of the simplest and would probably edify a Trappist monk. Breakfast usually consisted of a bowl of oatmeal or hominy. If we received any milk, it would have to be in the oatmeal or in the thin coffee or tea served at all meals. For variety, there was a single pat of butter or oleo with bread on Fridays and three hot dogs, which we called weenies, on Sunday morning. We surely looked forward to Sundays. However, during the week, many a lad would bet away his weenies or promise them in return for some other consideration. I'm sure that Babe would have been involved in this "action."

Lunch was a bowl of soup and bread. The bread was usually home baked and heavy, our own students being the bakers. At times it was

Ten-year-old Arthur Sterne (*left*) of St. Mary's presents a straw basket filled with money as a token offering to the girls of the Philadelphia orphanage that housed the Babe Ruth Band during its tour with the Babe in 1920. Arthur later became Brother John Joseph Sterne, the author of this Foreword (courtesy of Xaverian Brothers Heritage Collection).

necessary to buy regular bread which we called City Bread. That was before the invention of bread slicing. Supper was usually more soup and bread, though again on Sunday there was a change: three slices of baloney. Our simple food was supplemented by packages from home for some of us, or candy from the school canteen if we had the money for it. On Sundays when visitors came, the yards were filled with youngsters and their packages, the envy of the others.

Though the food seems scanty, there was little sickness and much energy, and the school infirmary had few occupants. I, myself, was not sick once in all the four years that I was there.

The key to our lives was held by the various Brothers. Dressed in their long black cassocks or habits, a large rosary chapelet dangling from the left side of a black cloth belt or cincture, a small crucifix barely visible on the chest, and a white collar to relieve the black, these Brothers were with us at all times.

The thirty or so Brothers assigned to St. Mary's during my boyhood were our teachers, counselors, supervisors, disciplinarians, friends, and often as not, our parents as far as guidance and care were concerned. From the beginning, I liked these men and never knew one who didn't seem to like me and my companions. Of course, they had to keep order, and at times, just as in any family or school, discipline was required, so the Brothers were not *always* smiling. Also, when so many youngsters from varied backgrounds played together every day, it was only natural that on occasion tempers would flare and fists would double up for a square-off. In no time, however, a Brother would be there separating the pugilists and perhaps taking names to be used when a regular boxing session was arranged for all to see. All in all, we got along fine and made lots of friends, some of them remaining such in future years, as I know from my own case.

There was one Brother not on the St. Mary's staff who had the most to say about my actually being accepted as a candidate for our congregation. His name was Brother Isidore Kuppel. I recall him as a smiling, rotund, back-slapping person whose favorite ejaculation was "By jacks." He usually wore a frock coat and somewhat baggy pants. Who was this unusual Brother? He was the Superior of all the Brothers in the American province that stretched in those days from New Hampshire to Virginia and out to Kentucky. His title was Provincial. His office was located nearby at Mt. St. Joseph College.

He used to visit the Brothers and would also come to the playground or wherever the children were. On one of these occasions, when I was a seventh grader, the following interchange took place. Frankly, I don't remember it, but Brother Isidore did and later laughed as he told me about it, usually in the presence of others. It seems that a group of us were gathered around this pleasant granddaddy of a man, when I stepped out in front of him and asked, "Can I be a Brother?" His reply, he asserted, was, "Yes, but you will have to wait until you graduate from the eighth grade." That's how my Xaverian journey started.

My love for music proved to be most fortunate for me at this time in my life. St. Mary's had an excellent band. In fact, before I lived there, it had three of them, from small lads to the older ones. My brother Buck was a clarinetist in the band when I arrived. And at age ten, I too was accepted and started to learn how to play the cornet. Over the years, especially when I worked with boys in summer camps, or when I belonged to several orchestras, my experience on the cornet or trumpet proved to be a valuable asset. But far more important than the music I learned was the influence exerted on me and on many other boys by the band director, Brother Simon Drury.

Yes, I was lucky to be allowed at only ten to start learning music and become a member of the school band. But this was no ordinary school band. It was highly skilled and widely recognized for its varied repertoire of classical, parade and popular music. Twice during Brother Simon's days the band won top honors in national competition held at Joliet, Illinois. On one of these occasions the massed bands played "Stars and Stripes Forever" under the baton of its composer, the famed John Philip Sousa.

My brother and I were two of the lucky "band boys" of St. Mary's Industrial School who traveled for three weeks in September of 1920 with the New York Yankees and their new star Babe Ruth as the team made its final western swing that season. This road trip scheduled them to play in Cleveland, Detroit, Chicago and St. Louis, and then back east for wind-ups in Philadelphia and New York. At age ten, I was one of the 49 boys on this trip, an experience brought about by a disaster.

For on April 24, 1919, a live coal had blown from a tinner's stove, landing under an eave and starting a fire at St. Mary's Industrial School, the Babe's alma mater, and at that time home for some seven hundred boys. Various projects had been initiated to raise money to rebuild the school. Since by 1920 Babe Ruth was a famous New York Yankee, someone had the idea of sending us 49 band boys on a trip with the ballclub of our famous alumnus. As a result, we lucky lads accompanied the Yanks on their last western road trip that September. Dressed in sailor suits, we were billed as Babe Ruth's Boys Band. Since in 1920 there were no commercial airlines, we boarded a train in Baltimore occupying a coach next to that of the ballplayers. I recall especially those thrilling games all of which saw us rooting for the Yankees. Babe hit eight home runs during that time. As there were 49 of us and he had already hit over forty homers, we cheered every time he went to bat. Sure enough, he hit his forty-ninth before our eyes! It was so high it looked as if it would never come down!

To raise money and justify our being on the trip, we moved around in the ball park and passed our white sailor hats for contributions following an appeal by the ballpark officials. Because of my nerve and youthful appearance, I became the best "money collector." Also, we played at a few businessmen's luncheons and gave several evening concerts, but, all in all, it was a ball! (Especially the boat trip with the Yankees on Labor Day weekend as we traveled from Cleveland to Detroit. To mark the end of summer, the Yankees had a "smashing" good time destroying every straw hat in sight or sending them sailing into the water a great distance away. As young boys, we identified with that!)

From St. Louis where the Browns (since moved to Baltimore as the Orioles) played, we came back east for another glorious week, this time in Philadelphia and New York. The Athletics were famous for their manager, Connie Mack. In New York, of course, the Yankees were back home, but home in 1920 was the Polo Grounds, since demolished.

Yes, that was a September to remember, especially by us youngsters who saw in the Babe another boy like ourselves.

It was in the "yards" that Babe displayed at an early age a natural talent for baseball. He played every position, but excelled particularly as a pitcher.

By the time he was 19, he had become a powerful home run hitter. Unknown to him, his future was being shaped by a successful baseball coach at nearby Mount St. Joseph's College, also operated by the Xaverian Brothers. This coach, Brother Gilbert Cairnes, was a friend of the owner of the Baltimore Orioles, Jack Dunn. Brother Gilbert, who had seen Babe play at St. Mary's, convinced Dunn to witness this young player in action. Dunn was impressed and signed Babe up.

Of importance to Babe was the influence of the Brothers, several of whom were of special help to the gradually budding baseball star. Heading the list was Brother Matthias Boutlier. Matt, as the Brothers called him, was a huge man physically, well over 6' 5" tall and possessing an imposing build. This popular man was known to the older boys as "Boss." The smaller lads really had little occasion to know him when I attended the school, though he seems to have influenced the Babe from an early age. Brother Matthias could hit a ball a mile high, and would delight the boys when he hit ball after ball, tossing them in the air with one hand and smacking the pellet up and out of sight with a fungo bat.

Brother Herman ran the leagues for the boys and played right in there with them, as did Brother Alban, a superior athlete. Of great influence in Babe Ruth's career was Brother Paul Scanlan, the superintendent of the school and the religious superior of the Brothers. I really loved this gentle, smiling man. He was aboard during our trip with the Yankees, and I can recall sitting beside him at times on the train. Since his was an administrative position, we seldom saw him in the daily life of the school, but I met with him on occasions such as when my mother came to see me and we would go to his office to pay the bill or have a chat.

Brother Paul came to know Ruth quite well as a person both before and after Babe signed his first contract and ventured out, green as grass, on his own.

As for myself, I was just a lucky kid who, as he nears ninety years, still has warm memories of those days with Babe and the other Yankees. That occurred almost eighty years ago. Since then, I have been privileged to teach thousands of men when they were impressionable boys.

Today Babe Ruth is a legend nonpareil. He still grips the imagination of baseball fans, young and old, just as he did in those years when he whacked the ball out of the park with such regularity. One indication of his popularity when he was at the top of his career was the existence of a couple of songs by which fans expressed their regard for him. I will give you the words of those which the St. Mary's Band played and sang with gusto and affection. I remember the tunes and on occasion still delight grand-nephews and small fry in recalling the Babe. In recent years, when asked to tell students about him, I have found that modern teenagers also sense the legend of the man whose name has acquired a certain magical aura.

"The Babe Ruth Song" (Fast, march-like tune)

Look at him now, and think of all the games that Babe has won.
And how he knocks the homers when the Yankees need a run.
We know he's broken records and we're sure he'll break some more.
Can't you hear those bleachers roooaaaaarrr!
He hears the call and then the ball is sailing in the sky.
A mile away it kills a cow.
And if a bandit on the border gets a baseball in the eye,
Put the blame on Babe —**Look At Him NNNNOOOOOOWWWW!**

The other song I remember has a slow movement like a love song:

> Ruth, Ruth, oh you Babe Ruth,
> You are in all our dreams.
> Your kind face holds a place
> In ev'ry Yankee lad's dreams —
> They love you.
> Ruth, Ruth, oh you Babe Ruth,
> Idol of all our dreams,
> Heaven above alone knows the love
> We have for you,
> Babe Ruth, Babe Ruth

There is no doubt that millions of baseball fans loved the Babe. They marveled at his ability both as a pitcher and especially as the King of Swat. But they were taken more by his smile, his generous nature and his interest in people, especially kids in hospitals and orphanages, all of which endeared him to so many. And his faults, mostly those of a big kid, brought out the human side of the legend.

Babe Ruth never really knew his parents, for he seldom saw them as he was growing up. But he never forgot the Xaverian Brothers who represented both parents to him in his youth. He loved to come back to St. Mary's and treat the boys to a "scramble." He would load his pockets with nickels and dimes and throw them to the lads waiting to scramble for the change, which would bring them candy in the school shop. Or he would hit out mile-high fly balls as he had seen Brother Matthias do.

In particular, he never forgot Brother Matthias, who was so very special to Babe all his life. After Babe began to receive his player's checks, he loved to show his affection for his friend, on one occasion giving him a motorcycle, and later an expensive automobile.

The Brothers have long sponsored and operated St. Xavier High School, a large and prominent school in Louisville. When in town for exhibition games which the Yankees played in Louisville, Babe regularly visited not only the Brothers at St. Xavier, but the entire student body, inviting them to the game as his guests. Of course, he paid particular attention to Brother Pius, whom he knew from St. Mary's.

In the Heritage Collection of the Xaverian Brothers at the Ryken House retirement center in Louisville, there is a picture of St. Mary's and its famous alumnus. One would seem incomplete without the other. You will surely delight in the remembrances of Brother Gilbert which follow, as well as Harry Rothgerber's insightful commentary which captures the history and spirit of the Babe, the Brothers, and St. Mary's.

As for myself, I was stationed in Louisville as principal of St. Xavier when Babe died in 1948 and I viewed the news on the newfangled electronic contrivance called television. At St. Mary's, more than thirty years after he had left there, the Brothers assembled the boys to pray for the repose of his soul. Years later, I was able to visit the Babe's grave in New York. As I said a prayer for this legend of American sports, I thought of the words I sang many years before: "Idol of all our dreams, Heaven above alone knows the love we have for you, Babe Ruth, Babe Ruth."

Brother John Joseph Sterne, C.F.X.
Louisville, Kentucky, 1999

Introduction

by Harry Rothgerber

It would be an understatement to say that George Ruth, the original home run king, exhibited a severe pattern of irresponsible, antisocial and erratic behavior as a child and adolescent. Today, he would no doubt be labeled an "at-risk" child in a multiple-problem family. Indeed, even in his own era, when the state was just beginning to exercise its power as the guardian of social interests, young George was so "hard to handle" in the community that he was removed and placed in an institution at age seven. "I was a bad kid," begins Ruth's 1948 autobiography, published shortly before his death. That simple confession does not nearly describe the range of difficult behaviors exhibited by this one-of-a-kind man-child.

The man who was destined to become the Babe, the Sultan of Swat, the Bambino, the Colossus of Clout and a dozen other monikers, was born in a tenement home located at 216 Emory Street in Baltimore, Maryland, on February 6, 1895. (Until he applied for a passport for his 1934 barnstorming tour of Japan and viewed his birth certificate, he believed his birth to have occurred on February 7, 1894. Delighted at being a year younger than he reckoned, he continued to use the February 7 date for birthday parties.)

In Ruth's first autobiography (no doubt ghostwritten by Ford Frick, a New York sportswriter who later became president of the National League), George remembers "the dirty, traffic-crowded streets of Baltimore's river front," the drivers who whipped "at the legs of the kids who made the street their playground," "the shopkeepers who took bruising payment from our skins for the apples and fruit we 'snitched' from their stands," and "tossing overripe apples or eggs at a truck driver's head." Ruth concludes: "A rough, tough neighborhood, but I liked it."

Contrary to myth, Ruth was never "an orphan," at least not within the actual meaning of that word. Ruth's father was a saloon keeper, and the family resided in the living quarters over that business. His mother, Katie, who gave birth to the Babe when she was 20, apparently was chronically ill. She delivered eight children, but only Babe and younger sister Mamie survived.

Running one of the many neighborhood bars on Baltimore's impoverished, seedy waterfront was backbreaking work. Ruth wrote that his parents, "trying to eke out a living for all of us, worked 20 hours a day trying to make a go of the barroom." Even with Ruth's record as a poor historian who often embellished, confused or misstated the facts, this estimate of his parents' labors was probably correct. They were responsible for cooking, cleaning, tending bar and breaking up fights among the dockworkers, longshoremen and transient sailors.

George Herman Ruth, Sr., was born in Baltimore in 1871, and worked as a lightning rod installer before becoming a saloon keeper. He married Catherine "Katie" Schamberger in June 1894, and Babe came along about 7½ months later — a somewhat scandalous occurrence in those Victorian times. Although Babe's father was Protestant, Katie and her parents were devout Catholics and remained so. Babe, who was born in the home of his maternal grandparents (both of whom died before his 10th birthday), was baptized as a Catholic at the age of one month with his mother's sister listed as Godparent.

Katie eventually died in 1912, at the age of 38, of "exhaustion" and pulmonary disease in the Baltimore Municipal Tuberculosis Hospital. At the time of her death, Babe was a resident at St. Mary's Industrial School; there is no clear evidence that he attended the wake, funeral or burial.

Babe's father was hardly the image of a nurturing, responsible caregiver. There was little or no contact between father and son after Babe's placement in St. Mary's in 1902. Babe's signing as a professional in 1914 was quickly followed by his marriage only eight months later to a young coffee shop waitress. Meanwhile, Ruth Sr. had also remarried. There was little time for the father and son to associate with each other, given the circumstances, although a notable photograph was taken in December 1915, showing the uncanny resemblance between the two Ruth men as Babe helped his father tend bar amid holiday decorations.

It was in front of that saloon at Eutaw and Lombard streets on August 25, 1918 that the elder Ruth met his death in a confusing incident. This much is certain: a quarrel occurred between Ruth Sr. and "Doc" Sipes, his new brother-in-law. They fought outside; Ruth was knocked to the

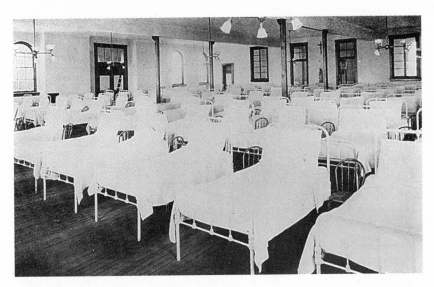

This is a typical dormitory for the younger boys, the type to which Babe would have been assigned during his early days at St. Mary's. All had a bed and a chair. Each boy made his own bed. Brothers told devout stories at bedtime, and all boys said three "Hail Mary's" before going to sleep. A night watchman was always present. (If the watchman was ill, one or two boys were chosen for this duty; they were then allowed to sleep later and received a big breakfast.) A former resident there, Brother John Joseph Sterne cannot recall ever having a locker. Washing areas were on the first floor (courtesy of Xaverian Brothers Heritage Collection).

pavement and fractured his skull. The police and a grand jury later brought no charges in the case, ruling self-defense.

A brief digression to the socio-legal world is necessary. In 1899, the first state-sanctioned juvenile court was created in Chicago. The "parens patriae" doctrine would soon sweep the country, infusing local cities and counties with the "child-saving" mission of special courts designed to act "in the best interest" of minors who were needy, neglected, delinquent and abandoned. A main tenet of this era of social enlightenment mandated that the state would intrude to help those children who couldn't help themselves or who were in need of the state's care, including delinquents.

Reflecting this trend that the state was the ultimate parent of all children in need of supervision, many so-called "orphanages" sprang up during the latter portion of the 19th century, especially those operated by and for the children of immigrant groups such as the Germans and Irish. During the time that Babe Ruth resided at St. Mary's Industrial School, there were 29 of these orphanages in Baltimore alone.

In his first autobiography, Ruth declared, "I don't know how I happened to be sent to St. Mary's." In fact, it appears that his parents probably just gave up on their severely acting-out child with his tantrums, truancy and back-talk and asked a justice of the peace to commit him. Maryland law at that time permitted commitments to St. Mary's of incorrigible children until the age of 21. Thus, George Ruth became what would be known in today's juvenile justice system as a "status offender" committed to a "private child care facility."

Later in life Ruth remembered, "I was listed as an incorrigible and I guess I was. Looking back on my early boyhood, I honestly don't remember being aware of the difference between right and wrong." St. Mary's Industrial School was a benevolent institution operated by the Xaverian Brothers, a Catholic religious order with Belgian origins. Ruth's biographers have referred to it as an orphanage, a religious home, a training school, a house of refuge, a reform school and even "a prison." In truth, it served the purposes of all these institutional settings, at least to some extent. Among the types of children who could be found there were delinquents committed by the courts, runaways, orphans, boys who were beyond the control of their parents, indigent youths whose parents could not afford to keep them at home, and children of parents who had separated or divorced. Quite a mixture of boys for the Xaverians to house, feed, clothe, train, discipline and educate!

Lou Leisman, a former resident of St. Mary's with the Babe, remembered how important Sunday visiting day was to the boys at that institution. In 1912, he mentioned to George that Lou's mother was ill and he had not seen her in two years. Leisman recalls, "Without batting an eye, the Babe replied: 'You're lucky, Fats. It's been ten years since I have seen my father.'" Babe's classmate went on to say that, indeed, he never saw Babe receive a visit from his parents, and he proceeded to recollect, "Babe would kid me and say, 'Well, I guess I am too big and ugly for anyone to come to see me. Maybe next time.' But the next time never came."

What more facts could a psycho-social researcher from the late 20th century desire in order to complete an evaluation of seven-year-old George Ruth! The following descriptive phrases could be applied to the young child: cultural and behavioral poverty, poor eating habits, poor hygiene, illegitimacy, poor housing, at least nine household moves, low class, intrafamily religious conflict, severe and chronic parental illness, dysfunctional family relationships, financial problems, smoking, drinking, incorrigibility and truancy. (He also refused to attend school on any type of consistent basis.) His life — and baseball history — might have turned out very differently without the influence of a group of devout and disciplined men, the Brothers of Francis Xavier.

* * *

If Babe Ruth was the epic hero who forced major league baseball back on the right track after a dangerous veer from the good graces of favorable public opinion due to the "Black Sox" scandal, then the Xaverians were the surrogate parents who nurtured that Babe. Numerous strange twists of fate connected Ruth to this congregation of holy men whose aspirations dated to the 1830s.

The Xaverian Brothers' Foundation Day is listed as June 5, 1839, since this was the day that founder Theodore James Ryken (Rijken), a humble Hollander, established himself in a house in Bruges, Belgium. Ryken was invested in the holy habit in 1843, and, after years of patient and prayerful work, he opened the Brothers' first schools in Belgium in 1844. By 1846 he had recruited nine other men to struggle with him. Ryken took Brother Francis Xavier, C.F.X. (Congregation of the Brothers of Francis Xavier) as his religious name.

Numerous Ruth biographers and commentators over the years have referred to these holy men as "priests." In a 1998 Ruth pictorial cowritten by his daughter Julia, the Xaverians are referred to as "a Catholic Order of Jesuit Missionaries." That is totally incorrect. Xaverian Brothers are neither priests nor students for the priesthood. They cannot celebrate Mass or bestow sacramental privileges as can Catholic priests. However, Brothers are not ordinary laymen, for they are members of a religious order or congregation. They belong to a *religious state*, a form of life approved by the Catholic Church, in which some of the faithful establish themselves in a permanent society in order to direct their lives more perfectly to God, their final end, by means of the three vows of poverty, chastity and obedience. Thus, the Xaverians are a religious order devoted to the teaching and moral development of youth.

After engaging in several years of professional training and special studies in the Saint Trond Normal School, this small band of Brothers was fairly well established, and a group of them traveled from Bruges to Bury, England, to open a school. Obviously, this was a stepping stone to America — a place to refine teaching skills, to better learn the subtle nuances of the English language, and to raise money for a missionary venture.

After a number of years in England, fate intervened in the person of Bishop Martin J. Spalding of the diocese of Louisville, Kentucky. In 1853,

while looking for recruits in Belgium, the American bishop was introduced to Brother Francis Xavier and was greatly impressed. So much so, in fact, that Bishop Spalding extended a warm invitation for the Xaverians to come to Louisville the following year to establish the Congregation in America. Brother Francis Xavier eagerly accepted this offer and signed an agreement to come to Louisville, although the Brothers' funds for traveling were virtually nonexistent.

In 1854 the Brothers arrived in America and soon had taken up quarters in Louisville, where they opened two schools. The years that followed were hard ones, and the survival of the Brothers' mission in America was often in doubt. In 1860, however, the Brothers opened four new schools in Louisville, and in 1861 they welcomed their first new postulant, or recruit, into the Congregation. By 1863, the Xaverians numbered 16, and in 1864, they opened St. Xavier's Institute on Broadway, the precursor of the flagship school of the Order, St. Xavier High School, today nationally recognized for excellence.

By 1929, when Babe Ruth clouted 46 home runs, the ranks of the Brothers had grown to more than six hundred. From a few boys in a few schools, the Xaverians were educating over ten thousand young men.

* * *

In 1864, Martin John Spalding was transferred from the Louisville diocese to become Archbishop of Baltimore. It took him only a short while to assess the pitiful condition of Baltimore's indigent children. It was painful for him to see the city's needy, neglected, dependent, abandoned and delinquent children turned out on the street after becoming too large for the Catholic Sisters to care for in their institutions. Thus, in 1866, he established the boys' school and training center known as St. Mary's Industrial School. Who else would the venerable Archbishop select to staff this institution but the Xaverians?

Contrary to the opinions that have surfaced in various writings, St. Mary's was not a prison, reformatory, asylum, or sweatshop where residents were physically mistreated. It is true that the school — originally run by priests and laymen of the diocese — suffered hardships in its early years, including a year of deadly typhus, near-bankruptcy, and a disastrous

Opposite: A typical class for younger boys at St. Mary's. The identity of the Brother is not known. Notice the size of the boys' ties and the slates and slate pencils being used. Brother John Joseph Sterne recalls using the sleeve of his jacket to clean his slate. Fifty-four boys in this class — a lot to handle (courtesy of Xaverian Brothers Heritage Collection).

This view of St. Mary's recreational area was taken prior to the disastrous fire. The "big yard" for older boys is on the right; the "little yard" for younger boys appears on the left. The road separating the two yards was the site of the Babe's "punishment by isolation" when he ran away before the big game against Mount St. Joseph's College. The building at the far right housed the tailor shop where the Babe worked. The main buildings were destroyed in the 1919 fire (courtesy of Xaverian Brothers Heritage Collection).

four-year period when the school was actually managed by a diocesan priest. Eventually, however, the Xaverians were given complete authority, and the picture changed significantly, espcially with the arrival of Brother Dominic (Patrick O'Connell) of County Cork, Ireland.

Brother Dominic served as superintendent from 1887 to 1907 (the last five years coinciding with Babe Ruth's early years at the school). Before Brother Dominic's term the management plan for the residents — many of whom were older, hardened delinquents — was based on secular facilities of a similar nature in the area. Sometimes boys were committed to the facility until the age of 20 or 21 and were consequently more difficult to supervise and control. Brother Dominic brought an end to any philosophy of harshness. He removed outward signs of institutionalism by discarding uniforms and discontinuing the use of disciplinary cells. Any stigma from being a resident of St. Mary's was gradually eliminated, and the facility

The utter devastation of St. Mary's Industrial School caused by the fire of April 24, 1919. This view is from the rear of the main buildings and shows the collapse of the flag pole/cross (courtesy of Xaverian Brothers Heritage Collection).

began receiving exemplary grades during inspections by city and state child welfare personnel.

It was on April 24, 1919, some five years after the Babe left St. Mary's, that tragedy struck. That afternoon when all the boys were in their yards, smoke began to billow from the roof. A live coal had been blown under the eaves from a tinner's stove and burned for hours before detection. Two Baltimore firefighters lost their lives in the ensuing effort to halt the conflagration. Soon St. Mary's ceased to exist. Allegedly fireproof buildings were no more. Only the chapel and several outbuildings in the yard were spared.

By October 1919, the outbuildings in St. Mary's yard had been remodeled into temporary dormitories and classrooms, and all the boys returned to the grounds. Two large buildings were built with Brother Paul Scanlon's architectural designs in mind to meet all the needs of the residents; upon their completion, the outbuildings were abandoned by the boys to their original use. The new St. Mary's had been born.

Financially, the school was in dire straits as a result of the fire. Insur-

The "Babe Ruth Boys Band" traveled with the Babe during the last western road trip of the 1920 American League season. Taken in front of the St. Mary's bandstand, the photo shows four future Xaverians, including Brother John Joseph Sterne (*seated, far right*), the author of this book's Foreword. Brother Simon Drury is seated in the center (courtesy of Xaverian Brothers Heritage Collection).

ance covered only a portion of the loss. There was no endowment in existence. The Brothers depended heavily on private efforts and contributions. Enter the Babe.

As related by Brother John Joseph Sterne in the Foreword, Babe Ruth was mightily upset on hearing news of the devastating fire. Then a member of the Boston Red Sox, he vowed to assist his old school. By the time he hatched his plan, the Babe was a Yankee. During the last road trip of the 1920 season, Babe sponsored the St. Mary's Band to travel with the Yankees as "Babe Ruth's Boys Band." Giving concerts at the ball parks before the game, the boys would later circulate among the patrons, collecting change and bills in their sailor hats. Not only was a goodly sum of cash received, but the free publicity was invaluable. By this effort, the Babe gave much back to his alma mater, of which he was always proud.

*   *   *

No other person was as responsible for the development of George Herman Ruth's natural talents as Brother Matthias, of whom Ruth said, "It was at St. Mary's that I met and learned to love the greatest man I've ever known." Under different circumstances, Brother Matthias' skills with a baseball bat may have taken him to the pinnacle of success in the sports world.

Born Martin L. Boutlier in Cape Breton, Canada, in 1872, "Big Matt" or "The Boss" became a legendary figure in the annals of Xaverianism. Estimates of his height range from six feet four to six feet six inches and his weight has been reckoned from 225 to 300 pounds. One thing is for sure: Photos show that he was large enough to tower over Ruth (himself an imposing man), and he was all coordinated muscle, according to the Xaverian Brother' Menology. For 38 years he was associated with St. Mary's, mostly as prefect of discipline, around whom life revolved at that institution. He dealt with the toughest boys, many of whom were wards of the court, in a fair, consistent manner which won the respect of all. Ruth was evidently an exception in one way, as evidenced by these remarks: "I don't know why, but he singled me out when I first came to St. Mary's. It wasn't that I was his 'pet.' But he concentrated on me, probably because I needed it. He studied what few gifts I had and drew these out of me and amplified them. He always built me." In her biography of her late husband, Mrs. Claire Ruth observed, "When Babe Ruth was 23, the world loved him. When he was 13, only Brother Matthias loved him."

Brother Matthias displayed a shambling gait and a quiet and diffident manner, but no one ever forgot that he was a disciplinarian. Brother Thomas More Page, later a provincial and superior general of the Xaverians, was a young resident at St. Mary's and remembered incidents from the early 1920s:

> What I think every boy who was at St. Mary's at the time will remember are the Sunday evenings after supper whenever the news got around that Brother Matthias would be hitting baseballs. Then, every boy in the school from all the five yards would gather in the upper yard, over 500 of us, awaiting the occasion. He would stand at the bottom of the steps, and with what seemed like an effortless motion, hit the ball with the fungo bat in his right hand only, while up and up the ball seemed to soar, almost out of sight, and then when it came down there was a mad scramble for it. We knew the end was coming to this extraordinary exhibition when he hit one ball after the other in rapid succession, and the balls kept falling down like snow flakes over the entire yard. What made possessing one of these balls important was that we knew that they had come from Babe Ruth.

A former St. Mary's resident once wrote about Matthias: "He was calm, considerate and gave everyone a fair break. But, brother, if you ever crossed him you were sure in trouble."

Brother Gilbert is often credited by Ruth's early biographers with

Brother Matthias looms in the left rear of this view of the Babe Ruth Boys Band in front of the girls' orphanage where they stayed in Philadelphia, prior to the Yankees' contest with Connie Mack's Athletics. Playing drum on the far right was Sammy West, who received much attention from photographers due to his likeness to the Babe. One boy, Lawrence Lockwood (later of the U.S. Navy Band) was playing solo clarinet at a concert in Lowell, Massachusetts, when his pants fell down! Brother John Joseph Sterne's natural brother Buck looks protectively over his sibling's right shoulder (courtesy of Xaverian Brothers Heritage Collection).

being Babe's baseball coach at St. Mary's, but that is incorrect. George Ruth was a left-handed catcher with a right-hander's glove for Brother Matthias, who also was responsible for converting the lad to a pitcher, and for pushing him into competition with much older boys. Ruth himself later recalled, "Brother Matthias had the right idea about training a baseball club. He made every boy on the team play every position in the game, including the bench. A kid might pitch a game one day and find himself behind the bat the next, or perhaps out in the sun-field. You see, Brother Matthias' idea was to fit a boy to jump in in an emergency and make good. So whatever I may have done at bat or on the mound or in the outfield or even on the bases, I owe directly to Brother Matthias."

Brother Matthias Boutlier (or Boutelier) was born at Lingan, Cape Breton, Canada, on July 11, 1872. This photo was taken around 1893 after his period of noviceship and training had been completed. Following a brief stay in Louisville, he was transferred to St. Mary's Industrial School in 1894. He devoted 38 years of his life to that school (courtesy of Xaverian Brothers Heritage Collection).

Above all, Matthias was a man of faith and humility. His sleeping room at St. Mary's was six-and-a-half feet square. Because he needed an extra long bed, the door to his room hung on the outside of the jamb, so as to allow more room for a place to sleep.

From the Ryken House retirement home for Xaverians in Louisville, Brother Thomas More Page recalls that Brother Matthias "inspired awe in all the boys which was demonstrated by an incident which became a legend, and which every boy even in my day knew about. While on retreat at nearby Mount St. Joseph's, Matthias got an urgent call from Brother Paul, the superintendent, that there was a riot brewing among the older boys in what was referred to as the Big Yard. When the boys saw Matthias at the head of the steps overlooking the yard, they immediately dispersed without saying a single word." Ruth also related this story in his autobiography, saying that Matthias "leaped in his carriage, laid a whip on the old plug that pulled it and drove very fast. ... [A] great silence came over the yard and the trouble stopped immediately."

In what may have been a lifelong testament to his desire to emulate Matthias, the Babe developed the same odd, pigeon-toed, minced-step style of walking and running which the good Brother displayed. It served them both very well.

In her 1959 book, Claire Ruth recalled, "Many times when the Babe was in a jam the Yankees got Brother Matthias up to New York to speak to the Babe." She also recited the amazing tale that Brother Matthias "knew Babe, too, because he gently, but firmly, talked Babe out of an ambition to be a priest that came upon my husband when he was about 15. This is advice no Catholic man gives lightly to a Catholic youth. ... But he saw no call."

It was only after Brother Matthias was stationed at St. John's Prep in Danvers, Massachusetts, around 1935, that interviews with him brought out his essential supporting role as a surrogate father to the Babe. But the Bambino never forgot what Matthias' friendship and guidance meant to him. Shortly before his final days, Ruth mused, "I had drifted away from the church during my harum-scarum early years in the majors. I'd go to Mass now and then and, believe me, I never missed a night without saying my prayers. But I wasn't the Catholic I had been at St. Mary's, especially after Brother Matthias died."

A kindly humanitarian, Brother Matthias not only devoted his professional life to helping troubled boys, but he assisted his fellow Xaverians in their darkest hours. In Peabody, Massachusetts, a Brother Marcus contracted pernicious anemia and gradually wasted away to death. His gentle and dedicated nurse was none other than the community giant, Brother Matthias.

* * *

"Brother Matthias and Brother Gilbert were as different as a boiled potato and a pizza," wrote Tom Shehan, a former sportswriter for *The Boston Evening Transcript*. As much as Matthias was reserved and constrained, so Gilbert—the Babe's other great influence and the author of this memoir—had "the gift of gab" and was sought constantly as an after-dinner speaker.

On June 15, 1882, the Cairnes family arrived in Boston after a long journey over the Atlantic from Liverpool on the ship *Missouri*. Irish-born, the Cairnes elders had emigrated to England following the potato famine of 1850. Edward Cairnes came to America wishful for a livelihood that would hold together body and soul; his first job was as an ice-cutter, and he soon found a niche in construction as a licensed engineer with the nickname "Dynamite."

In 1884, Edward's second child was delivered in Somerville, Massachusetts. Born as Phillip F. Cairnes, Brother Gilbert was the second oldest of twelve children (six boys and six girls). He would receive the nickname "Bud" from family members.

As a youth, Brother Gilbert was described as "mindful in manners and conduct, and a joy to everyone. He was not rough, nor boisterous, nor quarrelsome; maybe more gentle than most youngsters, a distinction sometimes not worth having among boys. He had a cheerful, humorous personality, a good character along with natural refinement and keen judgment. He was well liked with the group at school."

Brother Gilbert attended St. Joseph's, a Xaverian-staffed parish elementary school, and he entered the novitiate in 1901. His destination when he left Massachusetts was Mount St. Joseph College, and his train arrived at Camden Station in Baltimore. (Coincidentally, Camden Yards is the site of the current Oriole Park, home of the Baltimore Orioles.)

After earning his holy habit, Brother Gilbert's first teaching assignment was at St. Xavier's in Louisville, where he taught math and English from 1903 to 1908, prior to his transfer to Mount St. Joseph's College in Baltimore. Earlier, he had received his bachelor's degree from Mount St. Joseph's.

One of the first Xaverians to earn a master's degree (Catholic University, 1916), Brother Gilbert was also a gifted baseball coach. Being quite the garrulous Irishman, Gilbert found it easy to "make connections," and was friendly with many baseball entrepreneurs of that era, including Jack

Brother Gilbert and one of his Mount St. Joseph's teams stand in front of the main administration building, a favorite site for "official" photographs on campus. The building exists no more, having been replaced years ago. The young black lad is probably a "mascot," common for that era. The Mount's teams were consistently among the best amateur teams in the East, winning the national Catholic Collegiate Championship in 1915 (27–2) and 1916 (courtesy of Xaverian Brothers Heritage Collection).

Dunn of the Baltimore Orioles. While at "The Mount," Brother Gilbert was instrumental in the signing of St. Mary's resident George Ruth to his first professional contract by Dunn, whose Orioles played in the International League.

In 1915, Gilbert's Mount St. Joseph's College baseball team played 29 games against the best collegiate teams in the country, including Boston College, Fordham, Holy Cross, Georgetown, NYU, Villanova and Maryland. In winning the Eastern College Championship, they lost only to the Naval Academy (5–4) and an exhibition game with the Richmond team of the International League, then managed by Jack Dunn. As a coach, Brother Gilbert was called a perfectionist and a strategist who played for runs in bunches at a time when most coaches played for one run at a time. As a person, he always kept up with his old players and protégés. His philosophy of competition was captured in his remarks from a later address entitled "With God We Shall Win," delivered shortly after the Japanese sneak attack of Pearl Harbor: "No, definitely, there can be no doubt about the final result of this conflict. We've developed here in the states what's known among the athletes as a winning spirit. We are not good losers; we are hard losers. The American boy has never known the insensate apathy of the defeatist. Courage is his birthright, his legacy."

One New York publication, *The Tablet*, once described him in this manner: "As a religious Superior, Brother Gilbert was particularly the friend of his youthful confreres, guiding and encouraging them with unfailing patience and cheerfulness. He had the gift of making everyone feel the warmth of his personal interest." Another testimonial was given by famed sportswriter Jesse Linthicum of the *Baltimore Sun*, who said, "Brother Gilbert devoted most of his life to the welfare of young people. A friend once commented that he excelled both at 'making athletes out of boys and making men of character out of athletes.' Sports enthusiasts who knew him said frequently that if he had given all his time to athletics he could have been one of the country's outstanding coaches."

Sportswriter H.G. Salsinger, who wrote about Babe in 1948 in a story entitled "I Remember Babe" (as part of Dan Daniel's biography of Ruth), had some interesting comments: "Brother Gilbert got him his chance with Jack Dunn's Baltimore Orioles and acted as his spiritual guide in later years. When the Babe went on his much advertised spending spree in Cuba, it was Brother Gilbert who went to Cuba and brought the Babe back home.

"At times when the Babe got too much out of hand, Ed Barrow would send a hurry call to Baltimore for Brother Gilbert and Brother Gilbert always responded. He had more influence over Ruth than anyone else."

Gilbert was also an enthusiastic teacher, gentle but firm in giving correction, patient and sympathetic with slow learners, and generous with his praise for those who tried. At age 35, he was described by a former student as a commanding figure of a man well over six feet with a prominent forehead and dark hair that was beginning to recede and thin even then. As a teaching principal, his methods were sometimes unique. The same student, who later became Brother Jogues, recalled, "Sometimes his recitation periods in biology were a game of baseball," in which students would choose up sides and fire questions at the other side with Brother as the "umpire" who kept all the students' "batting averages" in his official "scorebook." The runs were posted on the blackboard inning by inning, and the boys learned painlessly as they played.

Each day on entering the classroom, he would greet his students with a long, drawn out "Good mawn-n-n-ing." He was seldom, if ever, out of humor, and occasionally would sing a stanza of "Good morning, Mr. Zipp, Zipp, Zipp" after his greeting. After these pleasantries and the daily prayer were over, he would boom out, "Who's got 'em all?"— meaning the problems he had assigned for homework.

Another former student, Brother Gerald Edward, wrote of his first encounter with the Xaverian Brothers in 1926 as he rushed to the bakery after Sunday Mass:

> The figure I saw directly in front of me in the middle of the cleared lane made me catch my breath a little, for he looked ten feet tall, dressed in a long, black cassock surmounted with a narrow white collar. Rosary beads swished at his side, looking cable-sized to my startled gaze. Speechless, I looked at this smiling giant (actually my giant was Brother Gilbert, first Xaverian Superior of Mission High, about six feet five, but from my vantage point ten feet at least). ... As Brother Gilbert passed me, I got a whiff of piney shaving lotion and as I looked up, nose wrinkling, I received a friendly, big-handed pat on the head ... destiny beckoned on the day I saw my first Xaverian.

Brother Gilbert was an outstanding administrator who inspired loyalty and devotion at the schools in which he served, including: St. Francis DeSales High School/Assumption Academy in Utica, New York, (first principal, 1917–1920); Old Point Comfort High School, Fortress Monroe, Virginia (principal, 1920–1921); Leonard Hall High School, Leonardtown, Maryland (principal, 1921–1922); St. John's Prep, Danvers, Massachusetts (instructor and baseball coach, 1922–1926); Our Lady of Perpetual Help High School, Roxbury, Massachusetts (first principal, 1926–1932); Immaculate Conception High School, Malden, Massachusetts (first principal, 1932–1938); St. Michael's Diocesan High School (instructor, 1938–1939); Keith Academy, Lowell, Massachusetts (instructor, 1939–1947). His Boston terrier "Mugsie" became part of the Xaverian folklore in Roxbury, and Malden's football stadium was named in Brother's honor, as was the gymnasium at St. John's Preparatory School in Danvers, Massachusetts. The Xaverian Menology observes that "Brother Gilbert's was the great heart; anybody in or out of the community could enlist his assistance."

Gilbert's sportswriter friend George A. Gagan of *The Lowell Telegraph* declared, "There was an intense humanness about Brother Gilbert. He possessed the humility, the understanding, the manliness, the zest for life which inspired respect for his great talents and reverence for the habit he wore. I will always remember his vigorous stride, his hearty handshake, his boyish grin and happy vibrant laughter." According to Charles B. McGhee of Lynn, Massachusetts, "His friends were not all of his own faith. They were numbered by thousands in the Protestant and Jewish faiths, and he was a living example of tolerance — he exemplified everything that is good in America." Charles E. Gallagher of Lynn observed that "Brother Gilbert was never stationed in Lynn, nor was he born here, but it is safe to wager that few men could call more Lynn residents by their first name than this popular Catholic educator."

Many anecdotes about Gilbert have survived the years. As an American Province delegate to the Order's General Chapter meeting, on his first trip to Europe, he was not interested much in "the glory that was Rome." As he made progress up through Italy to Florence, Venice and Milan, he took it all in stride. When he finally reached Switzerland, from the train window he caught sight of a hunting dog and said, "I'm going to like this place."

On Flag Day, 1931, Brother Gilbert was principal speaker at the Kiwanis Club in Boston at a time when American morale was at a low ebb from the Great Depression. His patriotic speech rejuvenated his listeners' sagging spirits. Within a week, Brother had received and fulfilled over a hundred requests for copies of his Flag Day Address.

There is no question that Brother had a certain way at winning people over from discouragement to trust, hope and optimism. In 1946, Brother Gilbert received a telephone call, asking him to come quickly to one of the suburban towns of Boston. A young man of his acquaintance was contemplating suicide. Brother hastened to the home of his sick friend and persuaded the distraught young man not to carry out his plan. Two years later, this same young man stood before Brother Gilbert's bier in Lowell, shaken with grief, sobbing his thanks to a real friend.

Then, in 1947, Brother Gilbert dropped into Peabody from Lowell, a distance of 30 miles, to confer with Brother Alban on data for his "Life of Babe Ruth." Following the interview, Brother Gilbert, rather than inconvenience anyone, declined the offer of a ride to Lowell in the school truck. "I'll get back all right," he said. Brother Gilbert, 62 years old and wearing clerical garb, thumbed his way back to Lowell.

One very cold day in midwinter, Brother Gilbert chanced to see a little girl sobbing convulsively while she struggled along a sidewalk in Cambridge, Massachusetts. Her hands were too cold and stiff to remove her skates and she was pleadingly calling for her mother. Brother Gilbert was always deeply touched at suffering, more especially when the victim was a helpless child. He immediately sprang to the middle of the road and halted an approaching taxi. After helping the confused child into the cab he instructed the driver to take the child home with all possible speed. Only upon Brother's insistence did the driver accept the taxi fare. "She's my special guest," Brother laughingly remarked, "and I want her to get the best care."

Before the site was cleared for a Federal Housing Project in Roxbury, Massachusetts, the homes on the land were tenanted by poor people who lived within a stone's throw of the Brothers' house. One afternoon while Brother Gilbert was strolling through a poor neighborhood, he espied a child in tears, lying prostrate on the sidewalk. The child had been sent to a nearby store for a half-dozen eggs and tripped as he mounted the curbstone. All the eggs were broken and the frightened, sobbing child was too much hurt to arise. Brother hastened to his assistance, lifted him to his feet, patted him reassuringly on the head, slipped him 50 cents and smilingly sent him back to the store for "some eggs that wouldn't break."

Rarely did Brother Gilbert attend the theater, certainly not more than once a year and then only as an accommodation to a friend who wanted companionship. Contrary to general belief, during the last six years of his life he witnessed very few major league baseball games. But he did find supreme pleasure in the seclusion of his home, sitting in the kitchen talking quietly with his father, then in his late eighties. Hour after hour, the two would chat and exchange wisecracks, never tiring of each other's company. His father's early exploits and escapades, dating back 70 years, fascinated the Brother. Those were quiet, peaceful sessions, removed from the turmoil of banquets and athletic contests, but Brother loved those sessions. If the conversation lagged, as conversation often does, they would resort to a game of cribbage or pinochle and every game was spirited and bitterly fought, for, be it said, that in all forms of sport, indoor as well as outdoor, Brother Gilbert was a keen competitor. Following his father's death in April 1946, Brother Gilbert seemed to become more reserved and less facetious.

Shortly before Brother Gilbert died, he was working zealously on his life story of Babe Ruth. A confrere, after proofreading some of the pages, remarked that he could find no reference to or provision for a picture of the man who was writing the story of the "Babe." Brother Gilbert looked up at his colleague and replied: "It doesn't concern me whether or not people know that Brother Gilbert wrote this book. What matters to me is that they know one of the Xaverian Brothers did the job."

Throughout the years, Brother maintained an active interest in many facets of baseball. He worked constantly on gathering information and refining his memoirs of "the Babe." Gilbert was an active and insightful scout. Joe Coleman of Arlington, Massachusetts, one of Connie Mack's better pitching prospects, was recommended to the Athletics by Brother Gilbert. Coleman played his high school ball at Malden Catholic where Brother Gilbert was once the principal. Also, Brother Gilbert recommended Larry Stone of Dover, New Hampshire, to the Boston Braves. Stone, a pitcher, was a Braves farmhand, but never had the fine future forecast for him by Brother Gilbert. Jackie Campbell, at one time one of the brightest college prospects in America as a member of the Notre Dame pitching staff, was a protégé of Brother's at Keith Academy and was regarded as one of the greatest high school pitchers in the history of Massachusetts.

One of Brother's last public appearances came at the testimonial dinner to old-time Red Sox star, Duffy Lewis, then traveling secretary for the Boston Braves. Brother Gilbert delivered the invocation at the dinner. At one time Gilbert had a chance to become owner of either the Newark or Jersey City ball clubs, but he turned down the opportunity to remain a religious. In the course of his lifetime Brother Gilbert delivered more than 1,000 speeches, many about his most famous discovery, George Herman Ruth.

Those who played baseball for Keith Academy between 1939 and 1947 will recall that Brother Gilbert was usually on the players' bench. He was influential in pushing many local players on to higher education via athletic scholarships. He actively participated in the Lowell community and was especially loved by fellow Irish Catholics.

Over the years, this Xaverian was also called upon to lecture on Irish history, his speeches being considered brilliant. He had a certain magic with words to fit them into colorful and thought-provoking phrases.

One of Gilbert's younger brothers was Joe Cairnes, formerly the president of Lou Perini's Boston/Milwaukee Braves before taking command of Perini's major project of building houses on former swampland in West Palm Beach, Florida. In a 1988 interview, Joe remembered his brother this way:

> Although he was consecrated to the spiritual life, Brother Gilbert was also dedicated to helping young men improve their material existence and to this end he loved sports, especially baseball.
>
> In the years preceding World War I, Brother Gilbert was stationed at Mount St. Joseph's College in Baltimore, Maryland. In addition, he coached the school's baseball team, which won national championships in 1915 and 1916. At the outset of the war, many of the players entered the Armed Services and the team was disbanded. Soon after, the college became a high school.

The fact that "the Mount" won national championships two years in a row is not of earth-shaking importance. However, the success of Brother Gilbert's teams assume a different significance when it is pointed out that the squad was comprised of only 12 men, and they had to travel from city to city on each of six consecutive days. Obviously, with a squad of twelve, several of them had to be multi-position men. At least one had to be a backup catcher.

Tourney teams they played included: Villanova, Seton Hall, NYU, Boston College, Fordham and St. John's. A total of twenty-nine games was played each year, with no Sunday contests. We didn't even play golf on Sundays in those days, and travel was by street car and train.

A summary of the precepts which motivated Brother Gilbert in his religious life can be found in the following poem, which he placed on his desk throughout his career as a Xaverian Brother:

OTHERS

Lord help me to live from day to day
    In such a self-forgetful way
Than even when I kneel to pray
    My prayer shall be for ... "OTHERS."

Help me in all the work I do
    Ever to be sincerely and true
And I know that all I do for YOU
    Must need be done for ... "OTHERS."

Let self be crucified and slain
    And buried deep; and all in vain
My efforts be to rise again
    Unless to live for ... "OTHERS."

And when my work on earth is done
    And my new work in Heaven begun
May I forget the crown I've won
    While thinking still of ... "OTHERS."

"OTHERS," Lord, yes "OTHERS!"
    Let this my motto be.
Help me to live for others
    That I may live for Thee.

— by MEIGS (first name unknown)

*   *   *

Although Brothers Matthias and Gilbert played major roles in the life of resident George Ruth — the strapping young lad, prone to temperamental outbursts in his early days and heavy hitting on the Big Yard as he grew older — it must be remembered that there were approximately 30 Xaverians at St. Mary's altogether. Several of these other Brothers played key roles in the task of supervising and training him during his impressionable years.

John T. Bannon was born in Monkwearmouth, England, in 1886 and was renamed as Brother Alban (frequently misspelled "Albin" by Ruth biographers). He became a superior athlete as he grew older, and he especially enjoyed the American national pastime. For 27 years at St. Mary's, he starred as a player (primarily a first baseman) and as a coach.

Matthias was the Brother in charge of all the boys' physical education; thus, he and Alban, the primary coach, established a league of the older and best boys. Each of these teams had a major-league nickname, and the level of play was of a higher quality, motivated by the Brothers. The popular version of how Ruth became a pitcher is that Matthias forced him to take the mound after catcher Ruth mocked his own team's pitcher who was taking a shellacking at the time. Ruth's pitching debut was a success, of course. But another version of events says that the regular St. Mary's Red Sox pitcher, Congo Kirby, was on the bench for reasons of discipline, and Ruth convinced Brother Alban to allow him to pitch one game. The result was better than one could hope for from a left-handed catcher!

Like most Xaverians, Alban enjoyed following the exploits of Ruth as they both grew older, and Alban was consulted frequently by Brother Gilbert as the latter worked on his Ruth stories. Tragically, Brother Alban developed diabetes later in life and suffered the amputation of both his legs at the knees to prevent the spread of gangrene. He spent the final 17 years of his life in close proximity to his bedroom due to this condition, a heavy blow to someone who was formerly a star athlete.

Brother Herman, born in Fort Sanders, Wyoming, as William Bahr, was another baseball athlete of equal magnitude with Brothers Alban and Matthias. Originally, he was a schoolboy from nearby Mount St. Joseph's who joined the Xaverian novitiate at age 16. The Brothers' Menology declares that "As a young teacher and well into middle age, he was the object of awesome wonder at recess time when he handled a baseball. One of his protégés was George Herman Ruth who became the home-run king."

The young and athletic Herman has been referred to as perhaps Ruth's closest pal among the Brothers. Herman was in charge of the boys in the yards during recreation time and was St. Mary's athletic director. He frequently engaged in baseball activities with the Babe, and he literally batted his way into Ruth's heart. It should be noted that George Herman Ruth selected his middle name out of deference to the Brother who mentored him when he was studying to receive the Catholic sacrament of Confirmation. (Although his father's middle name was Herman, Babe's birth certificate is silent as to Babe's middle name and his baptismal certificate announces his name merely as "George Ruth." However, the Confirmation Register of May 9, 1907, plainly lists his "Confirmation name" as Herman.) Ruth biographer H.G. Salsinger, a sportswriter, wrote, "Brother Herman was the real discoverer of Ruth. He taught him and supervised his development." (Coincidentally, Ruth was confirmed in the Chapel of St. Mary's by James Cardinal Gibbons; after St. Mary's closed in 1950, a new school on those grounds was established, and flourishes to this day, named Cardinal Gibbons High School.)

As Brother Herman grew older, he was stricken with arthritis and was hampered greatly, but he never lost his smile or friendly welcoming to others. He died in Baltimore in 1956 after celebrating his 60th year as a Xaverian.

Brother Paul's (Peter Scanlon) role in Ruth's development as a person cannot be understated. His 18-year tenure as superintendent of St. Mary's has already been discussed.

Paul was born in Lawrence, Massachusetts, in 1864 and entered the Xaverian order at age 21. He left St. Mary's in 1925 after being chosen the fourth American Provincial, a post which was long overdue him. In 1928, he was chosen the Supervisor General of the Brothers in Rome. During his time in that position, the Xaverians began a new missionary province in the Belgian Congo.

One story indicates how fond Ruth was of Brother Paul, and the influence that Paul had on him in later years. Legend has it that when he once hit a record-breaking homer for the Yankees, he dashed straight to the clubhouse after touching home plate and called Baltimore on the phone. Ruth immediately told Brother Paul all the details of his smash. And, later, when the Babe courted trouble, it is said that Brother Paul boarded a train to New York to give Ruth "a talking to," which worked wonders, of course.

Most importantly, it was Brother Paul who approved the signing of Babe's first contract and his "adoption" by Jack Dunn of the Orioles in 1914. Later, Paul was one of the chaperones for the St. Mary's band boys as they traveled the circuit with the Yankees in September 1920.

Brother Paul passed away in Old Point Comfort, Virginia, in 1950, after serving almost 65 years in the Congregation of the Brothers of St. Francis Xavier.

Brother Herman was strikingly handsome and a superior athlete in his youth. The Babe confided once to Brother Bruno that he took "Herman" as his confirmation name out of his respect and love for this Xaverian. Born in an army camp on an Indian reservation in Fort Sanders, Wyoming, in 1879, he could not find a record of his baptism at his Xaverian Diamond Jubilee (courtesy of Xaverian Brothers Heritage Collection).

Brother Albert, born Peter M. Griffies, has also been referred to as the "sports supervisor" at St. Mary's, where he spent 23 of his 54 years as a Xaverian Brother, beginning in 1910. Although not much is recorded about his relationship with Ruth, the Bambino must have towered over this tiny man who possessed "Christ-like kindness."

One aggressive athlete who influenced the Babe was Brother Felix, of

Wilmington, North Carolina, who was assigned to St. Mary's for three years, during which time he taught 78 boys from 6:45 to 9:20 A.M. and 5:50 to 7:30 P.M. His other assignment was to supervise the oldest and toughest boys in the shirt factory and "house" tailor shop. At the age of 30, he was horribly stricken with tuberculosis. While stationed at Newton Highlands, Massachusetts, in later years, he remained avidly interested in sports, and he insisted on being carried down to the playing fields by his colleagues. Brother Felix died at age 36, after writing an autobiography entitled *The Weed That Grows in God's Garden*.

*   *   *

The official seal or coat of arms of the Congregation of the Xaverian Brothers contains the Latin words "Concordia Res Parvae Crescunt" — "by harmony small things grow." The choice of this motto is appropriate as it relates to the Xaverian influence on young George Herman Ruth. He met, observed and knew all of these purposeful religious men who possessed a lifelong dedication to the ideals of their Congregation. Each Brother, in his own individual way and in unity of purpose with his colleagues, provided a source of inspiration for the emerging Babe.

CHAPTER ONE

Presenting Babe Ruth

INTRODUCTORY NOTE BY HARRY ROTHGERBER

It should be kept clearly in mind that the early 1900s provided a primitive frame of reference for the exploits of our hero in this tale, Babe Ruth. Only 19 years before his birth did our country celebrate the 100th birthday of its founding. If the republic could be given a human likeness then, it was a teenaged boy, feeling his oats, roaming the countryside in search of trouble and amusement.

Only 30 years prior to the Babe's birth did America's bloody, brutal Civil War cease, and, along with it, slavery as an institution. However, blacks were still brutalized, lynched and considered to be subhuman specimens by the majority of whites. The upper classes of women were treated romantically and with polite deference while the average working woman or working-class housewife struggled in pitiful conditions both at work and at home. No female, regardless of her "station" in life, had the right to vote. Jews, other minorities and anyone "different" fared little better.

The early 20th century was on the fringe of the transportation and technology eras, but the term "mass media," if used then, would only have referred to newspapers, dime-store novels and word-of-mouth. People were required to *read* and then think about what they read. It was a world without television or even talking motion pictures. Radio, airplanes, automobiles and silent films were in their infancy.

The concept of professional sports teams was also a relatively new one. Men were groomed or recruited to play baseball for their companies, churches, towns or cities. Prosperous men sponsored them, and as the wealth of the owners increased so did the quality of players, until baseball competition burst forth in the large cities.

Heroes of that era were most likely to be valorous soldiers or courageous politicians. However, as athletic competition in baseball grew between cities, so did the stature of the men who formed the team's starting nine. And for all of the idolatry which sprang up around established stars such as Christy Mathewson, Honus Wagner and Ty Cobb, the United States had never seen a true, living, breathing sports-cultural icon such as George Herman Ruth. He was a "first," a "one-and-only," a "natural" before Malamud considered writing about Roy Hobbs and Wonderboy.

The most wondrous thing about the Babe was his lack of pretense — please ignore the wags who say it was a lack of intelligence — and the fact that, in his stardom, he never grew out of his childhood. He was both a man's man *and* a boy's boy at the same time. In her remembrance of her father, Dorothy Ruth Pirone told of his enjoyment in listening to "Gangbusters," "The Shadow," "The Lone Ranger" and other favorites on his Philco radio. Furthermore, she commented, "The walls of his room were bare save for a plaque of St. Theresa, which was draped with two sets of rosary beads, given to him by the brothers of St. Mary's Industrial School for Boys, where he spent the better part of his youth." But it wasn't the better part, is was the *best* part of his childhood. And what boy's mother couldn't forgive the wild transgressions of the marvelous player called the "Bambino" and "The Big Baboon," when she heard about those homemade rosary beads on the wall!

Brother Gilbert's description of Babe as a "legend" is at once accurate and understated. It took a man larger than life to tap Queen Wilhelmina of the Netherlands on the shoulder and say, "Hiya, Queenie," and to greet President Calvin Coolidge on a sweltering afternoon by declaring, "Hot as hell, ain't it, Prez?" And don't forget the countless unpublicized side trips Ruth made to orphanages, hospitals and homes for the less fortunate children. With each visit he reclaimed his past and he reaffirmed his future: to be the best baseball player of all time.

And all of this began with the astounding salary of $600 for his first year! In that era, no multi-millionaire athletes graced the diamond or gridiron, and basketball was just beginning to come into popularity. The inherent "fun" of baseball had not been overcome by the business aspects and media domination that is often prevalent

Opposite: A Xaverian in his cassock supervises this St. Mary's game from a position on the first base line. This has to be a pre-fire photo, since no grandstands existed after 1919. The boys at St. Mary's were "baseball-crazy," and they played year-round, weather permitting (courtesy of Xaverian Brothers Heritage Collection).

George Ruth is in the middle of his St. Mary's teammates in a photo taken around 1912. The young man in the upper left has consistently been identified as Fritz Maisel, born in 1889 and a future major leaguer of some note, but his age at the time of this photograph would suggest this identification is incorrect. Maisel was a Yankee infielder from 1913 to 1917 and led the American League in stolen bases with 74 (a Yankee best for 71 years) in 1914. Fritz Maisel's brother George, born in 1892, played four seasons from 1913 to 1922 with three professional clubs. William "Chuck" Wortman was another St. Mary's alumnus who played in the "bigs," aiding the Cubs from 1916 to 1918, including one World Series. *Front row* (*left to right*): Sid Owens, Dizzy Tate. *Center row:* Jack Machen, Babe Ruth, Bru Bock. *Back row:* Fritz Maisel[?], Ben Romans, Cocky Nitch (courtesy of National Baseball Hall of Fame).

today. In plain words, players often performed for the sheer joy of doing so, and they considered themselves lucky to be paid. The reserve clause in the player contracts enabled the club owners to collectively control their athletes. Although fatally flawed, this system did foster stability in team rosters from year-to-year, thereby allowing fan loyalty to develop for individual players and for the hometown team. America's love affair with baseball was in full bloom by Ruth's era.

The opening pages of Brother Gilbert's memoirs leave no room for doubt as to whose side he is on! He will not be an apologist for Ruth, although he does recognize the humanity that Babe displayed in his meanderings into lust, gluttony and licentiousness.

Inherent in each line that Brother Gilbert writes is the argument that the Babe is certainly the most remarkable player of all time, the most superb batsman, an almost unparalleled pitcher and the player with the greatest impact on the game itself. The reasons for those conclusions are multitudinous and will be explored in later chapters.

The measure of a professional athlete is often how he is described by his contemporaries on the playing field. What did Ruth's friends and foes observe about him? Here is a sampling:

The Babe was always friendly, a real nice guy who'd go out of his way anytime to do you a favor. [Jimmy Austin, third baseman, Highlanders, Browns, 1909–1929.]

You know, I saw it all happen, from beginning to end. But sometimes I still can't believe what I saw: this nineteen-year-old kid, crude, poorly educated, only lightly brushed by the social veneer we call civilization, gradually transformed into the idol of American youth and the symbol of baseball the world over — a man loved by more people and with an intensity of feeling that perhaps has never been equaled before or since. I saw a man transformed from a human being into something pretty close to a god. [Harry Hooper, outfielder, Red Sox, White Sox 1909–1925. Hall of Fame.]

Ruth was great too, but he was different. Totally different — easygoing, friendly. There was only one Babe Ruth. He went on the ball field like he was playing in a cow pasture, with cows for an audience. He never knew what fear or nervousness was. He played by instinct, sheer instinct. He wasn't smart, he didn't have any education, but he never made a wrong move on a baseball field.

One of the greatest pitchers of all time, and then he became a great judge of a fly ball, never threw to the wrong base when he was playing the outfield, terrific arm, good base runner, could hit the ball twice as far as any other human being. He was like a damn animal. He had that instinct. They know when it's going to rain, things like that. Nature, that was Ruth!" [Rube Bressler, pitcher, A's , Reds, 1914–1920.]

Babe Ruth could hit a ball so hard, and so far, that it was sometimes hard to believe your eyes. We used to absolutely marvel at his hits. Tremendous wallops. You can't imagine the balls he hit. And before that he was a great pitcher, too. Really great.

My God, if he was playing today! Nowadays they hit about 1,500 home runs a season in the American League. If Babe was good relative to everyone else today, like he used to be, he'd hit *over* 200 homers a season. That'll give an idea of how the big fellow dominated baseball back then. Take Mantle, Mays, Killebrew and anybody else you want to name today, and *add them all up*, and they still won't match Ruth's home runs relative to the rest of the league! [Sam Jones, pitcher, Indians, Red Sox, Yankees, Browns, Nationals, White Sox, 1914–1935.]

His next to last game he played was against us. We were playin' Pittsburgh. He didn't play the whole game, either. He got three home runs and played to the eighth inning, I think. Two of 'em were hit really hard. The old boy must've been something to see 'cause when I saw him, he was through and he still hit three home runs. [Gus Suhr, first baseman, Pirates, Phillies, 1930–1940.]

I loved baseball. Babe Ruth was one of my idols. That's why I got such a thrill catching against him about two weeks after I got out of college. [Gene Desautels, catcher, Tigers, Red Sox, Indians, A's, 1930–1946.]

About anything you say about Babe Ruth is true. He was a lone wolf, I would say, but a very nice man. He was a gentleman, but everybody knows that his morals were terrible and he drank a lot, which you couldn't stop him. A guy performs and hits all the home runs, you can't stop him. [Tot Pressnell, pitcher, Dodgers, Cubs, 1938–1942.]

And finally, to counterbalance the saintly opinions above:

An amazingly graceful fellow for one so huge. After his death, the writers were calling him the greatest ballplayer of all time, but these people never saw him play, or me. It is true that no one ever hit the ball harder, but he was not the greatest. In the 1930's when the idea for the Hall of Fame came up, the voters had seen us play. Both he and I had been retired for only a short while and I received more votes, more than Ruth or anyone. They saw me play and they agreed I was better. [Ty Cobb, outfielder, Tigers, A's, 1905–1928. Hall of Fame.]

Somebody wanted to know once how many times Mickey Mantle, Billy Martin, and I got fined. All I could think of to answer was, more times than Babe Ruth. [Whitey Ford, pitcher, Yankees, 1950–1967. Hall of Fame.]

In addition to being a "natural," endowed with physical attributes and abilities "far beyond those of mortal men," the Babe's appearance was indicative of superb timing. What decade other than the Roaring Twenties could have given rise to this legend! Ford Frick once said of Ruth, "He was the right man, in the right place, at the right time."

As this opening commentary comes to a close, and you prepare to begin your journey with Brother Gilbert and his stylistic prose, let us ponder the words of a *fictional* Ruth, created by C. Brooke Rothwell in his essay entitled "The Never-Before-Collected Works of Babe Ruth," as it appeared in *The Best of Spitball, The Literary Baseball Magazine*. Comments the fictional Ruth:

> Somebody asked me when I was real young what I wanted to be when I grew up. I was so struck by the idea that I instantly put it out of my head. I think because I never wanted to do anything right 'cept play ball. I mean I never thought of growing up in the sense that I always wanted to feel the same way I always remembered feeling. Lou was quoted as being "the luckiest guy on earth." Maybe he hung out with me too much cause I consider myself to be the most absurdly fortunate guy to have slid into the 20th century safe.

*   *   *

FROM THE MEMOIRS OF BROTHER GILBERT

A Legend for the American Boy

There are many teen aged boys in the United States who cannot tell you what office Harry Truman holds. There were those during World War I who would flunk the question: Who is President? Indeed there are those right now who, questioned at a remote distance from the place in point, might conjecture that Long Island Sound is an explosion; or that Lincoln, Nebraska is either a hideous malady or an Indian named after our Civil War President; that Hollywood is a yule log; that the Cunard Line, a rope; New Orleans' levee, a city tax. But since 1919, there has not been an inhabitant of the United States and the Pacific Archipelagoes, including habitual truants, but could authoritatively harangue in his own peculiar vernacular the record of the achievements in baseball of one George Herman "Babe" Ruth.

The lads do not know — nor do they care — whether Ruth came from Eden by way of Sweden, or from Bavaria by way of Batavia. To many of Babe's ardent admirers, such knowledge is inconsequential. As far as they are concerned, those places are evidently in the Texas League, where, the lads surmise, all the players are obliged to hit hump-back liners. Anyhow they argue that geography is of no use to prospective left fielders; and, if it is necessary, they feel that they'll learn it later through the windows of

Pullman cars. All young athletes approach the study of geography in an attitude of defense. In the first place, they feel that the book is too ungainly to carry home; and that confirms their original suspicion that geography is obviously the invention of school masters, whose sole ambition is to extract fun from the life of school boys — to prolong their stay in the drill room of the dental clinic.

Even students of ancient history have felt a sickening feeling of lassitude at the mention of such names as Aristides and Themistocles. Why bother with them? They had never walked up to the plate in a World's Series with St. Louis, exchanged defiant glances with the pitcher, taken a toe hold, and blasted the speeding pellet into an unexplored county in Missouri. Sophocles had never faced Walter Johnson or Lefty Grove in a clutch; two on, two out, two runs behind in the ninth inning. Sophocles had never seen that fast one sizzling up there, the size of a Carter's Little Liver Pill, with a whistle on it louder than a siren, only to have it explode into a curve that was designed to cross the plate. Indeed, he hadn't. But Babe Ruth had. The Babe had met that exploding curve with the mighty swish of his timber, flush on the label, and then saw it disappear beyond yonder barrier to the joy and the tumultuous acclaim of 70,000 hoarse throats that continued the mighty roar until their adenoids were sunburnt.

Were American boys offered the choice of being the equal of Plato in the Academy, Cicero in the Senate or Babe Ruth in baseball, the decision would be spontaneously and sonorously snapped in favor of Babe Ruth in baseball. Nor am I certain that the youngsters could resist casting a cynical leer at the one who, to them, had the consummate effrontery to insult their idol with such a notoriously unfair comparison. In street corner vernacular, those fribbles had never made the big leagues, nor were their batting averages, or even their names in the record books. Piffle! And while their conclusions are unquestionably at polar distances with our convictions (and perchance their own), nevertheless, they often arrived at them because such conclusions definitely suited their tastes and had the universal sanction of kids who play ball. Babe Ruth, they knew, could pulverize that agate, and he had never heard of those fellows. Well, if he had heard of them, he, too, was perhaps irked at them for doing things that inspired men to write books about them. To alleviate an otherwise unpleasant situation, and perhaps massage their strained consciences with balm, Babe Ruth was in town with the Yanks. Oh, boy!

Here was visual education, real, live, vital learning — the kind that teacher so zealously commended yesterday — served with a thunderous thump. Here was a spectacle devoutly to be desired; an afternoon at a ball game in which Babe Ruth participated — no inhibitions, just a succession of cheers and thrills, with the safety valve wide open. Nor could one in sound mind ignore the important truth that the social prestige of one who had seen Babe Ruth would be given a more-than-negligible thrust with the lads who played on the back lot. Certain it is that he, himself, would now be able to bat with authority. While demonstrating Ruth's stance and swing, he'd be the cynosure of his pop-eyed teammates. Such familiarity with the technique of the Babe might qualify him for the captaincy of the Budding Violets.

And yet, withal, there was a boding of compunction in the astonishment and delight with which Tommy hoped to be ravished. Daddy might discover that Tommy appropriated a holiday to himself. That would be bad; unfair to organized fun. Such a contingency was not included in the plans of Tommy's post-game jollity. It suggested the warrantable suspicion that Daddy would require Tommy to expose the sacred precincts of his anatomy to papa's irate glare, while papa applied the family ferule with vim, vigor, vitality and heinous accuracy to cheeks that never had been blessed with a toothache. Such uninvited exercise on papa's part would dull Tommy's urge, for several days, to sit on hard bleacher seats.

But there was a chance — and what American lad is without optimism — that Daddy might miss the teacher's phone call concerning his absence. Huh, daddy himself often got a feeling of lonesomeness when Babe Ruth was in town — a lonesomeness that he mistook for sickness and oppressiveness that approached mental and physical stagnation — all caused by prolonged confinement. Obviously, the restorative to normalcy was fresh air and sun light at the ball park. If Daddy were at the ball park, the main artery of information, deleterious to Tommy's interest, would be closed. As Tommy appraised the merits of his chances, the odds were better than even in his favor. 'Twas worth the risk to see Babe Ruth swing from his heels.

About two years ago, Max Kase and Sam Cohen, two professional sports writers, came to visit me. Mr. Kase had decided to write a life of Babe Ruth, and he was desirous of getting some first hand information anent the Babe's school days. During the course of our rather pleasant afternoon's conversation, Mr. Kase remarked that the impulse to write the biography was sponsored by the universal welcome accorded the Babe on a recent trip that the two of them had made to Camp Dix. Mr. Kase had ushered, during World War II, all the first magnitude luminaries of the theatrical and movie world to the same camp, only to have them receive a decidedly tepid greeting. Whole clusters of top flight screen stars, according to Mr. Kase, carried only sufficient appeal to fill one half the spacious auditorium at Dix. But when the camp bulletin bruited the coming of Babe Ruth, although he had been out of baseball for ten years, the virile G.I.'s, the red-blood kids whose laboratory in life had been the corner lot, who grew up hanging cats over clothes lines, whose happy hunting grounds had been Yankee box scores, who delectated in prowess and who despised sham with the same intensity that they condemned the Pearl Harbor sneak, they honed their auditory nerves, and packed the place on the arrival of Ruth until one could not get a caraway seed with a trip hammer in that vast covered county. That was the tip off that Ruth is a man's man, even as he had been a ball-player's ball-player.

As I read history, I am often struck by the importance attached to tradition. Certain it is that coaches, before a big game, invariably respond to the impulse to tell their various teams about the heroic deeds of their alumni. Indeed, there is nothing that can so influence the young to dare nobly and to do bravely in ordeal like the contemplation of valor and tribulation of those who constitute an integral part of their own institution. To that end we relate to school children the intrepid reply that Commodore Jack Barry made when overtures were made to him for the surrender of the good ship Effingham, to wit, "There is not enough gold in all the realm of King George to buy a single hair of Jack Barry's head." Nor does the patriotism of the American boy suffer when he is informed that George Washington was offered a position of dignity and trust with handsome emolument if he would surrender the Continental Army, and the answer that he gave the next day flew blazing hot out of the mouths of his guns down on the field of Monmouth. Such examples of loyalty and courage fire youngsters to emulate in trying moments the valor of their ideals.

Athletic skill has given our boys courage, energy and the will to win; it came to them in dower from brave ancestors who had the courage to cross unknown seas, and then to wend their way into the trackless wilderness of the west to fix anew the outposts of civilization. They were great athletes indeed, and the heritages of their valor are kept alive by keeping our youth familiar with such traditions. Nor are the achievements of their leaders in competitive sports less inspiring.

Babe Ruth is an institution, an American institution, and it would be unfair to organized sports in these United States to willfully permit his memory and the inspiration of his courage to perish from the ideals of our American boys. Verily Babe Ruth is one of their heroes; his sympathy for children bears testimony to the beautiful truth that he has never outgrown their tastes. They have marked him as their very own. Well, he indulged in every popular sport indigenous to American life — Beano, Beating Red Lights, Duck on the Rock, Tying Tin Cans on Dog's Tails — in fact, he is adept at all these games, nor has his inveterate craving for hot dogs and ice cream, popular victuals with his cheering squads, minimized his popularity. It has merely accentuated their endorsement of Babe for a position of permanency in their alumni.

Yes, he belongs to the American boy. They paid for him in unashamed admiration and thunderous bursts of acclaim that amounted to adulation. 'Tis regrettable, to be sure, that the lads sometimes neglected family chores and other obligations — not out of contempt for authority, but rather out of an irresistible urge to see Babe Ruth play ball — even at the price of having a cudgel applied that same evening to the nadir anatomical periphery. And since he belongs to our young athletes, I intend to make this yarn a faithful narrative of the tastes that predominate the welter of his boyish activities as he mellowed into manhood. It will be written in a language intelligible to our youth, stripped of glamour and freed of all false dignities. There'll be no halo thrown around Ruth, nor do I intend gilding its outlines with diction that does not belong to the game, or to the man whom the boys love, George Herman "Babe" Ruth.

Ruth's life was without guile. It was a repudiation of those self-appointed members of the pre-sanctified, yet he endeared himself to a nation of men and boys who jeer pretense and who cheer sincerity. The American lad is something different, and so is Babe Ruth.

CHAPTER TWO

Last Days at St. Mary's

INTRODUCTORY NOTE BY HARRY ROTHGERBER

George Herman Ruth — raw, naive, crude, unsophisticated and only 19 years old — began his professional career with the Baltimore Orioles of the International League. Signed as a pitcher with a reputation for being a "very hard hitter," he had been "paroled" from St. Mary's Industrial School to begin his new career. Brother Paul retained custody over Ruth, who, as a ward of St. Mary's, officially remained under the guardianship of the Xaverians until age 21. Had Ruth failed, he would have returned to his job at the Baltimore institution's four-story shirt factory and to the "big yard" where the older and larger boys played top-quality amateur hardball.

How "Little George" Ruth came to the attention of the Baltimore Oriole's organizational genius Jack Dunn has been a matter of speculation and disagreement among Ruth biographers for many decades. Now the story is rooted in equal parts of myth, fact and legend, all revolving around Brother Gilbert.

The reader will recall how Joe Engel, the former major league pitcher and student at Mount St. Mary's in Emmittsburg, first saw Ruth in a freshman game. Engel soon after had a chance meeting with Dunn on the train to Washington and Baltimore, and he described a left-hander named "Ruth" from St. Mary's Industrial School who mowed the batters down and who beat the hell out of a bass drum. The year is uncertain, as is Dunn's reaction to this tidbit. Engel gives a compelling reminiscence which one is inclined to believe. After that incident, however, various stories have emerged about the events immediately preceding Ruth's signing.

One account has it that Brother Gilbert was mad at Brother Paul for the latter's refusal to "loan" Ruth to him for an upcoming "big game." In retaliation, Gilbert allegedly tipped Jack Dunn off so that St. Mary's would not have the big fellow's use either. Another report says that Brother Gilbert became aware that Dunn was on the trail of Brother's star pitcher Bill Morrisette. In order to keep Morrisette at Mount St. Joseph's, Gilbert tipped off Dunn about Ruth. One more scenario has Dunn "raiding" Brother Gilbert's college team's pitching staff to the extent that, rather than losing another lefty (Ford Meadows) to the Orioles, Brother Gilbert put Dunn on Ruth's trail.

All three stories are intriguing, fanciful accounts of what may have happened, but none should be taken very seriously, given the spiritual mission of the Xaverian Brothers and the sterling character traits possessed by Brother Gilbert. Deception and revenge surely play no part in the story of Ruth's signing. The Xaverians no doubt recognized the importance of matching a young lad with a job he could perform well, whether that be shirt-making or slugging a baseball. The Brothers at Mount St. Joseph's and St. Mary's Industrial School were close and friendly with each other. They helped each other in their more difficult tasks and they shared useful information. At some point, Brother Gilbert, a master judge of baseball talent in his own right, saw Ruth play, correctly assessed his unlimited potential and worked with Brothers Paul, Alban and Matthias to place him on a professional team. Naturally, the nearest and best known of the professional owners was Jack Dunn.

In *The Babe and I*, Babe's wife recalled, "Brother Gilbert told Dunn of Babe's remarkable skills. He surely also told his friend Dunn of Babe's almost as remarkable talent for misbehaving. But, like Brother Matthias…, Brother Gilbert told Dunn that the boy was decent beneath his waterfront exterior."

Although George had been a chronic truant who hated public school and who displayed incorrigible conduct to his parents, at St. Mary's he was one of the most popular among the approximately 900 boys there. In spite of (or because of) his size (6'2"), loud mouth and crude manners, he was a favorite of the younger boys ("minims"). Ruth allowed no bullying of small residents, spent his extra money on candy that he gave away to the orphan boys, and received Holy Communion at Mass several times each week. The Xaverian Brothers had provided him with a nurturing substitute family, and his "siblings," from their places in the refectories or dining halls, mourned his imminent departure.

One of the most interesting recollections of daily life at St. Mary's was penned in 1956 by Lou Leisman of Aberdeen, Maryland, entitled *I Was with Babe Ruth at St. Mary's*. Leisman spent six years with the Babe at the facility and was nicknamed "Fats" by him.

There were two recreational "yards" at St. Mary's: a "little yard" for those boys under 15 from dormitory #3, and a "big yard" for those over 15 years old from Dormitories #1 and #2. Ruth worked in the four-story shirt factory, where clothing was made to be sold eventually by an independent contractor. The laundry occupied the first floor, the "low City Tailor" shop the second, and the "high City Tailor" shop, where Babe made collars, the third.

Leisman recalls seeing a left-handed George Ruth perform behind the plate with a right-handed catcher's mitt by quickly switching gloves from one hand to the other and then firing the ball down to second base with his left hand. George was nicknamed "Niggerlips" due to his large and coarse facial features, which suggested an uncertain heritage. It was not a kindly sobriquet for the early 1900s. George's more famous nickname would not appear until 1914.

Once, shortly after he was transferred to the big yard, George was allowed to go to the St. James Home, located at High and Low streets in Baltimore. This placement could be described as a type of semi-independent living residence or a community-based group home. Boys who resided there were given the opportunity to earn money while they learned the ways of the world. George Ruth lasted there approximately two months before some neighborhood trouble with other boys necessitated his transfer back to St. Mary's, where he was placed in Dormitory #1. When he came back in his grey suit and black ball cap, hundreds of residents received him home with the chant, "Welcome Back, Niggerlips."

In what may have been a fanciful fabrication — Ruth always played fast and loose with the facts — he once told a Baltimore newspaper columnist that he could see better at the plate if he hadn't been hit in the eye with a brick during an altercation at St. Mary's. (This story was reported shortly after Ruth hit six homers in six at-bats in an exhibition series against his old Orioles team in Baltimore.)

At that time in baseball history, the Orioles with whom Ruth signed were not causing as big a stir in the Baltimore sports scene as their chief rivals from the Federal League, Ned Hanlon's Baltimore Terrapins. This third major league, which lasted for two full seasons, was consistently more popular with the fans and media in Baltimore than the minor league Orioles.

These Orioles whom "little" George was about to join were not the ancestors of the major league Orioles, currently ensconced in Oriole Park at Camden Yards and featuring Cal Ripken, Jr. The modern-day Baltimore club is the progeny of the hapless St. Louis Browns, who left that city at the end of the 1953 season for greener outfields and new fans in Memorial Stadium, where the team played until 1991.

The Xaverian Brothers maintained close supervision while the boys were instructed in a trade. Babe Ruth began his vocational tailoring work in the cutting department and worked his way up to the finishing department shown here. The Babe became an expert shirt maker who later astounded his wife when he used his experience and manual dexterity to make a perfect shirt collar. The ubiquitous Brother is present in the background (courtesy of Xaverian Brothers Heritage Collection).

However, minor league baseball in the early 1900s should not be discredited. Oftentimes, teams such as the double-A (then the highest minor league classification) Orioles were the focus of baseball excitement in their communities.

Indeed, professional baseball in Baltimore began in 1900 with the major league American Association's Orioles, succeeded by the National League's Orioles from 1892 to 1899 and the American League's Orioles from 1901 to 1902. The National League Orioles were guided by the superb managerial talents of Hall-of-Famer Ned Hanlon, a part-owner and later president of that club. Dropped from the league after the 1899 season, the Orioles were scheduled to join a new major-league-version of the American Association, but that project never got off the ground. After the 1902 season, Hanlon bought the Montreal team franchise and moved it to Baltimore, where it remained for 51 seasons as a member of the new International League.

Eventually, Hanlon employed a master baseball strategist named John Joseph "Jack" Dunn, born in Pennsylvania in 1872. Dunn was a versatile, aggressive and brainy baseball player who discovered that he was fond of Baltimore after playing there with the Orioles in 1901.

Finishing up eight years in the majors, he took over the reins of the Providence Clamdiggers in 1905 and won the International League crown in his first year! Hanlon hired him in 1907, Dunn won the IL pennant for Baltimore in 1908, and Dunn purchased the Orioles from Hanlon in 1909.

Although Dunn proved to be an outstanding judge of baseball talent who possessed considerable managerial abilities (he generally was able to finish in the league's first division), the Orioles were not destined to win another IL crown until 1919. Dunn's ability to sign outstanding athletes and prevent them from being stolen by major league teams until he was ready to sell them for astronomical prices led to a dynasty of seven consecutive pennants (1919–1925). Furthermore, Dunn's championship teams rivaled the major league clubs in quality. He had a penchant for playing (and defeating) big league teams in exhibition games. Such victories increased his club's popularity at home and increased attendance at future games. Clearly, it was no fool with whom Brother Gilbert dealt in 1914 when George Ruth's athletic talents became too big for St. Mary's. Brother was no doubt sure that Ruth had another "protector" in Dunn, someone who would cultivate the lad's talents, acclimate him into the "real" world and see that he was paid generously for performing well. Babe later recalled, "I'll never forget the day Brother Gilbert called me over and introduced me to Jack. I was flabbergasted."

Coincidentally, future baseball executive and Hall of Famer Ed Barrow, with Jack Dunn's support, was named league president in 1910, a post which he held for seven years. Barrow would later become "secretary" (general manager) of the New York Yankees during their glory years in the 1920s. But Barrow had also been there at the beginning of Ruth's career and fondly remembered him breaking in as a pitcher for the Orioles in 1914.

At the time of Ruth's departure from St. Mary's, the shadow of Federal League loomed large over professional baseball, especially in Baltimore. This league had its roots in the United States League (USL), which operated in eight Eastern cities as an "outlaw league" in 1912. This meant that its players were not attached to any other professional teams, and, as such, it was outside the official organized baseball establishment. In spite of heavy financial losses, the USL opened the 1913 season with seven teams and with "the Federal League" as its new name. Six teams finished that baseball season, and the owners soon resolved to expand to "major league" status in 1914.

The baseball war was on. The next two seasons, 1914 and 1915, when Ruth was in his professional infancy, would feature raids on players, broken contracts, lawsuits, team jumping, league jumping, high salaries and aggressive recruitment of players. When the 1914 season opened in the eight-team Federal League, four of its clubs were located in cities with major "organized baseball" teams, and two other teams were challenging minor "organized baseball" teams.

In Baltimore, the emergence of the Federal's Baltimore Terrapins under the expert guidance of that city's beloved Ned Hanlon meant that Jack Dunn had his hands full in his fight for baseball and business survival. The popularity of the Terrapins was no more evident than on Opening Day, less than two months after Ruth had signed with the Orioles. Hanlon's Terrapins drew a crowd of approximately 30,000 to Terrapin Park (capacity 15–16,000 estimated) while the Orioles with Ruth drew only 1,500 fans across the street in broken-down Orioles' Park. Although Dunn vowed to put a better team on the field than the Terrapins, his team's dwindling attendance (which culminated early in the season when the league-leading Orioles played one home game before only 150 fans) made it necessary to start selling his better players to recoup losses. Eventually, "Dunnie's" Oriole team finished in sixth place, while the "Baltfeds," as the Terrapins were also called, closed in third place, 15 games above .500. "Organized baseball" was certainly losing this "Great War" on the ballfields of Baltimore.

In his 1928 book, the Babe wrote, "...I think of that day, back in 1914, when I signed my first contract and Brother Gilbert gave me his first words of fatherly advice:

"'Playing baseball on the sand lots is one thing George' he said. 'And playing professional baseball in something else. The sand lot game is just boyish fun. You can start and stop as you please. Professional baseball is a business. It's a job for men.' Never were truer words spoken than those."

After leaving St. Mary's that Friday, George would spend the weekend at his father's residence, located over his saloon. Ruth would meet owner-manager Jack Dunn on Monday, and he would be placed in the care of big Ben Egan for the trip to Fayetteville, North Carolina's most inland port, on the Cape Fear River. (The rest of the team would follow later with Dunn.)

George and "Iggan" instantly liked each other. Both were big, brawling athletes, competitors filled with humor. Ruth's experiences and background at all-boy St Mary's translated well into the all-male world of baseball, and his statistics would eventually far surpass those of Egan, who hit .165 in 121 games for two major league teams in four seasons from 1908 to 1915.

* * *

From the Memoirs of Brother Gilbert

Departure for Training Camp

As mentioned before, Babe Ruth was signed to his first contract on the afternoon of February 22, 1914. Until the hour of his signing, Ruth had not the slightest inkling that the day of his departure was so near at hand.

At dinner on March 2nd, Brother Paul, superintendent of St. Mary's, a man whose gentleness and tender solicitude for the under-privileged admirably qualified him for the office, personally conducted George Ruth on a tour through the various dining rooms. It was what Ruth's buddies hoped would happen. He was bidding adieu to his brothers in affection, the pals of his childhood, and these are the brightest memories that cluster about life. Many of these boys were orphans, and orphans feel much more keenly the loss of a friend than do those endowed with the luxuries of parental protection. His old cheering squads wished to release a chorus of approval in a final farewell to their idol. And George Ruth had known and loved, since his days in the Minims' Yard, the sympathy and the applause of those kids. Ruth had come up through the three yards. He had been a dust-hawk, a dish washer, and a dodger.

At the School, a dodger is not a member of the Brooklyn Team. A dodger is a waiter, who combines the speed and grace of an ice follies skater with the manual flippancy of an adept juggler. If the reader saw a team of dodgers at St. Mary's dashing between tables at meal time, he would verily appreciate the significance of the appellation.

Ruth would prefer being spared the ordeal of that farewell tour. Bear in mind that he was leaving the place that had been to him a school, a workshop, a playground and a home since he was eight years of age.

"I hate to say good bye to the fellahs," he half-sobbed, as he and Brother Paul walked out of the office.

"Oh, cheer up, George. The boys expect your coming, and they would forgive neither you nor me, if I let you go away without seeing them. Besides, the training trip will last only a month or two and you'll be back to see them soon. They will follow you through the papers, and your success will be their joy and inspiration. Don't let them down."

"Brother Paul, every time that I go to bat, I'll be thinking of the kids. I hope that I can do something to make them happy."

"You will, George."

"I'll do my darndest, Brother."

"And, by the way, my dear boy, you are taking with you the well-wishes of everyone here at the School, and of those who have gone before you. And that includes the Brothers too."

"Well, Brother Paul, I hope that they do not forget to say a prayer that I play good."

"You mean play well. Good is an adjective and well is an adverb in the sense employed."

"Brother Matthias taught me about that, but well don't make sense when I am hittin' good. Adjectives and adverbs always did get me mixed up. I always thought that I'd be a motorman or a fireman and adjectives don't help those fellahs. If I don't make good, may I come back to visit the boys?"

"You'll make good, my boy. Of that I am sure."

At that moment, Brother Paul threw open the door of the Minims' Refectory. The presence of the Superintendent was a signal for silence; the presence of Ruth always a signal for a deafening din, an overt contradiction of personalities. The dodgers slammed on the brakes, forks were suspended between plate and mouth. It was not necessary for the Prefect to tap the bell for silence. Silence struck with a thud.

As Ruth stood, head bowed, twiddling his thumbs, Brother Paul broke the ominous silence. His remarks were a twit to George, a mild hosing that he hoped would lift Ruth from the doldrums.

"Boys, this afternoon George Ruth will leave us to go in training with the Baltimore Orioles at Fayetteville, North Carolina. This great timid child" — "babe" would have been more apt — "is fearful that he cannot cope with the superior skill of the professional athletes. It is his wish that you say a prayer for his success. Will you do that for him?" The thunderous affirmatives that followed — yes Brother, you betcher, I'll say so — fairly rattled the rafters of the whole plant. These youngsters loved Ruth. And why not? Had not he pilfered candy to treat them, thereby hazarding a chance of being thrown off the baseball team for the season? Hadn't Ruth asked George Lee, Assistant Baker and ball player extraordinary, to bring down a pan of rolls, dressed with molasses, every afternoon for distribution in the Minims' Yard? When they played outside teams, it was this same big, good-natured Bambino who knocked the ball over the center field fence and sent them up to supper laughing and shouting. Who'd take the blame now for the lifted shirts that were used to make tails for their kites? Memories quickly flooded their young minds and when Brother Paul, twitting again asked: "After he returns to Baltimore, as a full-fledged member of the Orioles, and he comes out to visit us, shall we let him in?"

A pathetic note was sounded in response when one badly deformed child, who had been a special object of Ruth's affection, blurted in dolorous tones, "Don't let him go." Sensing the impending gloom, Brother Paul in a reassuring conclusion said, "Boys, if ever George is out of employment, he can always return to the School, and I will provide him with permanent employment. We want men working here whom you children love." The tears of these children were far more eloquent in their silence than were all the oratorical eulogies that were thundered at Ruth from head tables during his luminous career.

Of necessity, Ruth continued to hang his head; his eyes were misty. As Brother Paul turned to the door, Ruth turned, too, blubbering as he did so: "Good bye, kids, I'll do my best for you. When I am going up to bat, I'll be thinking of you."

The shouts in the first refectory prepared the lads in the second one for his advent. As he and Brother Paul entered, a voluminous ovation greeted them.

Brother Paul spoke of the approaching departure of Ruth, and "Boots" Murray shouted "When he goes to bat hereafter, we won't have to stop our ball games in the second yard to keep from being killed."

"Piggy" Kearns yelled, "Hit 'em out in front, Old Pig Iron."

Both remarks helped Ruth relax, and he turned loose a broad grin.

"Piggy" Kearns, quite a pitcher himself, contributed further to Ruth's comfort by tossing in a loud aside: "It's tough to see that chum go, but it's nice to know that I won't have to pitch to him anymore. Lefty Ruth is one corner sewer on judging curved balls." Kearns' mispronunciation of connoisseur was not an inadvertence. He had his vocal sights trained on the right word, but the target jumped as he fired. That's a charitable explanation.

Someone called on Ruth for a speech. For the first time he raised his eyes, surveyed his field of co-workers and athletic competitors and gurgled: "Fellahs, you're all great pals; but I am really too full of utterance."

"Too full" suggested only one condition to Jack Ellis, who promptly opened his pipes: "So they feed you good when you're leaving, huh? Well, you shouldn't have eaten so much." No notice was taken of Jack Ellis, and the lads rose as a unit to give George Ruth a vigorous round of applause.

He was now on the way to his own refectory, where his own gang was preparing to turn on the heat, but not the tears. Knowing that Lefty Ruth could take it, his friends gloried in the privilege of needling him. By unanimous consent "Keyhole" Smith was appointed to make the farewell remarks. "Keyhole" was long on courage; but short, pathetically short, on oratory.

Through the "Keyhole" came: "Lefty, I ain't much of a speecher, but we all sure do wish you 'Good Luck'."

"What are you much of?" from one of the lads.

"I am much of a wrestler," from the "Keyhole."

"Then wrestle him."

"No; it's the first time that I ever saw him all dressed up, and wearing a necktie. I sure don't aim to spoil those nice fixins. Ruth is too good a guy. Anyhow, when I bit him last week, he said that he would never wrestle me again only on Fridays and Fast Days."

"Hey, Ruth," enquired "Lefty" McDonald, "Did the Brothers have to throw you to put that tie on you?"

"Pretty Face" Schraffer, automotive speed merchant and Beau Brummel, on his own account, who had never before seen George arranged in such gala splendor, ventured the warning: "Don't get all fouled up in this new error (era) of romances or you'll come back with a Frau and two hearts that beat the rent."

"That's right" chirped the taciturn Roussey, "They make good money in baseball, but they don't always make enough of it."

"Congo" Kirby looked on in silent awe, and Brother Alban, who recounted for me these various commentaries, called on "Congo" for a speech. He and Ruth were long-time buddies.

"Lefty, you're a great fellow and a corker ball player. Just don't choke up down there. Keep your Adam's apple out of your mouth and you will never bite the worm. I hate like _____ well, I'll miss you, but I'm pullin for you to make good."

As a chorus of clamors for a speech from Ruth followed, he made his first public address in that deep barrel-tone voice that has always been an organic part of him: "Fellahs, you're one bunch of swell guys. We've had lotsa fun together, and we've had lotsa tough battles together, and there isn't one squawker or one mean guy in the whole bunch of you. Now that I am leaving, I want to tell you fellahs that the big thing I learned from all of you is to play fair in everything that I do, and to try to be the good guy that you fellahs and the Brothers taught me to be. I am no goody-goody myself, but I sure do intend to make good, so that a lot of you swell fellahs will get the same chance that I am getting. You deserve it, too, because a lot of you are better ball players than I am. Gee, I sure do wish that some of you fellahs were going with me, then I know that I would make good. And, hey, when I come back to Baltimore, I'll come right out to the School and tell ya all about it. S'long, fellahs!"

Be it to the eternal credit of George H. Ruth that the first post card that he sent to the writer contained a deep-seated longing to help his friends. Forgetful of any gratitude to me, and equally forgetful of himself, he merely wrote: "Dear Brother: There are about six more fellows at the School that can make this club. Try to help them. Yours truly, Geo. Ruth."

Characteristic of Ruth's transparent simplicity was his letter, at the same time to Brother Alban, the man who first called my attention to the potentialities of Ruth. Terse as usual, Ruth never had much to say and less to write.

"Dear Brother Alban:

I am making good in everything that they have down here — basketball, baseball and running. Get Bro. Gilbert to send down some more boys from the School. Yours truly, Geo. Ruth." (On rainy days, the squad played a little basketball in the Armory, and the running represents the spring tests held at the park.)

The point is that Ruth knew that Brother Alban would rejoice in whatever successes Ruth had. The first sentence represents his boyish glee at giving happiness to another. That sentence served as a safety valve to the boyish jubilation within him. 'Twas the equivalent of his writing, "The mercury of my happiness is running high." But it was Ruth's natural way. As a growing kid, he got a thrill out of the simplest of joys. Observe, too, that in the ecstasy of his own achievement, he was not unmindful of those who desired a chance to share his opportunities. A desire to do for others is the truest barometric reading of genuine education. The selfish, even though blessed with an arabesque of learning, have never known the thrill of such kindly impulses. Ruth felt that joy often.

Brother Paul took the big boy down town and attired him in parade pomp. With a huge new suitcase, bursting at the seams, Ruth was equipped in duplicates and triplicates from toes to nose. He had everything, save the tall hat and the sash, while his embarrassment provided the Technicolor.

"Brother Paul, we forgot to get a baseball suit. I would not wish to play in these clothes," said Ruth.

"The Orioles will furnish your uniform. They have their own uniforms, George."

"Where will I live when I am down there?"

"The Orioles will live at Hotel Fayetteville; your meals will be paid for by the club. That reminds me that I have some money for you. During the training season, you will not be paid. After the season opens, your salary begins."

"How about bats and balls, Brother Paul? Do the players make 'em like we did at the School? I can sew 'em good."

"My boy, your chief duty will be to do as you are told. Keep your ears open and your mouth shut."

"Yes, Brother."

George was about to have his first train ride. Later he confessed that on reaching the waiting room of the Union Station in Baltimore, he wondered how they were going to board a train in there. At Union Station, the trains run underground.

Jack Dunn was present, merely to see the battery men off. To keep the contentious Federal Leaguers away from his infielders and outfielders prompted him to abide their arrival in town. As he scanned the flexible streamlined Ruth, Dunnie's face beamed radiantly. He even chewed his gum faster, always a tip that his eyes were ready to laugh at what he beheld.

"Hello, Brother," greeted Dunnie. "This kid looks good." Still making a mental appraisal of Ruth, he grinned: "Boy, I know that I am going to like you. Work out slowly until I get there; I don't want you to have a sore arm when I reach camp."

"I won't, Mr. Dunn. Since I signed with you, I have played eight games."

"You did what?"

"Yes, Mr. Dunn, I played eight games."

"What position did you play?"

"I pitched two full games. I caught two games, played shortstop two games, one game at first base. In the other game, I played the whole nine positions, one inning at each position. Brother Matthias told me to do that so that I would be ready for any place that you want me to play. Our club is leading the league."

"And your arm is not sore?"

"No sir, Mr. Dunn. We had some snow this winter and I was Commander of Fort McHenry in the snowball fights. My arm doesn't get sore."

"Brother, one thing about this mustang: he is not an alibi artist. Most beginners sob a swan song; but this kid, like frog legs, is ready to go. By the way, I had a feed of frog legs in Ganzhorn's last week; they give that Friday-law an awful licking."

Dunnie paged Ben Egan, the arch-comedian and first string catcher.

"Ben, this is George Ruth, and I like him. Don't you put a saddle on him and ride him to Fayetteville."

"Gee, Dunnie, that's a tough prescription. I can see that he is a nice boy; he looks like promising entertainment material. George, do you sleep well on trains?"

"I never been on one, Mr. Iggan."

"Dunnie, this boy is as polite as a pickpocket. He is a grand boy and a big boy. Shall I give him the first watch to keep that thieving porter away from the boys' shoes? He is strong and well knit."

"Now let this boy alone; he's my boy."

"Then that goes. Nice meeting you. George; I'll whisper some advice to you on the train."

Egan had an uncanny genius for tantalizing youngsters, for concocting the wildest and weirdest schemes that would enmesh them in difficulties, and for placing quicksand on all passages of escape. Like Ruth, Egan is a big, powerful good-natured fellow and while he willingly takes a joke on himself, it has become notorious that he has a horrible way of getting even. No trick, however trite, was spared. Some of the rookies were early in the hammock; others were appointed to keep watch on the Pullman Porter during the night to frustrate any attempt to steal the players' shoes, and when he finally did take them — for the purpose of polishing — they sonorously gave the alarm; others had as assignment to hold a watch, and call off the hours to prevent their riding past their destination. Egan played no favorites. He treated 'em all alike — like Rubes. Being in charge of the rookies was grilled quail on buttered toast to Egan. Even so, he melted with affection for the real follow-through fellows like George Ruth who obeyed his preposterous orders with modest puerile simplicity. For twelve years, George Ruth had learned to respect authority. Egan and the callused veterans, observing Ruth's willingness to comply, learned to like and admire him. Long before the athletes donned their uniforms for the first time in the spring of 1914, George Ruth was firmly entrenched in the affection of the entire party.

CHAPTER THREE

Life Outside St. Mary's

INTRODUCTORY NOTE BY HARRY ROTHGERBER

Thus was "little" George Ruth plucked out of St. Mary's, his periodic home for 12 years, and placed in the care, custody and control of baseball master Jack "Dunnie" Dunn and veteran Arthur "Ben" Egan, the Orioles' catcher and leader on the field.

Egan was born in 1883 in Augusta, New York, and had already served brief stints in the American League for the Philadelphia A's by the time he met Ruth. Sportswriter Lee Allen quoted Egan as remembering, "It would be pleasant to say that I developed Ruth as a pitcher, but that would be hogwash. Babe knew how to pitch the first day I saw him. I didn't have to tell him anything. He knew how to hold runners on base, and he knew how to work on the hitters, so I'd say he was a pretty good pitcher — on his own."

There was some brief dissension in that training camp at Fayetteville when Egan and coach Sam Steinman had a difference of opinion over indoor workouts. Egan recalled that owner Dunn had given control of the Orioles to Egan, and the catcher was quick to summon the owner to North Carolina to straighten things out.

Both the horse and bicycle incidents recalled by Brother Gilbert were reported to Dunn by Egan, who observed that "Ruth wasn't a bad kid, just wild."

Ruth was lucky to have a mentor and friend such as "Iggan" early in his career. Ben was a mainstay on some outstanding Oriole teams from 1910 to 1921, including the first International League team to win 100 games (1919). The affable Egan's name was forever linked with Ruth's from that training camp and from his later sale to the Red Sox, in which Egan was also included.

Ben Egan was soon traded by Boston and he played for the

Cleveland Indians in 1914–15. After his playing career ended, he became a coach with the White Sox under Eddie Collins and with Washington under Bucky Harris, both Hall of Famers. After that, Egan managed in the minor leagues for many years up to the early 1940s.

Ruth later stated, "Egan was my special friend. In my day you'd get a swift kick sooner than you'd get a word of encouragement. But even if Egan played jokes and tricks on me he took my part if other players went too far, and as he did most of my catching he gave me my first signs and a lot of good pointers."

Although teammates only for a few months with the Orioles, Egan inextricably became part of the Ruthian legend. When the catcher died in Sherrill, New York, 54 years later, the nearby *Utica Daily Press* announced his passing with the headline, "Ben Egan, 84, Dies; Babe Ruth's Catcher."

Having left the highly restrictive confines of St. Mary's Industrial School, and no longer under the watchful eyes of the Xaverian Brothers, George Ruth began to carve out his legendary status in American sports and popular culture.

Anecdotes about Ruth's appetite are not entirely exaggerated. In 1914, Ruth was a growing boy whose previous eating habits had been controlled by an institutional schedule. As a professional ballplayer, his appetite for food and drink became prodigious. Consuming six hot dogs and six soda pops as a mid-afternoon snack was not unusual for Ruth. Later, beer would become his beverage of choice with large repasts. In this way, Ruth was not unlike Fatty Arbuckle, the hugely rotund silent film superstar comedian of that era, who is referred to in this chapter. (As Babe grew older, these indulgences would be paid for dearly during lengthy and grueling spring workouts down south before spring training.)

In his autobiography, Ruth recalled that he was unable to believe when he first heard that the Orioles paid for the players' meals: "I was on my third stack of wheat cakes and third order of ham, and hadn't even come up for air, when I realized that some of the other fellows were watching me. I looked at them silently and kept chewing." Sportswriter Roger Pippen said, "I wouldn't have believed it if I hadn't seen it."

"Ruthian excess" surely describes the reports of the habits of the big fellow: A breakfast consisting of an 18-egg omelet, three huge slices of ham and copious amounts of toast and coffee; a dinner of an entire capon, potatoes, vegetables, beans, bread, pie and ice cream; a whole custard pie for dessert; a midnight snack of six club sandwiches, a platter of pigs knuckles and a pitcher of beer; and, an after-midnight snack of six ham-and-cheese sandwiches and six sodas. Other "snacks" consisted of a two-pound steak with a quart of chili sauce as flavoring, or hot dogs, peanuts and ice cream during an actual game. Over the years, nicotine became a constant companion, in the form of chewing tobacco, cigarettes, cigars, pipe tobacco and snuff, in enormous quantity. Belching and farting at will also appeared to be popular habits with the Babe.

Daughter Dorothy remembered, "One time my father came down with another serious stomach ache after eating eight or nine hot dogs, a few bags of peanuts and an apple, washing it all down with five sodas. As he finished chugging down a pint of bicarbonate of soda, he sheepishly explained, 'I'm sure it was that apple which upset my stomach.'"

Newspapermen referred kindly to Ruth's eating habits as "careless" or "indiscreet." In 1925, they called the serious ailment which hospitalized Ruth "the stomach ache heard 'round the world," indicating that the diagnosis was a combination of influenza and indigestion from overeating. (Later writers have suggested that the actual culprit may have been a sexually-transmitted disease!)

The Babe's ghostwriters were good to him in their accounts of his eating habits. In an amusing explanation of his conditioning and training, Ruth, in his second autobiography, tells of a 1926 meeting with Dr. H. Austin Cossitt, a specialist on glands and the digestive tract: "He quickly learned I had collected a fine series of germ life in my intestines. I think a lot of it contributed to my poor play and rotten disposition the year before. Dr. Cossitt and his staff got rid of the germs. It was a job. In the course of moving around the country, eating tons of this and that, I had committed a kind of internal hari-kari."

Ford Frick is protective of Ruth to the point of hilarity in Babe's 1928 book, which has Ruth telling about a Yankee pitcher who ate himself out of the league, with the Babe concluding, "In avoiding excess weight the first thing to get right is the diet." He went on to say, "I used to have quite an appetite myself. I was cursed with an iron constitution. And I really mean cursed. For my constitution was so strong that I could commit those excesses of eating without apparent harm for several years. When I did begin to have trouble, I had it in bunches and job lots.... Eating, beyond a certain point, is a matter of habit. It isn't necessary, and it isn't healthful." While these warnings may have been suitable for the reading public, children and wannabe athletes at that time, the truth suffered upon their publication.

Bill (or Billie) Morrisette, who appears in the Buzzards-Sparrows game as a right-fielder for the losing team, was a Baltimore boy who played a significant role in an earlier Ruthian episode of note. That first "Big Game" of George's career occurred at the end of the 1913 season.

Morrisette pitched for Mount St. Joseph's, where Brother Gilbert was athletic director and coach. This right-handed pitcher, who specialized in a then-legal spitball, had an outstanding season, barely missing several no-hitters and racking up many strikeouts. In similar fashion, Ruth had excelled at St. Mary's. Thus, a September game matching the two Xaverian schools was arranged, to be played on St. Mary's home field.

The game had been scheduled a month in advance, and excitement was running high at St. Mary's. However, approximately ten days after the game was announced, Ruth ran away from the school. The boys were shocked and saddened. Lou Leisman said, "Probably the strain he was going through in waiting for the game to be played caused him to become emotionally upset." The school probation officer and watchman searched for Ruth in Baltimore. Finally, the boys were told that Ruth had voluntarily returned. It is uncertain if he came back on his own accord, but he did face punishment for his actions. For five days, George was unable to take part in recreational activities, and he was made to stand on the road separating the big yard and little yard. When the five days were over, Brother Matthias allowed Ruth to resume practicing with the team. Elation and anticipation were restored to the St. Mary's boys.

The game was played in the big yard, which was gaily decorated with flags and bunting. A huge crowd, including most of the Brothers, was on hand. It appears that, for some reason unknown, Brother Gilbert probably missed the game, and he doesn't mention it in any of his memoirs or reminiscences. Leisman says that Jack Dunn was present at this game, but that is very doubtful.

In any event, Ruth was up to the occasion, striking out 14 batters in a six-or-eight-to-nothing shutout of Morrisette's team. Little George had proven himself in leading St. Mary's to the biggest victory in their school's athletic history. And, of course, Dunn later signed both of these dueling pitchers during the winter of 1913-1914.

Morrisette went on to play very briefly with the Phillies and Tigers on three occasions from 1915 to 1920. Poor historian as he was, Ruth does not mention Billie's name in his autobiographies.

Baseball at that time was dull in many respects. The emphasis was on "brainy" managers such as the Giant's John McGraw, who coaxed his players' crude gloves, monstrous bats, sacrifices, bunts and steals into a 1-0 victory. Due to dead and doctored baseballs and an abundance of "spitballers," home runs were not plentiful, and place hitters were generally prized over power hitters. The thought of actually measuring a home-run blast had only recently been considered.

Not a day goes by in the modern baseball era without mention of a stupendous circuit clout that measured over 450 feet after being crushed by McGwire, Sosa, Griffey, Belle, or Gonzalez (take your choice of them or two dozen others). Take note, though, that the original precedent-setter was the Babe. His daughter Dorothy Ruth Pirone proudly boasted, "Babe was not only hitting home runs more frequently than anyone in history, he was also hitting them farther and harder than anyone had ever thought possible. The home runs were hit so far and so high that some of them were literally hit clean out of sight. Because of Dad's awesome power, it became necessary to extend the foul lines, which normally ended at field level, all the way to the roof!" Indeed, this was not an exaggeration.

Pippen's measurement of Ruth's first homer in Fayetteville was allegedly conducted with the benefit of a handy, nearby tape measure; but, even if the Baltimore writer enlarged on the deed, it was still a colossal blast. Ruth himself said, "The ball cleared the right-field fence and landed in a cornfield beyond. I don't have to tell you what it did to me, inside, but the effect on Dunnie and the others was easy to see, too. They estimated that it had carried about 350 feet. I guess that doesn't sound like much in these days of the stitched golf ball ... [but] this was long before anybody heard of the lively ball, when a guy like Frank Baker could win the title of 'Home Run Baker' with eight to twelve home runs a season."

The Babe's lengthy homers opened the door to a new dimension of pleasure for fandom from the time he was a pitcher and a raw rookie until he was over-the-hill and near retirement. Those players who espoused the philosophy of Wee Willie Keeler — "Hit 'em where they ain't" — still had a place on the baseball stage, but not in the spotlight. The upcoming era faced by young Babe would see the ball being made "livelier" by the manufacturers, as well as the elimination of "trick" pitches such as the spitball, emery ball and various trick deliveries. This era belonged to the long-baller, of whom the prototype was Babe Ruth.

In 1935, 21 years after Ruth's cornfield clout, days before his retirement, he hit his last homer — number 714 — by jacking the ball over the rightfield grandstand and completely out of Forbes Field in Pittsburgh. He was the first person to do so. The hit was measured at 600 feet!

A New York Yankee teammate of Ruth's once remarked, "Babe Ruth wasn't born — he fell out of a tree." Well, that teammate should have seen the Babe in his first training camp!

Baltimore . International.
1914

By a quirk of fate, George Ruth began his journey to greatness in the small, sleepy town of Fayetteville, North Carolina. The Orioles were not a "farm" team, as we know them today, owned and operated in conjunction with a major league club. The concept of a major league club utilizing teams in the "bushes" to develop talent would not be realized until some years in the future, primarily under Branch Rickey's guiding hand. Traveling for spring training to Florida or Arizona was also the exception during Ruth's early years.

In Ruth's first ghostwritten book, published in 1928, he never mentions Fayetteville, or his experiences there. The town fared vastly better by his final testament, released shortly before his death in 1948. Babe recalled, "I got to some bigger places than Fayetteville ... but darn few as exciting. It was the place where Jim Thorpe, one of my sports heroes, had played a little pro baseball during his summer vacations from Carlisle (Pennsylvania)." Always the kidder, Ruth noted that he was extremely surprised at how much warmer it was in Fayetteville, compared to Baltimore. "I began to think I should have paid more attention to geography at St. Mary's," he quipped. "At Fayetteville, Dunnie saw to it that we took things easy for a long time. I haven't got the best memory in the world, but it is easy to recall those early days at my first spring training camp," Ruth recollected.

Indeed, George Ruth's "coming-out" exploits at the North Carolina camp as reported by Brother Gilbert ensured that the locals would long remember him, whether or not he succeeded at the sport.

The Orioles were initially welcomed by Mayor John Underwood; worked out inside the largest building in town, the armory; and, due to the poor, changeable weather, even accepted a basketball challenge from the boys who comprised the Fayetteville High School varsity team. (The Orioles triumphed 8–6, with outstanding contributions from Ruth.) On the eve of their departure, the townspeople gave the Orioles a rousing party, featuring a speech by the mayor. In their final game in Fayetteville that spring, Dunnie's son Jack Jr. was shooing away two cows that had intruded into his left field position when that momentary distraction enabled the batter to come all the way home on a hit to Junior's field!

Opposite: The cast of characters from Babe's first professional experience with the minor league Baltimore Orioles include: (*from far right*) the Babe, quite a cut-up at 19; catcher Ben Egan, a master practical joker in his own right; coach Jack Dunn, a superb judge of talent; Dunn's son, Jack Jr., for some reason out of uniform; and infielder Neal Ball, who is remembered for something other than his career .251 batting average in seven professional seasons — he is credited with the first unassisted triple play in major league history in 1909 (courtesy of National Baseball Hall of Fame).

Ruth's arrival at the Lafayette Hotel and his play at the Cape Fear Fairgrounds' baseball field signaled the emergence of a new era. Rodger H. Pippen, who later became sports editor of the *Baltimore News-Post*, was a young reporter covering the Orioles when he was asked to fill in for an intrasquad game in March of 1914. Decades later, he addressed an already-deceased Ruth: "I played in that first game with you and measured that first home run you ever hit. It was a long, long drive into a cornfield with a dead ball. And you know, Babe, that as close as possible to the spot where that sphere landed, the citizens of that North Carolina town have erected a plaque of copper on what is now a public highway."

Even though Ruth spent less than a month in Fayetteville, over 10,000 citizens would turn out in 1952 for the public dedication of the plaque which Pippen described.

*   *   *

FROM THE MEMOIRS OF BROTHER GILBERT

First Training Trip

On the morning of March 3, 1914, the athletes and their coaches detrained at Fayetteville, North Carolina. Several days of rain and wet grounds followed. During that time, the boys worked out in the armory. The Baltimore papers carried not one mention of Ruth, other than to say that a left-hander, by the name of "Frank" Ruth, who played with the Baltimore amateurs, was at camp. The presence of erstwhile stars so dominated press reports that Ruth was a guy named Frank, not Joe.

On March 7th a practice game was played. From then on, the central theme in all camp bulletins from Fayetteville was George Ruth. He was no longer Frank from the sand lots. Details poured in concerning his age, weight, height, whether he rode a bike or carried his lunch, whether he liked his cereal rare, medium or crispy. Instantly, it became vital to know that he wore a left-hand hat, a left-hand tie, used a left-hand fountain pen, although at that time, Ruth's ensemble included none of the three. Sun-up, he laboriously regaled himself in shoes, pants and shirt, with some buttons, and bolted for the railroad station to watch the trains. He loved to imagine that they would be thundering past St. Mary's that afternoon. Back to breakfast, he ran the gamut — and I might add, the waiter — bow-legged.

Breakfast, by the way, was not one of the chores distasteful to Ruth. The big fellow had just left an institution, where menus were not part of the daily routine. Indeed, in the school dining room, a sustained vigilance had to be maintained by the Prefect as an insurance that all guests, in reaching for their uncounted calories, keep at least one foot on the floor. George Ruth's interest in menus approached something less than total indifference. Sitting always at the same table, Ruth had the same waiter during the training season. Fast on the food, he was generally waiting for the dining room door to open. One morning he returned from the railroad station a trifle late. With the same mincing steps that characterized his approach to the big league plate in later years, he eased his way with equally dire purpose to his breakfast plate. Temporarily busy with several huge feeders, the waiter failed to notice the arrival of the young titan. Ben Egan, ever solicitous for the welfare of promising recruits, notified the waiter that Ruth was here and suggested that a menu be given him. With an expression of amazement that Egan, one of Ruth's party, should be so ill-informed concerning Ruth's dietary tastes, the waiter counseled hastily: "Mr. Rufe don't want no menu; I jest walk up to him and say, 'What will you have for breakfast, Mr. Rufe?' and he say, 'Fetch it.'"

Fun-provoking Egan, quizzically inquired whether "Fetch it" were a cereal or a meat.

"'Fetch it', Mr. Man, is everything that I can pile on that tray," rejoined the waiter. And I might add here that both plates — home plate and the dining room plate — remained equally alluring to George Ruth across the years of his stellar athletic career. Whenever he approached either one of them, he took a toe hold and never backed away until havoc was wrought.

That afternoon the first message of the coming of Ruth was broadcast to the world by two young sports writers, Rodger Pippen and Jesse Linthicum of the *Baltimore News-Post* and the *Baltimore Sun* respectively. That each was blessed with more than passing acumen is attested to by the fact that today each one of them is Sports Editor-in-Chief of his paper.

As stated above, little cognizance was taken of Ruth during the rainy days that preceded the scrub game. Both Pippen and Linthicum knew every worthwhile amateur in Baltimore. Jesse Linthicum had been most liberal in the space that he allotted to the amateurs and Rodger Pippen had starred on the best amateur teams in Baltimore, a place where sterling young ball players abound. In the big leagues at that time, from the Baltimore lots, were such brilliant performers as Fritz Maisel, captain of the Yanks; Willie Wortman, short-stop for the Cubs; Buck Herzog, second baseman for the Giants; Home Run Baker, third baseman for the Athletics; George Maisel, outfielder for the Cubs; Nick Maddox, three game winner for Pittsburgh in a previous World's Series; Butch Schmidt, first baseman for the Champion 1914 Braves; "Lefty" Russell, the original $12,000 beauty, and others whose names I cannot recall at this writing. Yes, Linthicum and Pippen knew the Baltimore athletes, since there were potential stars among them, yet they had never heard of Ruth. 'Twas natural, then, for them to ignore Ruth in pre-season dope. The grounds had been too wet for practice, and erstwhile big leaguers graced the roster.

The two advance notices that came to the Baltimore papers concerning Ruth followed after the prowess of the veterans had been duly recounted. In his roster of players, Jesse Linthicum, never having heard of Ruth, wrote in listing the players who would take part in the first practice:

"George Henry Ruth, of Baltimore, age 19, weight 165 pounds, is 6 ft. 1½ inches tall. He is right handed. Ruth is a single man. He played with Baltimore amateur teams last season."

Rodger Pippen's first announcement covered a little more ground. Despite the fact that he had not, at that time, seen Ruth in a uniform, he made bold to prognosticate: "A young fledgling here from St. Mary's Industrial School, given to Dunnie by Brother Gilbert, might grow to a full grown Oriole before we break camp." I have always felt that that generous observation was sponsored more as a courtesy to me than by any potential that Rodger hoped to discover in Ruth later.

In the very first game that Ruth played with Baltimore he crashed the headlines. After March 7, 1914, George Ruth was no longer regarded as a mere tourist at camp. In baseball vernacular, a tourist is one who bides his time until the manager can find a place in a lower league for his prospect to mature. Followers of the Orioles who anxiously awaited the season's first box score, were greeted as they turned to the sports page of the *Baltimore Sun* of Sunday, March 8, 1914, with Ruth's first bow in headlines:

HOMER BY RUTH FEATURE OF GAME

Fayetteville, N.C., March 7 — George Ruth, a pitcher Jack Dunn picked off the lots of Baltimore, is credited by Fayetteville fans with making the longest hit ever seen in their park. In the Orioles first game of the season this afternoon, with Cottrell on second base, Ruth leaned on a fast ball and easily circled the bases before Billie Morrisette had picked it up in deep right field.

Jim Thorpe, the famous Indian athlete, now a member of the New York Giants, held the previous record for a distant hit here.

	AB	R	H	O	A	E
Buzzards						
Hurney C	3	2	1	2	2	1
Jarman P-SS	4	2	1	0	0	0
Egan 1B	4	2	2	12	0	0
Cottrell 2B	4	3	3	2	3	0
Ruth SS-P	3	2	2	1	2	0
Russell 3B	4	0	1	2	1	0
Klinger LF	2	0	1	1	0	0
Pippen CF	3	2	2	0	1	0
Massena RF	3	2	1	1	0	0
Totals	30	15	11	21	9	1

	AB	R	H	O	A	E
Sparrows						
Potts C	4	2	2	3	2	0
Cranston P-CF	2	2	0	0	3	0
Steinman 1B	3	1	1	12	1	1
Danforth 2B	2	1	0	2	2	1
Lidgate SS	2	0	0	0	1	0
Lamotte 3B	3	2	1	4	0	0
Caporel LF	3	1	1	0	0	0
McKinley CF-P	3	0	1	0	1	0
Morrisette RF	3	0	1	0	0	0
Totals	25	9	7	21	10	2

BUZZARDS	1	7	4	0	0	0	3	15
SPARROWS	1	0	1	1	5	0	1	9

Two Base Hits — Egan, Morrisette, Pippen, Cottrell.
Three Base Hit — Pippen.
Home Run — Ruth.
Stolen Base — Pippen, Lidgate.
Base on balls — Off Jarman 3, off Cranston 3, off McKinley 1.
Struck Out — By Jarman 2, by Cranston 2, by Ruth 1.
Wild pitch — Jarman, Cranston.
Left on Bases — Buzzards 6, Sparrows 7.
Umpire — Fewster.

Local fans who watched the Birds play insist that Ruth's hit was much longer than the one made by Jim Thorpe. The ball sailed far over Morrisette's head, and landed in a corn field. The battle of the Buzzards and the Sparrows resulted in a 15 to 9 victory for the former, and Ruth's batting was easily the feature. He made two hits and scored as many runs. When not pitching, Ruth played shortstop very well, handling his three chances without a slip-up.

Ruth learned to play ball at St. Mary's Industrial School, and can play any position. He pitched the last inning of today's contest, and while one run was scored during his stay on the mound, he had little difficulty in disposing of the batters. The youngster is left handed, has plenty of speed and can bat from either side of the plate.

That covers about one half of Jesse Linthicum's first press release, and Ruth had already impressed himself on the game and on the fans. Observe that Ruth, a left hander, but a veritable ball hawk, played shortstop when not pitching.

A few years before Ruth hit the above-mentioned terrific homer, Jim Thorpe, playing in the Carolina Association, had hit a titanic circuit wallop to right field in the Fayetteville Park. The length of the hit had so impressed the patrons that one of them placed a marker at the spot where the ball had been picked up by the right fielder of the opposing club. The marker was intended as a reference for comparison with future gargantuan smashes. The first day that Ruth was permitted to hit in Fayetteville, the purpose of that marker was permanently destroyed. Ruth's clout screamed as it soared over Morrisette's head, and struck with a resounding thud in the soft mud of an adjacent cornfield. The recent rains denied it the growth of legs after it landed, and it settled in a cavity made by its own momentum. When Morrisette returned from the cornfield, wiping the mud off the ball, Ruth had already reached the players' bench with the terse comment, "Boy, he threw that pitch where I was swinging."

Rodger Pippen, the sports writer, and a distance hitter of some merit himself, was so awed by the power of Ruth's clout that he decided to make the blow the feature of his story for the day. To armor himself against the guffaws of the incredulous, he borrowed a tape measure to ascertain the distance — all carry — and reported to the *News-Post* that the ball had sailed 428 feet. As Rodger expected, the first one to question the accuracy of his measurements was his own Sports Editor who skeptically inquired, "How many inches are there to a foot in North Carolina ball parks?" Indeed, the Editor's doubts were not without justification, since in those days the players were using the dead ball, the one that is now cynically referred to by professional athletes as "the grapefruit." Bear in mind, too, that those were the years when outfield fences, even in big league parks, were rarely more than 275 feet from home plate. That poke was 153 feet beyond the established home run zone. Is it any wonder then, that when the news of it was picked up by the press, that it made the ears of baseball wizards, throughout the country, shoot out like block signals on a railroad? The following year, John McGraw of the Giants told this writer that when he heard of it, he scornfully remarked, "Josh Billings was right — dead right! — when he said, 'T'ain't so much harm in the world cause people know so much, no; but 'cause they know so much what ain't.'" That drive broadcast to fandom the coming of George H. Ruth, the full-grown Babe.

When Ruth, then a raw recruit unheralded and unsung, approached the plate, he was the only athlete in camp of whom nothing was known. The prophets had wasted none of their printer's ink on him. Apart from several carefully concealed squibs, the name Ruth might not suggest anything more than some winsome young lady with curly brown eyes and laughing blue hair. But since that time, it has suffused the mind of more than one ambitious young pitcher with visions of baseball parks back in the bush.

To dissipate ill-founded rumors, given currency after the vision of the sports world had been blessed with Ruth's rhythmic swing at the plate, it might be well to state here that Ruth's stance on that memorable day in 1914, and the one that he employed as he bowed off the stage at Pittsburgh years later, were identical. Rodger Pippen, Bill Morrisette, George Lee and others who saw him break in and who followed him closely across the years of his glamorous career, bear enthusiastic testimony to that statement. The late Jack Dunn, manager and owner of the Orioles that year pooh-poohed the suggestion of changing his stance. And when the final appraisal of great managers is made — if ever — Jack Dunn will be given a place in the front rank. The discerner of the luminaries of future diamond stars, Dunn had the perspective to recognize potential where it was most latent. "Don't tamper with Ruth," said Dunn to his coaches, "that fellow is a natural." And the writer is convinced that his stance never changed.

Dunn did not go to camp with the battery men who participated in the Sparrows vs. Buzzards practice game. He awaited the arrival of the infielders and outfielders. It was not until Tuesday, March 10, that he arrived to grade the worth of his men. The following day he sent the writer a letter urging him to come down to camp. Woven into the texture of that epistle were the following prophetic words: "That fellow, Ruth, is the greatest young ball player who ever reported to a training camp. If he doesn't let success go to his head, he'll become the greatest ball player of all time."

Success go to Ruth's head! In all of his years in baseball, he never took time to read a box score. Rarely did he concern himself with the names of the players on other American League clubs. Such matters were of no vital interest to him: his business was to hit the ball and win the game. Ruth needed more action than one gets from reading box scores. Illustrative of the above is the case of Eddie Collins and Max Bishop, both blond second basemen of the Philadelphia Athletics. When Ruth was sold to the Red Sox, Eddie Collins covered second for the Athletics. A good hitter, a superb fielder, he radiated confidence at bat, in the field and in his carriage. Collins' belief in himself, a quality so essential to the winning athlete that he was, merited for him the nickname of "Cocky." During the feverish days of the Federal League War, Collins was sold to the Chicago White Sox. A half dozen years later, Connie Mack bought Max Bishop, a blond-haired Baltimore boy, also a second baseman and a left-hand hitter, like Collins, from Jack Dunn's Baltimore Orioles. A hustler of the Collins type,

Bishop's bearing and mannerisms were not unlike those of his predeces-
sor. Between innings, Bishop raced to his post at second base. Invariably,
as Ruth passed him coming in from left field he greeted Bishop with, "Hi,
Cocky!" Max was not one to suggest a change in salutations. The only time
that he exercised his jaws was when chewing gum. A quiet chap, Max is a
dead ringer for the Arrow collar ad duke.

During Ruth's era as a Yank, the club had a young Polish catcher
named Stanislaus Grabowski. Bill Dickey's eminent services never allowed
Grabowski to get the prominence that his ability warranted. A likeable
boy, Grabowski was asked one day how the Babe treated him. "Very nicely,
indeed," was his quick response, "he never passes me without shouting,
'Hi, John!'" Names like Stanislaus, Arsenius and Pachonissis seemed to be
at polar distance with the names of athletes with whom he grew up at St.
Mary's. His memories were of such chaps as "Ike" Roussey, "Congo" Kirby,
"Skinny" McCall, "Jack" Morgan, George Lee, "Tom" Padgett, "Bill" Padgett, "Izzy" Katz, "Loose" Buttons, "Sour" Krause, "Pickles" Heintz, and
"Beans" Wagner. No, Ruth was not averse to people with long names; in
fact, he never fostered an aversion towards anyone. He was just a big,
good-natured fellow, who was too preoccupied to be bothered with lengthy
monikers.

Jack Dunn was ravished with genuine delight at the spectacle of a
good prospect. A single glance of Dunnie's critical eye sufficed for the grad-
ing of his pupils. During his first evening at Hotel Lafayette, he had been
furnished with glowing accounts of the hitting prowess, the sensational
fielding, the spectacular speed — and Ruth was fast — of his new prodigy,
who, although a left-hander, could play any one of the nine positions on
his club with grace, dexterity and finesse.

"Such pleasing chatter is a delectable training camp tonic, if true,"
said Dunnie, who definitely had no animated imagination. Jack Dunn liked
to see for himself with both eyes. On that account, he frequently scorned
all who wore a monocle with the cynical innuendo: "Those guys are fearful of seeing more at one time than they can understand." Scouts who
brought in drift wood, tourists and dead freight were habitually referred
to by Dunn as monocle wearers. "Tell me, Steinman, you think that Ruth
is such a sensation," continued Dunn, "Just how many hands has this guy
Ruth got?"

"Well," countered Steinie, "if you'll do me the courtesy of focusing
your optics on him in the dining room, you'll think that he is an octopus.
Personally, I rejoice in the fact that we are paying his board and not boarding him."

Since it was then after ten o'clock, and Ruth had turned in his borrowed bike for the night, he was seated in the lobby, laughing gleefully, as he poured gluttonously over a comic sheet. The other athletes were lounging about, some discussing the possibilities of certain recruits. Others were scanning the news from various big league camps, or reading sports periodicals anent the trade. Another one had that day received a first letter from his girl friend. With a far-away look in his eyes, he indifferently contemplated the interests of the group about him. Suddenly, his countenance assumed an expression of resigned complacency, while he solaced himself aloud, "Ah think I'll read it a-gain."

"Over there, luxuriating in the comics," observed Egan, "is your happy lambkin, Ruth, about as heavy with worry as he'll be tomorrow, with a count of two and two, when one of your young fork handlers is going to bend his number two pitch, knee high, over the outside corner."

"What'll he do then?" was Dunnie's skeptical inquiry.

"Oh, nothing more than foul one over the center fielder's head," conjectured Egan, who was no one's push-over in ludicrous debate. "I'll guarantee that when that pitch is coming on its perilous errand that Ruth will have a biting toe hold, his gun beautifully cocked, deep in his left shoulder, safety off, and that he'll follow that curve right down to his knees. What is more, if that kid elects to release the firing pin, there'll be poetry in the rhythmic coordination of his limbs and muscles. And while I have the floor, let me further add that the resounding thwack that follows will tickle your auditory nerves."

"What is this," Dunnie snapped, "college talk or baseball talk?"

"Baseball talk. If you want college talk, see Ensign Cottrell; he got another degree from Syracuse University last week. He now has more of the blame things than a thermometer."

"Yah, but he is not all college. Cottrell has more curves than a mountain trail."

"Well, we'll take him to the light tomorrow and have a long, lean look at him."

"Incidentally," interrupted Egan again, "I am advising you now to hire some young boys as retrievers of Ruth's shots. Morrisette, Russell and Danforth won't chase them. All three of them insist that not only their tonsils, but also their adenoids are sunburned from watching his drives go over their heads. I am glad that you are here to absorb the witty invectives of some of your outfielders. The other day I had Morrisette in right field, and he insisted that Ruth bat right-hand for a change. 'Let,' shouted Morrisette, 'some of the other gardeners leg it for a change.' And Russell shouted to me, 'Even though it is only batting practice, give Ruth a base on balls once in a while.'"

Dunnie forsook the monotony of that seminar for a brief conference with the idol of the camp.

"How do you feel, George?" was his greeting.

"Good, Mr. Dunn."

"Do you like it down here?"

"Yes, sir, Mr. Dunn; these fellows do all the things that I like to do, and they are a bunch of swell guys."

"Do you think that you can hit the pitching in this company?"

"Sometimes I hit pretty good. I got a good chunk of a couple the other day, Mr. Dunn."

"Well, George, go to bed now and get a lot of rest. And, say, don't ride that elevator alone anymore. The manager of the hotel told me that you came very close to being killed yesterday morning. An accident like that would give the hotel a bad name; and, from all accounts, rob me of a very promising young ball player. By the way, where do you go when you leave the hotel so early in the morning?"

"Oh, I just run down to the railroad station to watch the trains go by."

"Well, trot along to your bunk now. I am going to have you do a lot of hitting tomorrow, so pile up on your rest."

In Ruth's mad dash to get a flying start the previous morning, he threw the lever of the elevator without closing the door. The car started in relays of about one foot that were ominously spasmodic. Quickly sensing danger, Ruth tried to bring the car to a stop, but he could not budge the lever. With the top of the carriage not more than four feet above the floor of the third floor of the hotel, Ruth, in desperation, dived through the opening, the top of the elevator door brushing his back, and then, catching the heel of his right shoe, just as he extricated himself. He was split inches away from a broken back or the loss of a leg.

Asked afterwards why he hadn't closed the door before throwing the lever, Ruth nonchalantly replied as he hurried to the railroad station, "Those elevators aren't safe, when they are jerky, then you must leave the door open to be ready to jump."

When Jack Dunn awakened on the morning of March 10, 1914, he lay in bed for a few minutes reflecting on the enthusiastic accounts of that boy, Ruth, who Steinman, Egan, Cottrell and Pippen had unburdened themselves of the previous night. Apropos of nothing relevant to his roommate's musings, Dunnie blurted, "If those fellows were looking at that kid with their eyes, instead of the pious hopes, we are on our way to a pennant."

Before dressing, he jumped to the window, scanned the sky, and found it bathed in cerulean light. "Great!" chirped Dunnie, "this weather is not made by raw apprentices. Those people who get paid for telling people that it is going to rain, and keeping them away from my ball park, can't keep me from seeing Ruth today." Several moments of silence ensued, during which, it must be assumed, from the purport of his next remark, he indulged in the luxury of envisioning Ruth slapping the agate to new and unexplored regions of North Carolina: "We have only seventy dozen balls with us. I hope that he doesn't hit them all out of the state."

In the lobby of the hotel that morning, Dunnie was told that two prospective Orioles, Danny Murphy and Freddie Parent, had deserted his club to join the Federal League. Added to those rumors was the disturbing news that his brilliant young outfielder, George Twombly, from Medford, Massachusetts, was threatened with appendicitis. Painfully perturbed at these inauspicious reports, Dunnie nevertheless, ordered all players to be in uniform at the park by ten o'clock.

At the appointed hour, all batterymen, except Ruth, were ordered to the fielding positions while the regulars took their respective places in the temporary batting order. Due to Twombly's illness, Ruth was given his place in the fifth slot. Awaiting his turn at bat, the boys played "pepper" on the side. Bert Daniels led off, smashed five drives, dropped a bunt and sprinted around the bases. Ezra Midkiff, Neal Ball and Birdie Cree followed. Some of Cree's clouts were especially powerful. While they were being retrieved, Egan, ever the wag, was busy counseling Ruth that Cranston and Massena were going to be given pink slips that night, and that he would get one, too, if he did not paste that pellet far, wide and viciously. A pink slip escaped the ken of the Ruthian verbal repertoire.

"A pink slip," he frowned, "and what's that?'

"You don't know what a pink slip is?"

"No, Mr. Egan."

"Well," said Egan, sensing an opportunity for more comedy, "a pink slip is a garment that girls wear, and you'll be harnessed to one of them for the remainder of our training trip, if you don't go up there and swing from your heels."

Cree pushed his bunt, started sprinting. "No fun with a pink slip," growled Ruth in ill-concealed concern as he minced his way to the dish, twirling his bat is his left hand. "I want to ride that boy's bike tonight."

The gibes of the Chicago Cubs in a World's Series years later did not rile Ruth to a higher pitch of determination than did that final remark of Egan's.

Young Jarman, a big, promising Maryland boy, was on the turtle back pitching to the batters. Jack Dunn turned his head and grinned with suppressed glee, as he observed his outfielders retreat to remote battle stations. The first pitch was out of range and Ruth ignored it; the second was in range, and Ruth exploded it. The ball fairly screamed over Morrisette's head, who stood perfectly still, arms akimbo, and watched it sail. Finally, he cupped his hands at his mouth and yelled to Jack Dunn: "Wire the Raleigh club to put an outfielder in their ball park: it went that way." The eyes of the entire club were on the Manager, as he stood, transfixed, eyes surging, mouth agape, while following the carry of that tee shot.

Egan needled Ruth again, "Quit popping them up. Get a hold of that ball, or you'll get the pink slip before tonight."

Ruth turned, as he backed out of the batter's box, and in obvious dread of the pink slip, inquired, "What was wrong with that one?"

"Hit 'em out in front. You're a dead right field hitter — all the players are laughing at you."

The next one, a topped ball, was a feeble roller to the second baseman; but the third one really grew wings as it flew over Russell's head to deep center. When it landed, it galloped as if in abject fear of further punishment. Russell shouted to Dunn, "Who provides taxi fare for the fellows who retrieve his hits?" Those were the only long hits of his first time at bat in his manager's presence, but they were plenty long, and both Egan and Steinman knew that their estimates of Ruth's power had been justified. Two young boys returned the balls. After Ruth bunted, and started to circle the bases, Dunn who had watched operations from the first base coacher's box, call to him.

"Say, George, where did you get that bat that you've been using?"

"Over there in the bat rack, Mr. Dunn."

"Did you bring it with you?"

"No, sir."

"Those were mighty long hits that you cracked out there."

"Am I doing good, Mr. Dunn?"

"Boy, you are a soothing salve for my organs of vision, and a spring tonic for my digestive tract. You look great."

"Then I won't have to wear that pink slip tonight."

"What pink slip?"

"Mr. Iggan said that if I did not hit good that you were going to make me wear a pink slip." (To this day, Ruth's pronouncement of *Egan* is *Iggan*.)

"Listen, George, a pink slip is an outright release, and you'll not get one down here. When I release you, it'll be to a big league club for a price more fancy than telephone figures. In fact, it will be so fancy that it will look like the population of China."

"May I borrow that boy's bike again tonight?"

"Kid, when you get back to Baltimore, I'll buy a bike for you. Do what you like down here."

"Oh, gee!"

"Something else. Did you have an upper berth coming down here?"

"Yes, sir."

"Did Egan tell you to sleep in the hammock?"

"No, sir; he told me to sleep in my clothes."

"He did, eh? What did he tell you to put in the hammock?"

"Mr. Iggan told me to pull the ladder up that I used when climbing into the bunk, and to put it into the hammock."

"Oh, I knew darn well that he would have a good use for the hammock. Why did he tell you to sleep in your clothes?"

"So that during the night, the colored man could not swap my clothes with those of the little guy that Mr. Iggan calls Oliver Sudden."

"Oh, I see; It's all clear to me now. And what reason did he give you for telling you to pull the ladder up?"

"Well, Mr. Iggan whispered to me that Fatty Arbuckle was on the train, and that he had no bunk. He told me that when there is no bunk for a big shot, that the colored man makes the youngest rookie sleep double with him. Mr. Iggan said that if I'd hide the ladder Fatty would have to get in a lower."

"Ruth, by an chance has Egan told you that the fellow who rooms with you keeps a loaded thirty-eight under his pillow?"

"No, sir."

"Then Egan likes you."

"Yes, sir, Mr. Iggan is always helping me."

"I can appreciate that. Do you need anything in the way of tooth paste, shaving equipment, clothing — anything?"

"No, sir, my dad and Brother Paul took care of everything."

"Have you pajamas?"

"Yes, sir, but I don't use them."

"You don't use them! Why not?"

"Mr. Iggan told me that ball players never use pajamas — only in case of fire."

"Fine, you and Egan are hitting it off just right — for Egan. Now don't you pay any attention to Egan, only on the ballfield. A year ago, I had a fast ball pitcher who liked to drink beer — and don't you ever touch anything intoxicating. I promised the Brothers that I would not let you. Understand?"

"As I was saying" — Bang! Midkiff pulled a hot shot that whistled as it passed both Dunn and Ruth. "Hey, Midkiff! Don't hit this kid; he is the one who is going to take the crowds away from the Feds in Baltimore, and keep our turnstiles clicking. And don't kill me, because I'm the guy who writes the checks on the first and the fifteenth." Ruth did not save baseball for the Orioles that year, but he saved it for the American boys six years later.

"Well, to return to my story about the fast ball pitcher and Ben Egan. This pitcher really had it. He had it, and I mean he had zip. When he was right, the other club thought that he was flipping Carter's Little Liver Pills at them. We had just arrived in Rochester for a hectic session with John Ganzel's ball club. And last year, no club playing Rochester ever had an afternoon off, or an evening for that matter, because we played the game in our sleep the night before. Well, boy, we had our big ace, the speed king, pointed for that game to give us the jump in the series. We were stopping at the Cheltenham Hotel, and to make sure that he would be right, I had Egan rooming with him. But he fooled Egan and slipped out. Shortly after midnight of the day before he was to open the series, he groped his way into Egan's room. And that stupid fellow was somewhat more than incandescent. But Egan had prepared for just such a contingency. Out of the commode, Egan had taken the catcher, not the pitcher, and placed it at the foot of the other fellow's bed, not under it. Then he shook into it two sets of Seidlitz powders.

"As the fellow entered the room, Egan said to him, 'If you need the charlie during the night, just flip on the light; it's there.' After a moment's thought, that worthless fellow said, 'I need it now.' The effervescence that he saw so terrified him that he moaned and groaned throughout the night. Worry so weakened him that the next day he did not have enough speed for a change of pace. And, although he was a great help to us during the remainder of the season, I had to get rid of him. A fellow who is not his own boss, who lets his tastes control him, is no asset to a ball club. So have lots of fun, be a good boy, live right, and you'll reach the very top of your profession. Egan is a great kidder, but he also is a great fellow to have on a ball club. Don't worry about pink slips; you are the pet of the camp — all these fellows love you. When you get that toe hold, and start cowtailing, my eyes laugh."

"Thank you, Mr. Dunn, you're swell. I will follow your advice. I want to make good for the Brothers and for the boys at St. Mary's. You know, there are a lot more good ball players up there. Gee, I wish a lot of them were down here; they're good kids."

If any single factor robbed Ruth of determination at the plate, it was kindness. Forgiving by nature, George Ruth was an emotional kid, with a deep and an abiding sense of gratitude. The world was kind to him now, and he walked up to the plate visualizing the new bike that would be given to him in Baltimore. Yes, and the hilarious, mad races that he would enjoy, as he dashed out to the school every day after the game. Instead of having his mind on hitting the ball, it was down in the big yard at St. Mary's, sharing his joy with the boys. As a result, he hit three weak flies to the outfield and two grounders to the second baseman.

That afternoon, in a game between the Sparrows and the Buzzards, Ruth hit what Jack Dunn said afterwards was the longest drive that he had ever seen. He liked to tell that he had seen Delahanty, Lajoie, Brouthers and all the great power boys tag them, but their best never approached for distance the one that this kid hit in Oriole Park at Fayetteville. Reclining in his big chair, feet on the desk, Dunn gloried in recalling that wallop. "Fayetteville," he would say, "might be only a small town; but its people were the first paying customers to see the greatest ball player of my time." Nor did he ever grow unmindful of the remark of one of the little colored ball hawks whom he daily hired to chase foul balls and home runs. When the lad saw that one sail far out in the cornfield he groaned: "Mistah Dunn, I ain't gine chase that one, 'cause does I do, I ain't gine see no mo this yere ball game."

Ruth Is Nicknamed "Babe"

For years people have wondered when and where Ruth was first called "Babe." Reams of copy have been printed — all wild conjectures as to its inception. The Babe himself has never been able to give a satisfactory explanation of its origin. That is easy to explain, because he was fifty yards away and spread out like Central Park when the endearing moniker was handed to him. On Wednesday evening, March 18, 1914, in Fayetteville, Ruth left the dining room, and bolted down to the home of a boy, whose acquaintance he had made at the ball park. Every day the boy rode out to the park. One of Ruth's admirers, he told George that he could use the wheel after supper. On the evening mentioned above, Ruth was pedaling about town with what he thought was something better than ordinary efficiency. Knowing that the Orioles would all be seated in front of the hotel, and a bit proud of his progress; he decided to give the gang a free demonstration of his skill. As he passed the hotel, on the wrong side of the road, a la Bob Burman, he waved a hearty greeting to his teammates. A large truck that he did not see was bearing down on him. Only the frantic scream of one of the players saved his life. Swerving suddenly, he escaped the truck, but not the curbing on the opposite side. As he spread out on the street some of the players rushed toward him. Before they could cross the street, Ruth had brushed off the greater part of the dirt that he had accumulated in his slide and was up on the bike and pedaling toward the railroad station. Scout Steinman broke the awestricken silence: "If Manager Dunn does not shackle that new babe of his, he'll not be a Rube Waddell in the rough, he'll be a Babe Ruth in the cemetery." Rodger Pippen was standing next to Steinman when the remark was made. The next day, in Pippen's column, George Ruth was called "Babe" Ruth for the first time. The name caught on like a porous plaster and stuck like liquid cement. Most fortunate was it for the fandom of America that Steinman was out for a stroll with Pippen that evening, and most fortunate was it again that Rodger Pippen was sharp enough and quick enough to scoop the name.

Due to the preference that sports writers were giving the Federal League team, and the negligible space that was allotted the Orioles, little importance was attached to the roster of Orioles. In the same article appeared the notice that Jack Dunn had screamed as he watched the near accident: "That promise that I made to give Ruth a bike when we reach Baltimore doesn't go."

But from that day forward, the sports world knew George Herman Ruth as Babe Ruth. And by the way, that includes the Japs, who shrieked on charging into battle, "To Heck with Babe Ruth."

The name was appropriate. He has always been a real Babe. Each day revealed new wonders to him, new interests to arouse his excitement, and new nomenclatures. In his time, he battled against the slider, the sailer, the fadeaway, the spitter, the emery ball, the screw ball and the knuckler. All of them came up to test his vision and his timing and all were sent back, air mail, to convey to the world the arrival of Babe Ruth — a name synonymous with his game.

Original Drugstore Cowboy

Fayetteville became a grand vacationland to the newly branded Babe. No longer a maverick, his escapades brought nothing worse than uproarious laughter and kindly warnings from Dunn and the coaches. What a riot of revelry! Early morning trains, baseball all day, and the evenings for antics suggested by the buoyancy and the optimism of his effervescent youth. There were no bells regulating his daily routine, no 8:30 PM summons to night prayers and to bed. Full of health, energy, and craving for action, he was turned loose on pastures fertile with opportunity for adventures. Into them, he galloped without check or bit.

Babe Ruth had never ridden a horse, nor had he ever ridden a bike or a train for that matter, until he signed with the Orioles. Some of the players were already availing themselves of a riding school just outside the city. With amusement, Ruth watched several of the boys gallop past him one evening. They yelled words of recognition before disappearing in a cloud of dust. Oh boy! There was a real chance for a combination of conquest and daring, and George Ruth was not one to ignore either. On inquiry, he learned from Steinman the place and the rental price of the horses. On afterthought, sensing a reprimand from his boss, Steinman hurriedly sent word to the riding master that Ruth was to be given the smallest and gentlest horse in the barn. "Don't give that fellow, Ruth," advised Steinman, "anything more vicious than a saw horse or a hobby horse or he'll ride it back to Baltimore."

Desiring the good will of the Baltimore club, the stableman chose a large sized Shetland Pony for Ruth to ride. The pony had the gentility and timidity of a scholarly freshman. But Ruth was so left-sided that the animal shied nervously on being mounted from the wrong side. Indeed, it was almost necessary to throw the pony to get Ruth astride. Once up, he handled the whip as he did his bat, in his left hand. Evidently, the creature had never been punished on the left side before, and at the first tap, its rear end spun to meet its head. Ruth shouted orders in a strange terminology that were piously disobeyed. A few caracals that revealed a desire to discover Ruth's wishes followed. The excitement of the experience and the warmth of the day had both Ruth and the pony frothing at the bit. But not for long. Full of the conviction that he had a winner, Ruth struck out for the Main Stem to exhibit his horsemanship and to slake his thirst. He headed for a downtown drugstore, where the real party boys had already gathered for the evening to display their graces and make their playful observations. As Ruth approached the drugstore, it was obvious that in the bout between him and the critter, no holds were barred. His arms gripped the pony's neck in a strangle hold fashion, while his legs were locked in a winner-take-all clinch. Indeed, he was very much tangled up in that pony.

"Which one is the horse?" sneered a bystander.

"I take it," ventured another, "that he should be a sweet rider on his mother's side."

Ruth would not condescend to ignore them. Three sonorous shouts for ice cream cones brought nothing but the echoes of provoked merriment. Curb service was unknown then.

Remembering his difficulty in mounting, and fearful of being able to remount, Ruth ducked his head and urged his pony right up to the soda fountain. The sentiment of the crowd quickly oscillated in his favor. The jeers of a moment before became a chorus of generous cheers.

"Give me a large ice cream cone and one for my horse."

"We don't serve horses here," said the clerk.

Attracted by the crowd, a rotund, saffron-faced man emerged from the rear of the store and bellowed, "Put him out."

Emboldened by the plaudits of the crowd, Ruth, who never knew fear, snapped back, "You come outside and put me out."

By that time, the clerk, after handing Ruth the cone, took the horse by the bridle and led it to the street. Applause grew louder as Ruth tightened his embrace and the horse went away in a lame canter. Thus, the Babe led the field as the first Drugstore Cowboy. The next day, at the ball park, Ruth was as lame all over as a centipede with fallen arches.

If there are those who question the truth of the above episode, I respectfully refer the incredulous to the testimony of an eye witness, Mr. Rodger Pippen, Sports Editor of the *Baltimore News-Post*.

Appended here is the box score of the game in which Jack Dunn, Manager of the Orioles saw Ruth play.

Neal Ball, who played second base for the Regulars, is the same Ball, who, while playing second base for Cleveland, was the first major leaguer to make an unassisted triple play.

Newspaper comment: "The chief topic of conversation in camp is the terrific hitting of Lefty Ruth, the former St. Mary's School star. His work around short stop yesterday attracted the attention of everyone."

And again: "Jack Dunn is struck with the work of Ruth. The first time that he saw him in action, he predicted a great future for Lefty."

After the game, Steinman asked Ruth, "Are you afraid of those pitchers?"

"Naw, some of our teams up at school can best either one of these teams. If we had all those bats and balls and gloves to practice with, they couldn't get us out in one season."

Regulars	AB	H	O	A	E	Yanigans	AB	H	O	A	E
Daniels RF	4	2	2	1	0	Dunn, Jr. LF	6	2	3	0	0
Midkiff 3B	5	3	4	2	0	Schartuz CF	4	0	1	0	0
Ball 2B	5	1	5	3	1	Barrows RF	4	2	3	1	0
Cree CF	5	2	1	1	0	Ruth SS	5	3	1	1	0
Twombly LF	4	3	1	0	1	Egan C	5	2	6	1	1
Derrick SS	5	3	4	2	0	Steinman 1B	4	1	9	1	0
Gleichman 1B	4	2	5	3	2	Dunn, Sr. 2B	5	1	2	5	0
Lidgate C	3	1	4	1	0	Gerwig 3B	4	3	2	1	0
Davidson P	2	1	0	1	0	Klinglehoffer P	1	0	0	1	0
Jarman P	1	0	0	2	0	Morrisette P	2	2	0	2	0
McKinley P	1	0	1	1	1	Danforth P	2	1	0	2	0
Totals	39	18	27	17	5	Totals	42	17	27	15	1

Regulars	0	2	4	5	0	0	0	0	0	11
Yanigans	0	2	3	1	0	1	3	1	0	11

Two base hits — Morrisette, Cree (2), Gerwig, Steinman, Midkiff (2), Derrick.
Three base hits — Gerwig, Derrick, Daniels, Morrisette, Ruth. Home Run — Ruth

CHAPTER FOUR

Babe Beats Connie Mack's World Champions

INTRODUCTORY NOTE BY HARRY ROTHGERBER

One can hardly think of the name "Babe" without supplying "Ruth."

In the preceding chapter, Brother Gilbert was unerringly correct when he referred to the many conjectures as to the origin of Ruth's nickname. Although credence must be accorded to his account (of George Ruth's bicycle misadventure which caused Coach Steinman to make his Rube Waddell–"Babe" Ruth comparison, which, of course, was conveniently overheard by Baltimore sportswriter Roger Pippen who memorialized it the next day), that is only one of several "Babe" origins which have been perpetuated through the decades since. Let's examine what others say about the beginning of "Babe":

Kal Wagenheim, 1974 biographer: "A former St. Mary's inmate swears that he was called Babe the first day he arrived at the school, a frightened seven year old, and began to bawl."

Robert W. Creamer, 1974 biographer: "Generally, the veteran players looked on Ruth as something apart, a guileless child. Thus his nickname, Babe, which he had acquired by the end of the second week in camp, soon after the veterans arrived. Dunnie's Babe, they called him, meaning simply, Dunnie's baby. The nickname was a common one in those days for the young and innocent. Twombly's kid brother was called Babe. The Pittsburgh Pirates' baby-faced right hander, Babe Adams, was then in his sixth season in the major leagues. 'Babe' fit Dunn's prize; 'George' seemed too formal for him. By the middle of the third week of training the Baltimore papers were calling him Babe Ruth, and then the fans were, and soon everybody was."

Marshall Smelser, 1975 biographer: "Ruth got a nickname at Fayetteville. While veterans were baiting the rookies, Coach Sam Steinman warned them to go easy with Ruth. 'He's one of Jack Dunn's babes.' Roger Pippen, who covered the Oriole camp for a Baltimore paper, asked Steinman to explain. Steinman said Dunn had many very young players in camp but 'Ruth is the biggest and most promising babe in the lot.' Some of the players also had the mistaken idea that St. Mary's was a foundling home, so that anyone from there could be 'Babe.' The name stuck. Babe Ruth. Babe thought it was meant to be funny at first. If so, it soon lost its edge and became a useful proper noun."

Ken Sobol, 1974 biographer: "George or 'Babe,' as the Oriole players had nicknamed their new teenaged teammate...."

Guernsey Van Riper, Jr., 1954 (juvenile) biography: "Two of the Baltimore players watched the gangling boy. One of them shook his head. 'There comes Dunnie with another of his babes,' he said as George walked away."

Tom Meany, 1947 biographer: "For posterity let it be recorded that when Ruth arrived on the practice field at Fayetteville that march day in 1914, trotting after Dunnie, it was Steinman who observed, 'Here comes Jack with his newest babe.'"

Roger Pippen, sportswriter: "Babe Ruth made his debut in the fourth..." (*Baltimore American*, March 19, 1914, first time Ruth mentioned in print as "Babe").

Wagenheim (again): "'Roger,' said the scout [Steinman], 'Dunnie didn't get that fellow from St. Mary's, he got him from an infant asylum. We've got some real kids on this trip, and that Ruth is the biggest babe of the lot.'"

Let's end with Ruth himself, ever a confused historian when it comes to the facts:

Babe Ruth (1928): "A man named Steinam [sic], who was the coach of the Baltimore Orioles when I joined the club in 1914, gave me the nickname. The first day I reported at the clubhouse he said, 'Well, here's Jack's newest Babe now.'"

Babe Ruth (1930): "Jack Dunn took me down to the field, where the players were holding a morning workout, and turned me over to his coach — a man by the name of Steinam [sic]. He took a good look at me and then turned to the other players and said, 'Boys, here's Jack's new babe!'"

Babe Ruth (1948): "On that day, Dunn practically led me by the hand from the dressing room to the pitcher's box. I was as proud of my Orioles' uniform as I had been of my first long pants. Maybe I showed that pride in my face and the way I walked. 'Look at Dunnie and his new babe,' one of the older players yelled."

Babe Ruth (1948) version two (after the elevator incident): "Dunnie bawled me out until the stuffings ran out of me, and what he didn't say to me the older players said for him. But finally one of them took pity on me, shook his head and said, 'You're just a babe in the woods.' After that they called me Babe."

Oh, well, what difference does it make whether he is Babe, The Big Baboon, The Mauling Monarch, The Bambino, The Colossus of Clout, Cave-man, The Sultan of Swat, Bam, Big Bam, Gigge, The Wizard of Whack, The Behemoth of Biff, The Maharajah of Mash, The Goliath of Grand Slam, The Infant Swatigy, The Prince of Pounders or Jidge (as most of his teammates called him). In spite of the moniker "Babe" being used by more than 23 major leaguers over the years, our Babe was the first and last of his kind, and has been immortalized in the *Dictionary of American Slang* by the following:

> Babe (Capital B) A large fat man; esp. A large fat baseball player; used as a nickname. As irony, and because many fat men have baby faces. Reinforced as Babe Ruth, the baseball star of the 1920's who was a heavy set man.

The old saying that real life and fiction differ in that real life is often so unbelievable is certainly apropos to the Babe's games in Wilmington, North Carolina. The residents who journeyed out to see both of the Philadelphia big league teams battle Dunnie's Orioles witnessed the debut of the most acclaimed hitter-pitcher of the 20th century.

Wilmington is not far from Fayetteville, and, as North Carolina's principal deepwater port, it also sits on the Cape Fear River. It was a principal seaport of the South during the Civil War, and heavy fighting occurred at nearby Fort Fisher. Wilmington's history also saw it as the scene of Stamp Act resistance prior to the Revolutionary War and as the headquarters for an occupying army led by English Lord Cornwallis. None of this history prepared that town for the debut of Babe Ruth. Indeed, the current presence in Wilmington of the battleship U.S.S. *North Carolina* is as much of a testament to the fireworks provided by Ruth as the fact that this city is a leading port for wood pulp.

There were no pushover teams among the first major league clubs on which Ruth had ever laid eyes. The Philadelphia A's (Athletics), were the forerunner of the Kansas City A's and today's Oakland A's. As a charter member of the American League in 1901, this team was coached by one Cornelius McGilicuddy, better known as Connie Mack, Hall of Famer. This shrewd baseball strategist did not retire as coach until after the 1950 season, and spent an additional four years as part-owner of the club. During that period, only the Yankees won more pennants than did Mack, who garnered nine league and five World Series championships. Since Mack always thought of his 1912 third-place finishing A's as his best team of the decade, it was no surprise that they won the pennant in 1913 and then bested the Giants 4–1 in the World Series.

The A's were only the second big league team Ruth had ever seen. Their 3-4-5 hitters were Eddie Collins (.345 in 1913), Frank "Home Run" Baker (.336)—both Hall of Famers—and Stuffy McInnis (.326). The "One Hundred Thousand Dollar" infield of the "Mackmen" was completed by Jack Barry (.275). Outfielders Eddie Murphy (.295) and Rube Oldring (.283) were no slouches. Baker had captured his third home run race in a row with 12. Although Mack did not throw his best pitchers (Chief Bender, Eddie Plank, Bob Shawkey, Joe Bush) against the Orioles, still this was the World Series victor which had offensively decimated the Giants five months earlier, and which was destined to win the 1914 AL pennant with a 99–53 record. Ruth's future teammate in later Yankee years, Herb Pennock, pitched well for the A's that year, compiling an 11–4 slate. (The Boston Braves' 4–0 sweep of the A's in the 1914 World Series was one of the most miraculous underdog victories in the Fall Classic.) These A's were a team of destiny and history.

The Athletics' National League counterparts from the City of Brotherly Love, the Philadelphia Phillies, were bound for glory in their own right. A member of the "senior circuit" since 1883, the Phillies were coming off a runner-up finish (88–63) in 1913. They would finish in sixth place in 1914 (due to personnel battles with the Federal League) before winning the NL pennant with a 90–62 record under new manager Pat Moran, a former backup catcher, in 1915. This triumphant season is especially notable in Phillies' lore since it represents their only first-place finish between 1883 and 1950.

The Phillies' nucleus was comprised of excellent hitters. Sherry Magee (.306 in 1913, with a .479 slugging average) won the NL batting title in 1910 with a .331 average. Hans Lobert (.300), Dode Paskert (.262) and Fred Luderus (.262) were also reliable, game-tested veterans. It is not known for sure who pitched for the Phillies in the first game in which the Babe played against a major league team, but the next day's moundmen were average: Henry "Eddie" Matteson (3–2 in 1914) and Rube Marshall (6–7). It would certainly have tested Ruth had his opposite moundman been the Phillies' ace, Hall of Famer Grover Cleveland "Pete" Alexander (later portrayed by Ronald Reagan in a movie biography), who was to win 27 games in 1914.

Pat Moran played 14 years for three teams in the major leagues, primarily as a reserve catcher, with a career batting average of .235. Hanging up "the tools of ignorance" after the 1914 season, he managed for the next nine seasons in Philadelphia and Cincinnati, earning a .561 win-loss percentage, and pennants in both cities. Thus, in 1919, Moran piloted the Reds against the "Black Sox" in the notorious gambling-tainted World Series, won 5 games to 3 by the Reds. After arriving in Florida for spring training in 1924, Moran appeared in a debilitated state due to the effects of chronic alcoholism. He was taken to a hospital in Orlando, where he died of Bright's disease at the age of 48.

The role of Roger Pippen in all of these early goings-on should not be underestimated. In addition to being the first writer to chronicle Ruth's exploits, he was a superb athlete in his own right.

Pippen, then 26, wrote sports dispatches for the Baltimore Sun and filled in for the Orioles when they needed him. In his 1948 book, Babe refers to Pippen as "one of the Orioles." In the first Orioles' intrasquad game in which Ruth played, the Buzzards' 15–9 victory over the Sparrows, Pippen played errorless centerfield, went 2 for 3 with a double and triple, scored two runs and drove Ruth in once for an RBI. (The newspaperman also was cast in the role of Ruth's roommate, during that spring training trip, for reasons unknown.) Of that first game, Ruth recalled, "Pippen, who was made my roommate, and whose name I just couldn't remember as long as I roomed with him, helped tone me down and got me ready for my first game as a pro. And as things turned out, Roger drove out a double which scored me in the early innings with the first run of my 22 years in organized baseball."

Pippen, later the Sports Editor of the *Baltimore News-Post*, wrote gushingly to Ruth in a memorial column in 1955: "You stand immortal as a symbol of America.... Yours was the greatest of all 'rags to riches' stories. You started in baseball with ten cents and made millions. No great man ever fired the imagination of the populace as you did, a big, overgrown boy from a reform school."

* * *

From the Memoirs of Brother Gilbert

The Orioles Visit Wilmington

On March 18, 1914, the Orioles journeyed to Wilmington, N.C., for an exhibition game with the Phillies. Pat Moran was in the driver's seat at Philadelphia, and he had already pointed his team pennant-ward.

Having no inkling that he would pitch, Ruth ate about one dozen hot dogs and two quarts of ice cream before the game. Jack Dunn had told Moran that he was going to unveil a real kid against the Phillies. "Pat," said Dunn, "this kid is only nineteen years old, and for twelve years, until I picked him up two weeks ago, he had not been outside the yard of the Manual Training School. Your team today is the first big league club that he has ever seen."

"Don't regard me too lightly, Dunnie," said Pat. "I have a good club in the making. My first five hitters are 'Dode' Paskert, Hans Lobert, Fred Luderus, 'Sherry' Magee and 'Josh' Devore. They are names to be conjured within this hectic old game of ours; their gun sights are trained on fences. If he is a good kid, don't let these boys of mine break his heart. The way they are hitting will ruin him."

"No, Pat, the kid has no fear; he trains on hot dogs and ice cream. I am warning you now that he will beat you."

"Quit kidding, Dunnie. After these boys whistle a dozen by his ears, he'll lose those hot dogs, and some of the ice cream. What's the kid's name?"

"George Ruth. Doesn't sound tough, but tell the boys to start swinging as they leave the dugout. Get a good look at him, because before the season is over he'll be in your league or the American."

"Well, if he is that good, I'll needle the boys."

That afternoon George Ruth went the full distance to defeat the first major league team that he had ever seen, 4–3. Ruth walked off the field with Dunnie. Nearing the gate, Sherry Magee came almost alongside, and Ruth leaned over to Dunnie and whispered: "That big left fielder on their club is a pretty good hitter."

"What makes you think so?"

"I was bearing down, and I couldn't strike him out."

"Listen, George, that fellow is one of the greatest hitters in baseball. A few years ago he led the National League in hitting. From what I saw of him today, he is going to have another great year."

He had it. In 1914, Magee had more hits than any other player in the league — 171. He had the most doubles too — 39.

The very next day, Ruth was right back at the Phillies. He was so little concerned about the spring schedule that when the Phillies came on the field he looked them over for a minute or two and said, "Shucks, these are the same guys that we played yesterday. There's that guy who plays left field. I hope that I get another chance to pitch against him."

He did. In the sixth inning the Quakers were leading 6–0, four of their runs having been registered in that chapter. Dunnie was taxing his

Baltimore	AB	R	H	O	A	E		Phillies	AB	R	H	O	A	E
Daniels RF	5	0	2	0	0	0		Paskert CF	5	0	0	2	0	0
Midkiff 3B	5	0	4	1	1	0		Lobert 3B	4	0	0	2	0	0
Ball 2B	4	1	2	2	4	0		Luderus 1B	4	1	1	7	0	0
Cree CF	4	1	1	1	0	0		Magee LF	3	1	0	2	0	0
Twombly LF	4	1	2	1	1	0		Devore RF	3	2	3	2	0	0
Derrick SS	4	2	2	3	3	0		Murphy SS	4	0	1	1	3	0
Gleichman 1B	3	1	2	10	1	0		Irelan 2B	3	2	2	4	1	1
Egan C	3	1	1	5	2	0		Burns C	1	0	1	7	3	0
Lidgate C	1	0	0	3	0	0		Marshall P	1	0	0	0	2	0
Morrisette P	1	0	0	0	3	0		Matteson P	2	0	1	0	2	0
Klingle'fer P	1	0	0	0	0	0		*Reed	1	0	0	0	0	0
Ruth P	2	0	0	1	1	0								
Totals	37	7	16	27	16	0			31	6	9	27	11	1

*Batted for Matteson in the 8th

Orioles	0	0	0	0	0	3	0	4	0	7
Phillies	0	2	0	0	0	4	0	0	0	6

Three base hit — Murphy, Derrick, Gleichman, Egan.
Balk — Ruth.
Struck out — Matteson 7, Morrisette 1, Marshall 1, Matteson 5, Ruth 2.

---

wits. One out, a man on second, and Matteson who already had one hit, was at the plate. And the top of the bat to follow. "Smoke" Klinglehoffer couldn't fog 'em any more.

"Ruth," said Dunn, "it's early in the season and I don't want to make your arm sore. This game might be gone, but can you keep us from looking too bad? A bad beating, and the Baltimore papers, just to please the Feds, might put our box score in the obituary column." Klinglehoffer had been subpoenaed for jury duty.

"We'll beat those guys. Gimme that ball," said Ruth as he started for the turtle back without a warm up.

The Feds had no chance to gloat over obituaries. The next morning one of the Baltimore papers said:

"Babe Ruth saved the day when he rushed to the relief of 'Smoke' Klinglehoffer in the sixth, after four Quakers had dented the rubber. With one out, and a runner on second, Jack Dunn's promising young southpaw struck out Matteson and Paskert to end the inning. In the remaining three innings, Babe struck out three more, allowed two hits and no runs. Jubilant over the rescue work of Ruth, the Orioles scored three runs in the sixth and four more in the eighth to sew up the game."

Talking to Baltimore sports writers after the game, Pat Moran remarked: "Dunnie wasn't guessing when he said that kid with the girl's name would beat us. My boys report that he had plenty out there. Not a bad start. Saw a major league club yesterday for the first time, today for the second time and has two wins over us. He looks like Dunnie's next $12,000.00 beauty. For a kid just breaking in, he is far ahead of anything that I have ever seen for confidence and stamina. No club that I have ever seen will make that kid lose his dinner, even if it is hot dogs and ice cream."

Scarcely was the game finished, than Ruth went racing through the crowd to find his friend with the bike. Flushed with two straight victories over a major league club, the veteran Orioles and their manager were slowly walking off the field complimenting each other, and discussing the superlative ability and heroic gameness of "Merriwell" Ruth. In the midst of their jubilation and back-slapping, Ruth rushed by them, inquiring as he went: "Did you see the kid with the bike?" Awaiting their answer, he sprayed tobacco juice.

"Hey, George, come here," ordered Jack Dunn. "I saw him and he told me that you can't hit — that you are a phony. He told me that he is going to lend the bike to that big left fielder on that other club."

"The kid is right," said Ruth, "but I'll smack one for him tomorrow. He won't lend it to that palooka in the left field; he said that I can take it any time."

"That pitcher was too good for you today," twitted Dunn, who was in high glee over Ruth's pitching.

"He was nice to hit against, but he didn't throw 'em so I could get a good piece of the ball. Tomorrow, I'll hit good." Ruth was off.

"Imagine him saying, 'I didn't hit good today.' That ball that Devore caught on him in the eighth would be over the fence in any National or American League park."

"By the way, Dunnie," advised Egan, "watch that lad Ruth. For all that I know he is going off to pitch a game now. He doesn't need that bike to ride the elevator to his room."

"Maybe a double header for that matter," laughed Dunnie, "He is a hot spud, but he is the greatest kid ball player that I have ever seen."

"Not a hot spud, Dunnie, a hot gunner. He went in cold and fired BB shots to strike out Matteson and Paskert. When I was with the Athletics, Egan continued holding out his hand, 'my hand was never swollen like that in the spring. When I asked you to send in Lidgate, my hand could not hold any more.' 'Oh,' confirmed Lidgate, 'he was faster in the ninth than he was in the eighth. To protect that one run lead in the ninth, he really let 'em go. Although blinding fast, he is easy to catch, because he is never more than an inch or two from the corners.'"

"That is precisely what makes him a great pitcher," added Dunnie. "No matter what the count on the batter, he rears back and lets that agate go. No one gets anything soft to hit from him. A week from yesterday we play Connie Mack's World's Champs, the club that required only five games to clean up the giants last fall in the World's Series, and I'll give even money, that with a minor league club in back of him, he'll beat them. Don't any of you fellows tell him the club that he'll be pitching against."

Pat Moran's gun sights were not ill focused when he declared that he had a real club. The following year, 1915, he won the National League gonfalon. And the leading pitcher of the pennant winning Boston Red Sox and the American League, with eighteen wins and six defeats, his first full year in the majors, was none other than George "Babe" Ruth. The travesty of that setting is that Ruth was not chosen to pitch against the Phillies in the series. As a crude recruit the year before, he was instrumental in beating the Quakers the three Spring games that the Orioles played them. In the 1915 series, Ruth's name appeared in the box score only once, and then as a pinch hitter for Ernie Shore. Only twenty years old, Ruth was regarded by his great friend and coach, Bill Carrigan, as being too immature for the World's Series' contention. Perhaps he was, but this writer wonders if Pat Moran was of the same mind?

The Babe took on the world's champions at Wilmington, N.C., March 25, 1914. Although the day was bright, a heavy rain the night before left the field in a soggy condition. The Athletics knew of Ruth's triumph over their fellow townsmen, and they intended that Philadelphians should know of their superiority over the Phillies; sports writers agreed that the game would serve as a test of Ruth's mettle under fire. We'll let the *Baltimore Star* report the game.

BABE RUTH CONQUERS MACKMEN
THE KID GOES THE FULL DISTANCE

Wilmington, March 25 — Though touched for thirteen hits, the kid from St. Mary's was strong in the pinches.

With Babe Ruth pitching the entire game, the Orioles defeated the Athletics this afternoon 6-2. Fresh from the sandlots, the extraordinary recruit from St. Mary's, went bravely to his work of defeating the Champions of the World. He performed like an old master.

The hard-hitting Mackmen touched him for thirteen safeties, but the young southpaw kept the hits scattered. When in danger he was as tight as a drum. In the fifth inning with three men on the corners, up to the plate walked the mighty Schang. His gallant effort was a weak roller to Ruth to retire the side. Eddie Collins came up in the sixth with one man on base, score tied, and one out, and Ruth proceeded to strike him out. Frank Baker popped up to end the session. The mighty Rube Oldring ingloriously struck out with men on bases. In only three innings did the Champions get more than one hit off the benders of the Rookie Ruth. Home Run Baker was the only member of Connie's powerful organization to hit Ruth consistently. The Maryland slugger drew four safe blows out of five trips to the counter. At least four of the bingles were due to the heavy field. They were swinging bunts that would have been easy outs on a dry carpet.

No batters had a party at Ruth's expense. During their invasion of Dixie, the Mackmen had been hilariously cutting a wide swath through all opposition. When Connie invaded the territory of the Orioles, he decided to pit the prowess of two sterling youngsters, Boardwalk Brown and Herb Pennock, against the talent and stamina of Dunn's new sensation, George Ruth. For five innings Ruth and Brown locked horns in an animated fray. The honors were even, but Brown was supported by that historically famous Million Dollar Infield of McInnis, Collins, Barry and Baker, while Ruth's cardinal props were a minor league outfit. When Herb Pennock, the streamlined side wheeler from Bucknell, assumed the hurling responsibilities, the Athletics ran fresh out of resistance. The game lost its competitive spirit as Ruth dashed out in front of the youngster who was later to become his friend and teammate.

Throughout the contest, Ruth's coolness was refreshing. No more concerned than the horse on the weather vane until Baker got his third hit. Reaching the dugout, he sidled up to Ben Egan. "Ben (he wasn't mistering him any more), who is that big dark guy on third base? I can't get him out."

"That big dark guy on third base in only the famous Home Run Baker."

"Home Run Baker!" replied the perplexed Ruth. "Who the blazes is Home Run Baker?"

"Be at ease, kid," Egan consoled, "Home Run Baker is that big dark guy on third base, who finds pleasure in hitting home runs during World's Series on such a celebrated left hander as Rube Marquard. Those pop flies that he hit against you were only humpback liners. Be tough, bear down when he comes up to that dish. Are you afraid of him?"

"Am I afraid of him? I'll strike him out the next time."

As Roger Pippen wrote: "That courage alone was enough to make Dunn love the Boy." Jack Dunn condemned good losers; he called them human invertebrates — spineless Americans. (The attitude of our government at war would seem to indicate that our Army and Navy authorities approve of these sentiments.)

'Tis not odd that Ruth should survey Baker with awe and admiration. Ruth wished to discover that Baker had what he himself did not possess. Evidently he saw nothing, since Ruth later relegated Baker's records to the limbo of forgotten documents.

Old time pitchers recalling this lineup might well reverberate with shudders. There was a formidable array of talent. Opposing hurlers did not have a recess after getting by the first four hitters of that roster. I submit and depose and what-have-you that their bats were burdened with scornful insolence. If it be true that baseball is a game in which a tall man stands on a hill and fires hot shots at men who have only a stick with which to defend themselves, then I further depose that Connie's Athletics of that year, defended themselves offensively. Indeed I do.

The slogan of the Athletics that year was: "Trot 'em out and we'll take 'em." The only courtesy that that aggregation of brilliant brutes requested of the opposition was the joy of aggression. There was never a question in their minds as to whether or not they would win; their sole perplexity was when they would cease scoring. Be it to their glory that such a perplexity had its inception in a charitable impulse to spare the morale and masculine dignity of the opposition.

Over-confidence beat that club in the World's Series that year. The consensus of opinion among neutral baseball men and baseball experts was that the Athletics would take four straight from the Braves. The reverse happened. Accordingly, 1914 has become a red letter year in the history of the diamond. First, because of the Athletics' upset and dismemberment; secondly, because along came Ruth, the adult Babe. For the veterans who will recall it, and for the youngsters whose vision the spectacle has never blessed, I submit a complete box score of George Ruth's first game against an American League club. He was three weeks out of school!

After the game, Jack Dunn sent the writer another letter. Woven into the fabric of its theme was the prophetic observation: "This kid, Ruth, will become the greatest ball player of all time. Right now, he is better than any youngster that I have ever seen." Before concluding the letter, he asked the writer to correspond with Ruth and counsel him against becoming squirrel fodder. His final sentence before me now is: "Tell him to pay no heed to those darn Feds."

The box score:

Baltimore	AB	R	H	O	A	E
Daniels RF	5	2	1	4	0	0
Midkiff 3B	4	1	2	1	2	0
Ball 2B	4	1	1	4	1	0
Cree CF	5	0	2	1	0	0
Twombly LF	5	0	2	1	1	0
Derrick SS	3	1	1	1	6	1
Gleichman 1B	2	0	0	12	0	0
Egan C	4	0	1	3	0	0
Ruth P	4	1	0	0	3	1
Totals	36	6	10	27	13	2

Athletics	AB	R	H	O	A	E
Murphy RF	4	0	1	1	0	0
Oldring LF	5	0	1	0	0	0
Collins 2B	4	1	1	1	4	1
Baker 3B	5	0	4	3	1	0
McInnis 1B	5	0	1	15	0	0
Strunk CF	5	0	2	2	0	0
Barry SS	5	0	1	1	4	1
Schang C	3	1	1	2	0	1
Lapp C	1	0	0	2	0	0
Brown P	3	0	1	0	3	0
Pennock P	0	0	0	0	4	0
Totals	40	2	13	27	16	3

Baltimore	1	0	1	0	0	4	0	0	0	6
Athletics	0	1	1	0	0	0	0	0	0	2

Two base hit — Schang, Brown, Baker, Ball, Oldring, Strunk.
Stolen bases — Midkiff, Barry.
Base on balls — off Brown 2, Ruth 4, Pennock 2.
Batter hit — by Brown 1 (Ball).
Struck out — by Brown 2, by Ruth 3, by Pennock 1.
Passed ball — Schang.
Wild pitches — Ruth 1, Brown 2.
Left on bases — Baltimore 7, Athletics 13.
Umpires — Sibe and Steinman.

Friends have often hinted that had Ruth been a college man he would have been a galaxy of stars in himself. College men are often familiar with the accomplishments of professional stars. As a consequence, college men in initial encounters, frequently become palsied with fear. Ruth could not be awed into submission by the fame of his opponents. Having never heard of Connie Mack's champions, they were to him nothing more or less than a team of North Carolina Sand-lotters draped in fancy equipment. Judging by Ruth's standards, fellows attired according to Butterick's fashions were so many sissies — so much easy prey for a horny handed kid who had grown up where life was a biological struggle for existence. Granted that they had an "A" on their shirts, but Babe's best memory of "A" was on his school report and then it was for absence, not for scholarship. The Albrechts, too, a Baltimore semi-pro team that Babe piously beat once a month also had an "A." Babe's pal, Ike Roussey, played for them. At Ephrata, Pennsylvania, even at this remote date, Ike Roussey and Mark

McCarthy occasionally indulge in luxury of reveling in the memories of the Albrechts and Babe Ruth.

At times, there have appeared on the horizon of college athletics stars of genuine quality, who, unfortunately, knew so much about the ability of other athletes that it desiccated faith in themselves. Ruth was hampered by no such acumen. He possessed eminently the five essential assets of a stellar athlete — belief in his own personal worth, the courage to take a chance, the will to win, probity in competition, and a combination of superb power and litheness.

Never vain, Ruth had no fear of the crowd's derision. In the field or at bat, he concentrated on the game, not on how he was impressing spectators, and that explains much of his success. When he was struck out one day in Boston, the crowd cheered the pitcher. After the game Ruth was asked if the applause were for him or the pitcher. "What difference does it make?" he replied. "It's all just noise."

During 1913, the writer frequently went from Baltimore to Washington to see him play. During a spirited set-to with Walter Johnson one afternoon, Ruth struck out Bob Ganley, a dangerous hitter, with runners in striking distance of the plate. More to recall the feat, than to satisfy a curiosity, for every one knew Ganley, I asked: "Who was that fellow you struck out in the ninth to save the game ?"

"I dunno. Some one of those darn left handers," was his indifferent reply.

Babe Ruth was not proud. Pleased with his success on hitting a homer — and he loved a long one — he generously acknowledged the plaudits of the crowd; but Ruth's charity denied his gloating over the humiliation of his victim. For that, he was loved by all players.

One need not be hesitant in declaring that Ruth was a smart ball player. Shrewd critics have declared that they never saw Ruth throw to the wrong base. Rival players took no liberties with his judgment or his arm. Alert at all times, on the bases and in the field, Ruth played the game every minute. He was once asked why he did not shorten his grip, when he was two strikes, to avoid striking out. To get his reaction, it was intimated that other players did so.

"Why choke up? The third strike," he promptly responded, "can carry that agate as far as the first. Some of my longest hits have been made on the third strike, anyhow." He continued, "Those guys who shorten up are not team players; they are selfish individualists who would take a chance on hitting into a double play rather than face the shame of striking out. A club with two or three of those guys will be out of the race before the Fourth of July. They're quitters." And Ruth was right.

After the Orioles defeated the Athletics, Ruth was the favorite of the squad. Three weeks out of school, he was the ace pitcher of the Orioles. All five of those starting pitchers saw years of big league service too. They were Allen Russell, Dave Danforth, Bill Morrisette, Ensign Cottrell, and Ernie Shore. From that day forward, all newspaper bulletins had a Ruthian tang. Breaking camp, the team moved to Portsmouth, Virginia for an exhibition game before taking the best for Baltimore.

Portsmouth being the home town of Bill Morrisette, he was given the opportunity to display his wares before his town's people. Bill had only a mediocre day, and the fellow who rushed out to save his social and athletic prestige was George "Babe " Ruth. Needless to say, the Orioles won.

CHAPTER FIVE

Dunnie's Babe Attracts Attention

INTRODUCTORY NOTE BY HARRY ROTHGERBER

Noted Washington political columnist and baseball fan George F. Will once declared, "The future has a way of arriving unannounced." That sentiment accurately describes the return of the Babe to his native city in this chapter.

The casual observer may be surprised at the desire of Babe to return to St. Mary's to play ball for his school team. However, it is certain that he never forgot his alma mater nor the needs of those less fortunate. After his Red Sox triumphed in the 1915 World Series, one in which he played hardly at all, Ruth returned to St. Mary's 11 days later to lead St. Mary's to an impressive victory over the archrival Albrecht Athletic Club. Entertained by a brass band, a huge crowd of approximately 8,000 fans surrounded the playing field and watched as Babe pitched the entire game. During that game, Babe gave his brand new 2½ carat diamond ring to one of the Xaverians to look after. He had paid $500 for that piece of jewelry from his share of the World Series winnings. Unfortunately, when the Brother was engaged in crowd control, the ring was lost and never found!

On another occasion eight years later, Babe accepted an invitation in September from a local Philadelphia priest to play for Ascension Catholic against Lit Brothers, a well-regarded area amateur team. Ascension's Father Casey, who also served as unofficial chaplain for Connie Mack's Philadelphia Athletics, had gone into debt to build a small enclosed baseball field that was to be used for leagues, which the church would sponsor as a source of income. Father Casey rushed Ruth over to Ascension's field after one of Babe's teammates no-hit the A's in 83 minutes. Almost 10,000 people crowded the grandstand and neighborhood hillsides, fields and housetops to watch him play first base in a 2–1 losing effort. Babe was errorless in the field and hit an over-the-fence ground-rule double which some say traveled 600 feet or more. In the ninth inning, on second base after an opponent misjudged one of his lofty fly balls for a two-base error, Ruth engineered a double steal. The runner going from first to second was thrown out, but Babe went all the way home, scoring his team's only run on a sensational slide.

Later, the slugger signed autographs for every child who asked, and he also endorsed dozens of baseballs for the church, which sold them for $5, a sizable sum in those days.

(The next day, he hit his 230th career homer in the sixth inning against the host Athletics with no one on base. This was the same year that he batted .393, his personal season best, but lost the American League crown to Detroit's Harry Heilmann, who hit .403.)

Thus, once again, without regard to the possibility of personal injury, Babe reached out to assist those in need. By his actions one is reminded of the later words of his daughter Dorothy: "When Dad finally left St. Mary's Industrial School for good, people remarked that it was as if a caged animal had been set loose. He was spontaneous and wanted to sample everything life had to offer. Babe was no saint, but then he never tried to be someone or something that he wasn't."

About St. Mary's at that time, Ruth later commented: "I had kept in close contact with the school, and even then, before I was in the important money, had sent it some contributions. I wanted it to share my new prosperity. The kids I left behind took on a new importance for me ... kids happen to like me, feel natural around me. I'm the same around them. I've always felt cleaner after a session with kids. Wherever they've gathered, they've turned my thoughts back to St. Mary's and my early days in that institution."

In this chapter, Brother Gilbert describes more of Babe's early pitching encounters against superb teams with superlative personnel. The Brooklyn team was mentored by first-year manager Wilbert "Uncle Robbie" Robinson, a future Hall of Famer who had formerly been a crony of manager John McGraw with the Giants. Formerly known as the "Superbas," they were to become the "Robins" (in honor of Robinson), and only later would be popularly known as the "Trolley Dodgers," and finally just the "Dodgers." Under Uncle Robbie, the Dodgers would win league championships in 1916 and 1920. Ironically, Robinson had also been the player-manager of the Orioles in 1903 and 1904, their first two years in the International League. The Brooklyn team against which Ruth pitched featured Jake Daubert, National League batting champion of 1913 (.350) and 1914 (.329); the incomparable Casey Stengel (.316 in 1914), who was a top-quality outfielder before he became a Hall of Fame manager; Jack Dalton (.319); and illustrious outfielder and future Hall of Famer Zack Wheat (.319). This squad would finish the 1914 season with a 75–79 record, good for fifth place, as Robinson began the process of leading them back to the first division while playing their home games at Ebbetts Field, just opened for the 1913 season.

The Boston Braves (later to move to Milwaukee in 1953 and Atlanta in 1966) were next to be spanked by Dunnie's Babe. This special Braves team, coached by George Stallings, was to average over 88 wins over the next three seasons. During the regular 1914 season, the Braves began with a 4–18 record, and were 15 games behind the Giants in July before staging one of the greatest comebacks in league history by winning 52 of their last 66 games to finish 10½ games in front of the pack. The future Hall of Famers on the Braves' nine included second baseman Johnny Evers (the middle portion of the most celebrated double play combination in baseball history — the Cubs' "Tinker to Evers to Chance") and Rabbit Maranville, the zany shortstop. Butch Schmidt, a tall, sturdy lefty who hit .308 in 1913 and .285 in 1914, was born and also died in Baltimore. Fred Hoey, referred to as a writer and sportscaster by Brother Gilbert, had a brief career as a manager, taking over the New York Giants in mid-season of 1899, ultimately finishing 10th with a career mark of 31–55–1. (Hoey actually was totally unqualified to manage a ball team, having experience in little else than Tammany Hall politics at the time.) This was a Braves team which swept the Philadelphia A's in the 1914 World Series.

The story of the Orioles' game with the Giants is amusing, but not prophetic, for it was Ruth's "homer-ic" attitude which ultimately spelled doom for the low-scoring tactics of master strategist John J. McGraw, known as "Little Napoleon," the second-winningest manager of all time.

The Giants were coming off three consecutive pennants from 1911 to 1913, and would finish second in the National League in 1914 with an 84–70 record. Although their next pennant would not be claimed until 1917, the New Yorkers were always a difficult bunch under McGraw. Speedy outfielder Bob Bescher led the league in stolen bases from 1909 to 1912 and was an imposing figure at 6'1" and 200 lbs. His teammate George Burns twice led the league in steals, including 62 thefts in 1914, to go with his .303 batting average. Outfielder Red Murray was a career .270 hitter in 11 seasons with St. Louis and New York. Other Giant players of note were Fred Merkle, Fred Snodgrass and Chief Meyers. McGraw's pitching staff in 1914 was headed by Hall-of-Fame legends Christy Mathewson (24–13) and Rube Marquard (12–22), while the main moundman was Jeff Tesreau (26–10).

Thus, the Babe was in the process of being initiated into the fraternity of baseball by the best which that sport had to offer (or vice versa).

Once again, Brother Gilbert addresses the threat to "organized baseball" posed by the newly-formed Federal League, especially by the Baltimore Terrapins, coached by Otto "Dutch" Knabe. Primarily a second baseman, Knabe played in the majors for 11 years with the Pirates, Phillies, Terrapins and Cubs. His career batting average was .247 and he fielded his position at a .956 lifetime clip. Born in Carrick, Pennsylvania, he became the Terrapins' coach at age 30. Knabe led his "Baltfeds" to an 84–70 record and a third place finish in 1914 before huge, excited crowds of Baltimoreans in Terrapin Park, at what is now 29th and Vineyard. (This ballyard, built in 1914, had an estimated seating capacity of 16,000 with dimensions of 305, 412 and 310 feet from left to right field.) The 1915 Terrapins slipped to 47–107 during Knabe's final season as a player-manager.

However, the most important aspect of the Terrapins' brief existence did not result from their activities on the playing field, but rather in the courtroom. During the disintegration of the third major league, the Federal League sued the National League, alleging that "organized baseball" existed as a monopoly in violation of antitrust laws. The case wended its way torturously through the courts and ultimately concluded in the United States Supreme Court, where Justice Oliver Wendell Holmes wrote the opinion on behalf of a unanimous court. This decision upheld "organized baseball" by finding that it was not subject to the laws governing interstate commerce. Most importantly, Holmes also endorsed the so-called "reserve clause" which bound players to certain teams. While the reserve clause was ultimately struck down decades later through the legal efforts of Curt Flood, Dave McNally, Andy Messersmith and other players who followed, baseball's antitrust exemption is sill in effect today (despite occasional Congressional threats). Thus, even in those "good old days," the sport of baseball played between the foul lines was sometimes overshadowed by courtroom contests generated by the "business of baseball." Meanwhile, Ruth and his new-found Oriole teammates played across the street at American League (Oriole) Park, with dimensions of 300 feet in left and 350 in right field. The story is still told about one of rookie Ruth's rocket shots off the right field fence which hit with such force that it rebounded to and was played by the second baseman, much to the amazement of the Newark pitcher Al Schacht.

Back River Park, the site of Ruth's preseason exhibition game against the Dodgers, was in East Baltimore. It was actually a racetrack where all of the Orioles' Sunday games were played.

Eventually, after the Federals folded, Jack Dunn bought Terrapin Park and moved his Orioles there, long after Ruth had departed. Renamed Oriole Park, it was the home of minor league baseball in Baltimore until it burned to the ground in the early morning hours of July 4, 1944, the result of a holiday fireworks show.

Brother Gilbert has Jack Dunn, Jr., mention several players in a favorable comparison to his father and to Ruth. In the last chapter, Sherry Magee's abilities were touted (a career .291 hitter in 16 years with three major league teams). Mike "Highlonesome" Donlin was even more impressive statistically. This 5'9", 170 lb. outfielder spent 12 seasons from 1899 to 1914 in the majors, achieving a lifetime batting average of .334 with six teams. In 1905, he collected his highest season mark with a .356 average and a league-leading 124 runs. "Turkey Mike" Donlin was also quite a character. In 1906, he encountered trouble with the law when he hit a train conductor and pulled a gun on a porter during the off-season. After hitting .316 for McGraw's Giants in 1906, Donlin took the following year off to pursue a vaudeville career with his wife. The year after that, when fans in his own Polo Grounds began to make fun of him because of his vaudeville attempts, he went into the stands swinging, prompting the police to rescue him and to guard him for the remainder of the game. Several years later, Donlin quit the game for good to become a bit actor in motion pictures.

James "Cy" Seymour, born in Albany, New York, was a pitcher-outfielder like Ruth. In his 16 years with four teams he hit for a lifetime total of .304. With the Reds, he led the National League in 1905 with a mark of .377, a slugging average of .559, 219 hits and 121 RBIs. Spending his first five seasons as a pitcher, he achieved a career win-loss record of 61–56, leading the league in both walks (213) and strikeouts (239) during a 25–19 season for the Giants in 1898.

Dunnie Jr. had good reasons to single out these baseball men for not only their skills at the plate and on the mound, but for their strength of spirit and for the colorfulness of their personalities.

The mix-up over signals between Ruth and Egan in this chapter relates to the latter's desire to initiate a "pitchout." This is an effective defensive play in which the pitcher deliberately delivers the ball wide off the plate so that the batter can't reach it and won't swing at it. The catcher can then more easily snare the ball for a quick and accurate throw to break up an attempted hit-and-run or steal.

The possibility of Babe Ruth as one of Connie Mack's Philadelphia A's has intrigued many serious baseball fanatics through the years. Brother Gilbert expounds on some 1914 details in this chapter. The Babe's presence surely would have aided the A's in avoiding the consecutive eighth-place finishes which occurred from 1915 through 1921 (followed by an elevation to seventh in 1922). Indeed the A's went without a pennant between their superlative teams of 1914 and the club in 1929 which featured Jimmie Foxx (.354), Al Simmons (.365), Mickey Cochrane (.331), Jimmy Dykes (.327), Lefty Grove (20–6), George Earnshaw (24–8) and a host of others. Imagine Ruth on that team! However, the reality of Mack's situation in 1914 is that money, not pennant-producing players, was on his mind. The A's 1914 championship team was slowly breaking up due to defections to the Federals, retirement and a cash shortage (due to an all-time low attendance) which led to the sale of key players.

In fact, the Mackmen were not first in line to receive the services of the Babe — that honor belonged to the Cincinnati Reds. However, it appears that the Bambino's abilities received a negative report from an erstwhile Reds scout named Harry Stevens, who also recommended against the signing of Ernie Shore (career totals: 65–43 with a 2.45 ERA). Also interested in Ruth was John McGraw of the Giants, but he was never involved in serious negotiations. This led to bitter feelings by the Giants' skipper against Jack Dunn, who was an old friend up to that time.

Ironically, Ruth did play for Mack and his Athletics — in one game which occurred during the spring exhibition season. Ruth was in the midst of battling the illness and injury which would plague him for the entire 1925 season, his worst in the majors, and Yankee coach Miller Huggins at one point allowed him to play for the A's against the Milwaukee Brewers of the minor league American Association. Babe played left field and was zero for three in this game, which took place in Ft. Myers, Florida. Columnist Lee Allen of *The Sporting News* later reminisced that "Connie Mack always felt that Jack Dunn should have sold him Ruth in 1914, and it was probably not much of a consolation to have had him for that one afternoon, March 24, 1925."

* * *

FROM THE MEMOIRS OF BROTHER GILBERT

Orioles Return to Baltimore

And so the Oriole pageant moved to Baltimore to encounter Federal League resistance. 'Twas too much for them but not for Ruth. As he stepped on board the boat at Norfolk, he ejaculated: "All night on the boat, and tomorrow night at the School. Mr. Dunn, have we a game tomorrow?"

"No, we'll be idle tomorrow, but we'll work out from ten in the morning until two in the afternoon."

"That's good; I'll go home in the morning, but I'll be out to the School in time to play the afternoon game. My club out there is in first place."

"Don't you pitch out there. We have Brooklyn in here on Sunday, and I plan to have you beat them."

"Oh, Mr. Dunn, they're easy; I've beaten them often." Ruth referred to a semi-pro team that represented a section of Baltimore.

Sensing Ruth's faulty association of places and not caring to warn him that Brooklyn is a major league club, he agreed, "That's true, but they got some new players now. If you play at St. Mary's, don't pitch and don't catch; I don't want any broken fingers on my pitchers, not on your left hand anyhow."

"Yah, Mr. Dunn, but you taught me a lot of baseball that I want to teach to the kids."

"Stick to pitchin'; stay away from teachin'. Go up on deck now and watch the boats. If you keep your head, you'll own your own boat some day."

Passing Jack Dunn, Jr., his Dad said: "Ruth thinks that he has beaten the Brooklyn club often. 'Twould be a crime to disillusion the kid."

"If he hadn't beaten them often, it isn't his fault," returned young Jack. "One sure thing, he is always rearing to go. I have never yet seen you take him by the arm and weep into his ear, 'It's just another ball club. Pitch your natural game out there and you'll win.' Sufferin' fried tripe! You do that to some of you high-salaried college chaps, and after that some of them sag at the knees, and we have to carry them off the mound. I am partial to athletes like 'Sherry' Magee, Mike Donlin, Cy Seymour, my father and Babe Ruth, who are not terrified with too much learning."

"Son, you're wrong there. I regret that I did not have a chance to go to college."

With scarcely any formal education, Jack Dunn's brain was trigger quick. An analytic mind that split hairs in controversy with deadly precision, he ornamented every field of endeavor that he ever touched. Brilliant, impulsive and untiring, even his snap judgments were bulls-eyes. What Dr. Johnson wrote of Charles XII of Sweden might not inaptly be applied to the mentor of ten pennant winners, the wizard of the Orioles, Jack Dunn:

A frame of adamant, a soul of fire,
No dangers fright him, and no labors tire.

On the fifth day of April, down at Back River Park, Baltimore, George Ruth tamed the truculence of the Dodgers' bats, striking out five and allowing eight hits, for a comfortable triumph, and the name "Ruth" became so much an integral part of the Orioles, as it was to become in later years of the Red Sox and the Yankees.

A few days later, the Yankee game that Ruth was scheduled to pitch was rained out. That was the recess that Ruth was patiently awaiting. Although he had been out to St. Mary's whenever time permitted, and the lads were awed into ecstasies of envious delight as he recalled the places that he had seen and the escapades that thrilled him, he hadn't shown them anything. The rain game was the big chance. Some advance money enabled him to purchase an Indian Motorcycle for $115.00. He was beautifully prepped now for an excursion.

Shown how to start it, George was ready for the open road and the wind-blown boulevards. He was not the least interested in knowing how to stop it. In fact, he intended that it never should stop. According to Babe's plan that motorcycle had work to do. No matter how it plied its chore, it would still be too slow for him. With St. Mary's Industrial School as his destination he started a zig-zag course across downtown Baltimore. People stared in amazement and fear at the rough rider who could not stay on the beam. They felt that they had paid money to see shows that were a poorer exhibition of gallantry. Ruth was oblivious to everything, save the front wheel and the management of his intractable toy. Near the old City College on Howard Street, laborers were at work. A sign in front of them read: "SLOW — MEN WORKING." The sign jumped right in his path and over he went, still holding a tight grip on the reins of his iron colt. One of the men shouted something that had no meaning for Babe. But as he lifted the machine and remounted, he yelled: "When you didn't move the thing, I could see that you are all SLOW, without having that stupid sign to advertise your laziness."

Unmindful of rushing traffic, he turned into Fayette Street, bent on forward progress "in any direction." He made the turn at an angle that was horrifyingly variant to the street surface. A colored lad had started to cross Fayette Street, when he suddenly sensed with obvious concern, the approaching peril. With a face full of eyes popping like a pot of tapioca coming to a boil, the colored boy jumped the right way at the wrong moment. The inevitable collision followed. The colored boy hit the curbing on the seat that he carried for just such exigencies. Ruth himself was procumbent in the middle of the street, while the motorcycle chugging away for a much needed rest was between the two. Irked that another had the consummate effrontery to use Fayette Street when he was using both sides at the moment, Ruth demanded in sonorous tones: "Didn't you ever see a motorcycle before?" "Yas, sah, but when I saw them going, they always had a driver," answered the young boy, still using both hands to pamper bruises on hidden lobes.

"Well, this is a crazy Indian motorcycle."

"Yas, sah, the Indian is crazy, but the motorcycle ain't. I hears it trying to get up now, and I gets me outa here, 'fore the Indian gets on it."

Just before Ruth reached the end of the serpentine trail, the mailman's horse deposited a bunker of road apples at the gate next to a puddle caused by the afternoon rain. Good Brother Matthias was standing inside the gate contemplating its removal when up steamed his friend, Babe, aboard his stubborn vehicle, covering, as Brother Matthias later said, "three points of the compass with each revolution of the wheels."

With nice calculation, Ruth missed the road apples by the marginal thickness of the first coat of white paint, but he swan dived the puddle. Rising promptly, his gabardine trousers suggested that he had ferried his ark down the muddy Patapsco River.

"Oh, too bad!" moaned Babe's sympathetic friend. "Now you are wet and dirty."

"Yes, Brother, I wish someone had washed the water before throwing it next to those horse chestnuts."

"Why didn't you blow your horn, and those things would have hopped out of you way?" grinned the kindly Brother Matthias.

"Those things don't pay any attention to horns. It seems to me from the way Wilkins Avenue is polka-dotted with them, that they have got the right of way out here."

Still enjoying the colloquy, Brother Matthias further inquired, "Did you meet many of them on the way out?"

"Did I meet many of them? If any one asks me the way to the School, I am going to tell them to follow those things."

"Shall I assume that some of them were in your path?"

"Brother, I'll say that some of them were in my path; they were bouncin' across the street to get in front of me."

"Now, George, come inside. I'll get you a room, and take your trousers to the laundry, where they will be dried, cleaned and pressed in less than an hour."

"Thank you, Brother! I don't care anything about my trousers. I want to get down to the yard and give those fellahs some fun. This thing can run on its belly."

"As you approached the gate, I noticed as much."

Into the big yard went the idol of the kids, hair unkempt, clothes dirty — just as he had always looked after one of his wrestling bouts with "Keyhole" Smith. "Lefty" had come home as they knew him and loved him, and he brought something different. Syllables were split in halting conversations, hostilities in sports were abruptly suspended, punches in fights were stopped six inches from their targets. "Lefty" was back with a live bike, and there'd be more going on than the rent — the surge was on. No swarm of bees ever followed its queen in a more adoring formation. Those of the outer fringe who were denied the boast of having touched the turbulent mechanism, had touched someone, who had touched someone who had touched some who had touched the torturous instrument. It was another case of shake the hand that shook the hand, that shook the hand of George Washington. Nothing retarded the commotion, or the progress, of the army of 1200 around the yard until the supper bell halted proceedings. After supper, the panic was on again. Whole crowds were knocked down in the mad dash to go forward once more. Not since the Charge of the Light Brigade was more valor shown. Strong men wept as they were grounded in their desperate flight to reach the bleeding Indian. No time to wait for them; the show had to go on.

Once the motor started the mob came to a quick boil. The first session was, at best, but a blurred preview of the real thing. A constant staccato of clashing requests rent the air. "Hey, Lefty, I ain't had a," "Congo's out here," "When are you gonna let 'Keyhole'?" "Iron Man Scott's been on three times," "Hey" — "Hey" — "Hey." If three were on the motorcycle, each one had another on his shoulders. There was no room for it to fall. And so the merry chase continued without interruption until 8:30. At the sound of the bell, everything in the yard comes to a dead stop, a momentary silence follows, a second bell and all fall in line, thence to the Chapel for night prayers. That night there were infractions of the rule that the Prefects connived at. A few laggards remained behind to speak with Ruth.

"Aw, Lefty, I didn't get a ride," from one.

"Well, I can't get the whole herd on at once, can I?"

From another, "Ellis had four rides."

"You'll get a ride tomorrow."

"Yah, Lefty, but it might be broken tomorrow."

"If it's broken, I'll get another. Just be patient."

When the boys left the yard, Ike Roussey and Ruth took it for a few sprints around the yard, intended perhaps for a warm-up for bigger and better expeditions next evening. Over in a quiet corner of the machine shop, the two of them bedded it down for the night.

After supper the next evening, there were sometimes three, sometimes four astride the noisy contrivance, as the chug, chug, chug around the yard continued. Save to refuel, the pace and the chase never flagged. The Babe finally gave it to the Prefect of Discipline, Brother Matthias, who had been so thoughtful during the Babe's visits, to allow recreation periods to lag.

*   *   *

The pennant-winning Braves of 1914, barnstorming their way back to Boston, stopped at Baltimore for an exhibition game with the Orioles. In the Braves' entourage was Fred Hoey, well-known sports writer and broadcaster. The Braves having finished their infield workout, the Orioles were about to begin theirs, when a big left hander hopped out of the Oriole dugout and began warming up. Fred Hoey overheard the following dialogue:

"Who's the big 'palooka' that's going to toss them up for the Orioles?" queried one of the Boston scribes of Johnnie Evers who was swapping yarns with them.

"Oh," replied Johnnie as he glanced at Ruth, "That's some big hunkie that Jack Dunn pulled off the top of an ash can around here. No left hander has finished against us this spring."

"True, but that kid looks good," interposed one of the writers.

"They all look good until they get on that mound," volunteered Evers. "The Orioles' outfielders will have their tongues sunburnt before this fray is over. That kid will need the whole Baltimore Fire Department to put us out today. Along about the third inning Dunnie will send for the same ash can, tie it to the hunkie and farm him out to Centreville, Arizona, or some other no man's land. Dunnie picks up a lot of those kids, but they don't linger in his camp. None of them ever gets two pay days from that wise old bird."

Presently, Jack Dunn's big hunkie found his way out to the turtle back without a lantern or a compass, and the game got under way. The same big hunkie, according to Fred Hoey, not only shut out the Braves, 1–0, but he smote the two-bagger himself, in the fourth inning that chased home the only score of the game.

'Tis scarcely necessary for me to explain that the big hunkie was George Herman "Babe" Ruth.

Playing first base for the Braves that year was "Butch" Schmidt, a

Baltimorean, whose home is directly opposite Carroll Park, Baltimore. The game over, Schmidt was walking across the field, three paces in front of Ruth, when one of Schmidt's friends yelled at him: "Hey, Butch, go back to Carroll Park; your club can't beat the Orioles."

Knowing Carroll Park teams well, Ruth turned to Jack Dunn, "Mr. Dunn, are those guys from Carroll Park?"

"That's right, George; you didn't beat anything today. In four days, I'll put you against a real club — the New York Giants. Get ready."

Having disclaimed all credit for the development of Babe Ruth, I feel free to divulge Ben Egan's best story on the Babe. Egan jocosely adds, "Babe wants to kill me every time that I release it." The story had its inception during the impending Giants' game, just mentioned.

Led by John McGraw, the Giants came in the wake of the Braves. Realizing that all sentiment had oscillated to the Feds, Dunn decided to beat every big league club that he could in the hope of luring to his own turnstiles a decent quota of the cash customers. Should his trump cards lack the necessary allurements, strategy prompted his instigating competitive bidding for his youthful prodigy. He arranged, therefore, to let the money-eyed big league clubs get an eyeful of Babe Ruth. Dunnie nominated Babe Ruth to oppose the Giants.

Egan and McGraw were by birth up-state New Yorkers. 'Twas no secret that Ben was not averse to finding a place for himself on the Giants' roster. The speed king of the National League, Bob Bescher, was the lead-off hitter for the New Yorkers. The game would be close. With Ruth better than half right, the Giants would be pressing for runs. In fact, McGraw would be forced to release his speed. Bescher would get the green light to steal. A left-hander can hold a runner close to first base, and Egan knew that the throwing out of Bescher would not impair his own market value. If McGraw bought Ruth, he might ask the price tag on Ruth's catcher. Egan decided to groom Ruth for the culminating moment.

"Now, George, get me right on this thing. The first and third base coaches on the Giants are smart. They'll study your every movement for the one revealing flaw that will determine for them whether my signal called for a fast ball or a curve. We must cross them up."

"That's right, Ben. I want to beat these fellahs."

"You've got a great heart, Babe, and you will beat them. But we must not let Bescher steal. He burns gasoline when he runs. The guy can fly. If I can throw him out, McGraw will ask him, 'Where did you get that trunk that you're carrying?' And that will upset Bob."

"It's easy. See that clenched fist. When I crouch and clench that fist, ignore the signal that follows. What I want you to give me then is a waste ball. Get that?"

"That means, Ben, that after your fist is shut, no other signal means anything. A signal for a curve or a fast one is just a waist ball. Am I right?"

"Dead right, Babe. If you'll remember that, we'll shackle Bescher. You're a great kid and a smart kid, too, for my money. Five pitchers like you, and the Orioles would cap the pennant in any league on Planet Earth."

"Thanks, Ben! I'll give those guys the nine of hearts."

"That's just what I know you'll do. Go to it, Babe."

And he went to it. There was blood on every Ruthian pitch. Into the top of the ninth, the clubs breezed with the Orioles out in front 2–1. A pinch hitter for the Giants' pitcher flied out to Twombly in left, to start the final reel. With the count of two balls and two strikes, Bescher scratched an infield hit. Red Murray, a dangerous right-hand batsman, ambled up to the counter. To force Murray to bounce the ball into a double play, Ruth purposely kept his curves low. A brace of them failed to catch the corner of the plate. Egan realized that the setting was perfect for the hit-and-run play. Bescher would definitely dash on the next pitch. Egan would throw him out — two down. Egan placed his clenched fist in the glove for the waste ball. His signal for the fast ball which followed was glaringly obvious. Knowing, too, that Ruth would not dare to get himself three and nothing, Manager McGraw flashed the hit-and-run. Ruth whistled a bullet right through the slot. With a swish of his bat, Murray greeted it. The ball cleared the left field fence, landing in the middle of Greenmount Avenue. With the impact of the ball and bat no one in the park doubted the destination of that pellet.

Horror stricken, Ruth stared at Egan.

"What," asked Egan, "are you giving me the dirty look for? Do you think that I called for a bed pan?"

"You might, Ben, have a dirty look, but I did not give it to you," was Ruth's heart-broken response.

Making an effort to be conciliating, Egan asked, "Didn't I give you a signal for a waste ball?"

"Yes, and that is what I gave you," Ruth tartly answered, "a fast pitch waist-high right in there. You are bright enough to see the consequences of it, I hope."

"Wait a minute," interposed Egan.

"Wait nothing," bawled the incensed Ruth. "Get back in there and catch. I am sick and tired of second-guessing."

Nor would the Babe take further counsel from his battery mate, until Jack Dunn pointed out the difference between a waist ball and a waste ball.

"A waste ball," explained Dunn, "is a 'pitch-out'; a waist ball is one waist high."

When Babe apologized to Ben for permitting himself to get provoked, he added good naturedly: "Too darn bad, Ben, that you did not get a chance to learn spelling when you were a kid."

"Too bad, Babe, that the Brothers didn't teach you to ask questions."

"They knew that it wasn't necessary. Sometimes, Ben, just like it happened out there, I am not smart enough to know that I don't know a whole lot. If I ever learn that I am not too clever, I'll be a smart guy."

"Well, Babe, it takes a great kid to own up to that. And in my book that's just what you are — a great kid."

And because he confused a waist ball with a waste ball, Babe Ruth lost a game for the first time in professional ranks to the Giants 3–2.

In the spring of 1914, the sable clouds of a baseball war darkened the Oriole's horizon. Even Babe Ruth, who had lifted baseball from the contagion of the gamblers, could not save the Orioles. The Federal League had landed on the shores of the Chesapeake in the grand old metropolis of Maryland to invade the territory of the Orioles. Baltimoreans were athrob and agog with excitement at the restoration of their lost heritage, big league baseball. In the fall of 1902, the Baltimore American League franchise had been transferred to New York, the present Yankees. The transfer irked Marylanders, but the Federal League would redeem them and avenge them. The ransom price was the spewing of spleen on organized baseball, with Jack Dunn's Orioles as their immediate target. To the fans of Baltimore, Dunn's return from Fayetteville was meaningless. Spontaneously and unanimously, the denizens of Baltimore had voted the Orioles' conflict with the Feds no contest. The whole city marked time awaiting the arrival of Otto Knabe's Federal Leaguers. A pseudo-patriotic feeling for the Feds gripped the people, and organized baseball was regarded as a menace to the prosperity of Baltimore.

During those trying times, real baseball fans contemptuously asked, "Who are the Orioles?" Indeed, a letter addressed to "Ben Egan, c/o the Oriole Park" was returned to the sender for a more definite address. Even those who had passes refused to attend Dunn's games, lest they expose themselves to ridicule. The hot dog and deviled crab vendors jumped to the Feds, and the only spectators at Oriole games were the substitutes of both clubs.

To be sure, the story of the Feds is cold porridge now; they made a

very poor dessert. Their reign in Maryland was brief. Brief as it was,
though, it was sufficiently long to compel Jack Dunn to dissemble the great
machine that he had assembled in 1914. After nineteen games had been
played at home and about the same number on the road, he was obliged
to auction his stars to the highest bidders.

There are those who might wonder why Dunn did not shift his club
intact to Richmond. The answer is simple. It cost him $1,000.00 a day to
open his park. Not a wealthy man, he was heavily in debt. One afternoon
in Baltimore when Ruth shut out the Rochester club, there were exactly
eleven paid admissions. Baltimore had the greatest long distance hitter of
all time and did not give him a nod. And yet Baltimoreans are smart baseball people. Have no doubt about that. During Babe Ruth's three months
with the Baltimore club, less than 5,000 people attended their games.
Across the street, the Feds were playing to a packed house. Thousands of
Marylanders never saw Ruth until, in later years, they journeyed to Washington, and paid big league prices for a glimpse of him.

Dunn had open warfare on his hands. The Feds were dickering with
his players. Contracts were not legally binding. Players were in a position
to sell themselves to the Feds, and enticing overtures were made to desir-
able athletes. The allurements were not confined to the salary; the bonus
for jumping was all velvet. 'Twas not a secret that the Feds had designs on
Babe Ruth. Dunn could ill-afford to lose Ruth. Babe Ruth represented a
bale of the folding currency so necessary to rescue Dunn from financial
doom. Jack Dunn grew nervous. He asked this writer to urge Ruth to
remain in the fold. Ruth promised to do so. That was security for all who
knew the boy. Indeed, Ruth hurried to Jack Dunn and reported the Feds
advances. As he did so, Dunn flew into a rage. They had taken his patrons,
now they were after his players. Dunn had not taken the American League
franchise to New York, nor had he hampered the progress of the Feds.

"Babe," he asked, "have I treated you better than the terms of our contract?"

"Yes, you have, Mr. Dunn. I am very thankful for the two raises that
you have given to me since the season opened," answered Ruth.

"Good! Babe, I like you, and I'll see you through. Before this season
closes, I'll sell you to the big leagues. When you go up, I'll see that your
contract calls for double what you are getting here."

"Gee, that's fine, Mr. Dunn."

"Now, Babe, I am going to give you a chance to make a little quick
money."

"How is that, Mr. Dunn?"

Jack Dunn was well known in Baltimore amateur and professional baseball circles. The mutual respect that he and Brother Gilbert Cairnes had for each other led to Dunnie "adopting" the Babe from St. Mary's Industrial School in 1914. Everyone was delighted: the Babe had expected to stay there till age 21, Brother Gilbert delivered his charge into the hands of an honorable, respected, kindly coach, and Dunn, simply put, received the biggest "impact" player the sport ever encountered. Dunn died in Towson, Maryland, at the age of 50 in 1928 (courtesy of National Baseball Hall of Fame).

"When those Feds come after you again, I'll give you $100.00 for every punch in the jaw that you give them."

"Where are they now?" quickly inquired Babe.

"Don't go hunting them. Let them come to you."

On the side, Babe was advised by another to ignore the Feds; but to do no punching. He didn't.

Dunn was $3,000.00 short of funds to meet his second monthly payroll. Being already $15,000.00 in debt to Connie Mack, a loan that he made when purchasing the club, Dunnie was timid of asking Connie for more money. To supplement the payroll deficit, Dunn telephoned his request to Joe Lannin, owner of the Boston Red Sox, who promptly loaned and wired the money to Dunnie. Obviously such conditions could not continue. Instead of the prosperous year that Dunn had hoped for, he found himself skidding speedily and surely to bankruptcy.

Connie Mack still had his Champions, but Philadelphians were tired of watching him win. As a consequence, Connie, too, was making very little money. Baseball as a professional sport was unsettled. Investments in young athletes were risky. Magnates were not sure of the line-up of the following day; they did not know who would jump to the Feds overnight. To keep players in the fold, prohibitive terms had to be met, and dividends were sure to be lean. Such was the tension among baseball men, when Jack Dunn called Connie Mack on the phone and told him to rush over to Newark to see Ruth pitch.

"Connie," said Dunn, "I want you to have first chance at this boy; he goes on the block tomorrow." A double header was to be played that Sunday afternoon between Baltimore and Newark. Since Philadelphians did not have Sunday baseball at that time, Connie was free to go.

When Connie reached the Newark ball park, Dunnie almost sobbed: "I have to let this kid go. Look for yourself, Connie; he is the greatest left hander that I have ever seen." Ruth was already warmed up, and in a few minutes the game got underway. For the first and only time in his illustrious career, Babe Ruth was knocked out of the box in the first inning, and it was that memorable afternoon in Newark. Before one man was out, the Newark club had rattled three rifle shots against the left field fence. Dunnie promptly had him paged. As the crestfallen Ruth verily stumbled toward the dugout, Dunn, taking his arm, said: "Babe, rest yourself. You are going right back in the second game and you'll shut them out." Turning to Connie Mack: "Yours is not a wasted trip. I will let you see him in the second game of the double header. Ben Egan is calling for too many curve balls and the new ball is too smooth for Ruth to curve well. His curve is merely taking the hop off his fast one. Furthermore, Connie, I'll bet you a suit of clothes that Ruth will shut out the Newark club in the second game."

True to his word, Dunn sent Ruth back in quest of that promised shutout in the second game that afternoon. And just as he predicted, Ruth hung up nine horse collars on the Newark scoreboard. During the intermission between games, Dunn told Egan, "Don't you signal for a curve until the ball has been roughened up a bit. It'll hook better when there is friction on it." Connie had seen the boy knocked out of the box, had seen the same lion-hearted boy go right back and hand-cuff the club that had treated him so unceremoniously only a few hours before.

The game over, Connie said to Dunn, "Jack, he is all that you say he is — a great pitcher. In fact, Jack, he is worth much more than you are asking for him. Believe me when I tell you that though I hope to win the pennant this year, our club will lose money."

"Then if you don't take him," said Dunn, "Joe Lannin of the Boston Red Sox will be given the next chance."

CHAPTER SIX

Babe Is Sold to the Red Sox

INTRODUCTORY NOTE BY HARRY ROTHGERBER

Prominent baseball historian Donald Honig once wrote, "If Babe Ruth had not been born, it would have been impossible to invent him." That observation is proven true in this chapter.

The amusing tale recounted by Brother Gilbert of the Babe's motorcycle ride to St. Mary's, combined with prior tales about his harrowing bike rides and horse jaunts indoor, make it clear that a pattern was developing. This trend toward vehicular recklessness, wantonness, carelessness and just-plain-ignorance would remain ongoing for many years after the Babe graduated to full-fledged automobiles.

Recalling some of Babe's adventures in his "horseless carriages" lends a degree of insight into the vigorous manner in which he tackled the world, especially its highways. Babe was a risk-taker behind the wheel, and he lacked the skill in that position which he possessed standing at the plate ready to drive a baseball. Shortly after he first obtained his driver's license in the summer of 1914, he would travel at breakneck speeds from Providence, Rhode Island to Boston in order to spend time with his sweetheart, Helen Woodford (whom Babe mistakenly called "Woodring" in one of his books). His first serious mishap occurred near Cambridge, and his license was jeopardized as a result.

In 1917, with a young lady in his auto, he attempted to beat two trolley cars crossing in front of him; his vehicle was sandwiched between them into an unrecognizable piece of metal. Babe was not injured but his companion was treated at the local hospital. In fact, it became his modus operandi to "borrow" autos from the young women who had accompanied him during the evening. As his skills were honed and his reputation enlarged, it appears that the home-town police forces allowed his celebrity to affect their enforcement of the traffic laws. As often as not, police would watch over his car, wherever it was left.

After buying his first Packard, he bragged openly to teammates about his reckless driving at high speeds. Another time in Cambridge, his auto struck an elderly man who was trying to cross the street, and an upset Ruth took him to a nearby hospital where he was treated.

From his earliest days with the Red Sox, Babe was involved in the purchase and sale of numerous autos. It was the dawn of the age of mass production of motorized vehicles, and a decent six-cylinder auto averaged around $2,000, with a luxury vehicle costing in the range of $5,000. Over the years, for advertising purposes, he endorsed many makes of autos, including Studebakers, Oldsmobiles, Chevrolets and Cadillacs, but he especially enjoyed Packards. One particular Packard, very fast and maroon with 12 cylinders, became known as "the ghost of Riverside Drive" by Babe's Yankee teammates. Its cost was estimated at $7,000 to $10,000, and it was eventually wrecked when Ruth missed a turn when speeding from Washington to Philadelphia with his wife, a coach and two teammates on the Fourth of July. The mishap occurred in Wama, Pennsylvania, and no one was seriously harmed, although the press universally announced that he had been killed. This was the same Packard roadster which Ruth once drove without a radiator cap, resulting in the expected foaming and spewing of radiator fluids.

In Ruth's 1948 autobiography, he recalled his driving experiences: "I had a long, low Packard roadster, painted in a fire-engine red, and there wasn't any greater thrill in life for me than stepping on that baby's gas. During the 1921 season, I nearly killed myself and four others, in that car.... I hit a turn too fast and we started to skid. Finally we turned over and rolled like a ball, with bodies flying out of the car in every direction.... The car was completely wrecked. I just left it there and bought a new one. (Incidentally, I hit a home run against the Athletics the next day.)"

On one bizarre occasion in New York, Babe was jailed for one day for picking up his second speeding ticket in two months. (It was often estimated that he traveled up to 90 miles per hour on city streets.) In order to play in that day's home game, he donned his Yankee uniform under his business suit and when released, covered the nine miles to the ball field in an amazing eighteen minutes! Ruth remarked, "I'm going to have to go like hell to get to the game. Keeping you late like this makes you into a speeder."

In January 1924, Babe was taken into custody when stopped for speeding in Massachusetts, and it was discovered that he had possessed no valid driver's license for ten years. His punishment was a $70 fine.

All the way into the late 1930s, Babe was still making headlines with his driving, such as the time he bumped another car, failed to stop, and was apprehended by a police officer with a drawn gun on the Queensboro Bridge. (The complainant's loss was eventually repaid.)

Even when standing still, the Babe could be hell in an auto. Once he stopped his car on a busy Boston street and jumped out to chase a fellow ballplayer who had been slinging insults at him. Needless to say, the resultant mess included a traffic jam with yelling and cursing police. When he paid a visit in 1926 to revenue officials to check on a tax problem, Babe double-parked his car in front of the Massachusetts State House and was quite surprised to find a ticket and a traffic jam waiting for him — two hours later.

In Chapter Six of Brother Gilbert's memoirs, a number of additional personalities from baseball history — some significant and some minor — parade through the Babe's life.

Doc Adkins is mentioned as being associated with Guilford College, a church-related, liberal arts college in Greensboro, North Carolina. Doc was a "six-game wonder" in the majors as a pitcher, earning a 1–1 record with the 1902 Red Sox (with a 4.05 ERA) and gaining no decisions in 1903 with the Highlanders in the inaugural year of the New York Yankee franchise. Ironically, *The Babeball Encyclopedia* lists Doc (born Merle Theron Adkins) as having the primary nickname "Babe."

Irish immigrant Patrick Joseph "Patsy" Donovan, born in Queenstown in 1865, was an outfielder and manager in his major league career, which spanned from 1890 to 1911. In his 17 years as a player, he served Boston, Brooklyn, Pittsburgh, St. Louis and Washington, all of the National League; Louisville and Washington of the American Association; and Washington of the American League. From the years 1897 to 1911, he was manager of five professional teams in the National and American leagues. Despite being shuffled about between teams, cities, leagues and owners with regularity, Donovan worked to attain a career batting average of .300 with 2,246 hits, and he led the National League in steals in 1900. As a manager, he guided teams through 1,597 games, winning 684 of them, although never finishing above fourth place. The last team he managed was Boston during the 1910 and 1911 seasons, and he remained active scouting for the Red Sox in later years. All things considered, Patsy Donovan was a veritable fountain of baseball knowledge.

Two other "sale items" offered up by Jack Dunn in this chapter
are Ensign Cottrell and Birdie Cree. The former pitched for the
Pirates, Cubs, Phillies, Red Sox and Yankees during the five years he
performed in the majors, compiling a record of 1–2 in 12 games. In
a somewhat more active career, William Franklin "Birdie" Cree played
eight years in the outfield for one team, the Yankees, achieving a lifetime .292 average. A speedster at 5'6" tall and 150 lbs., he amassed
impressive totals in the stolen base and triple categories.

Ben Egan was the "throw-in" player in the major deal with the
Red Sox. Lee Allen reported in his *Sporting News* column the following comments by Egan: "A couple of days later, Dunnie said to
me, 'Ben, would you like to go to the big league?' 'If you can make a
deal, okay,' I said. So they made the deal. But I never played a game
for Boston. I was traded to Cleveland in a deal for Dean Gregg. When
I got to Cleveland, Jack Graney, the outfielder, said to me, 'Where in
the hell do you find pitchers like Ruth and Shore? I've looked at both
of them now, and I'm never going to get a hit off either one.'" (Egan
hit .227 for the Indians that year, appearing in 88 games. The next
year with Cleveland, in which he hit .108, was his last in the majors.
Pitcher Vean Gregg, who began the season going 9–3 for Cleveland,
was 3–4 with the Red Sox for the remainder of the season. Gregg's
career had been in steady decline since his first season, 1911, when he
debuted with a 23–7 record.)

Although himself young, Ernie Shore would also pitch well in
four seasons with Boston, going 58–33, with a 19–8 season in 1915.
At 6'4" and 220 lbs., the right-hander cut as imposing a figure as
Ruth. Shore's first effort in Fenway Park consisted of a two-hit, complete game, 2–1 victory over the Indians in which the twirler had a
no-hitter until the sixth inning.

Shore and Ruth would forever have their names linked due to
an unusual series of events that occurred on June 17, 1917. When Babe
walked the first Senator batter that day on four pitches, he took exception to the umpire's calls and eventually slugged the arbiter, leading
to banishment (and later a hefty fine and ten-day suspension). His
place on the mound was taken by Shore. The runner on first was
thrown out during a steal attempt, and Shore retired 26 batters in a
row for a rare perfect game! (Brother Gilbert's own words describe
this incident in Chapter Eight.)

Egan would later reflect: "If I have any regret, it is that I did not
recommend Ruth to John McGraw. What an attraction he would have
been for the Giants, and I think they could have used him. The Reds
had a crack at Ruth, though. They had the right to select two players
from Baltimore that year, and they passed up Ruth and Shore and

picked Claude Derrick, a shortstop, and an outfielder named George Twombly."

The Red Sox of that era were a tough veteran team with established stars. No doubt Ruth's brash attitude and disregard for convention colored their opinions of him quite negatively.

In 1937, centerfielder Tris Speaker was among the second group of players inducted into the Hall of Fame. A lifetime .345 hitter, he led the league in 1916 with .386 after being traded to Cleveland. He played his position so shallowly that at times he covered second base on sacrifices. Harry Hooper hit .281 during 17 years with the Red Sox and White Sox in the outfield. An outstanding defensive player, he possessed a powerful arm and played in four World Series. His induction into the Hall of Fame occurred in 1971. With Hooper and Speaker, Duffy Lewis completed one of the most potent and effective outfields in baseball history. He achieved a lifetime batting average of .284 over 11 years. Carl Mays pitched for 15 years, earning 207 victories and a lifetime ERA of 2.92. Everett Scott played steady at shortstop. Overall this team won 91 games in 1914 while finishing in second place behind Mack's A's.

The "John Igoe" to whom Brother Gilbert refers was a hustler supreme. As Ruth put it, "My 11 home runs in 1918 and my 29 consecutive scoreless innings had gotten me a lot of national publicity, and a kind of manager, named Johnny Igo [sic]. Igo thought it would be a great idea and a profitable one, if I became a boxer." Actually, Igoe was a druggist who lived in Boston. Somehow he became a close companion of the Babe's and his first business agent.

Under Igoe's prodding, Ruth held out for a larger salary one year with the Red Sox. Igoe also circulated rumors that Babe was training to fight prominent heavyweights Jack Dempsey and Gunboat Smith (These fights never took place — Igoe's maneuvers always occurred near the time for salary talks.) The Bostonian lined up a trip out west for the Babe in which Ruth played exhibition games with other major leaguers and toured numerous golf courses (allegedly hitting the ball 340 yards on one occasion). Ruth's passport paperwork for his 1920 barnstorming tour of Cuba was filled out by Igoe. The druggist-manager even negotiated for a series of motion pictures with his blossoming star. (These were never produced either.) For better or worse, Igoe pushed Babe to capitalize on his magnificent baseball prowess; thus, the Babe's fame off the field grew steadily. In 1921, Babe retained the Christy Walsh Syndicate to handle all of his business, financial and publicity matters, and this arrangement served him well till the end of his career.

Nine years of Brother Bruno's (James J. McCleary) teaching were

Ruths' last experience in the minor leagues was with the Providence Grays where he pitched for six weeks in August–September 1914. With Ruth hitting .300 and earning a record of 9–2 on the mound, the Grays won the International League pennant by four games. He then beat the Cubs in an exhibition game before rejoining the Boston club at the end of the season. The Babe spoke fondly about the lessons he learned from Providence Skipper Wild Bill Donovan (courtesy of National Baseball Hall of Fame).

spent at St. Joseph's in Somerville, Massachusetts, where he later met and counseled with Ruth. A native New Yorker, Bruno was a Xaverian for 40 years. He later taught for 20 years in Brooklyn and was a willing guide for any brother who wished to tour that borough. In Massachusetts, Bruno came to symbolize the description "Xaverian Brother." Again, Babe was lucky to be guided by the likes of this black-cassocked holy man.

Babe still received emotional support from his mentors in Baltimore. In his 1948 book he noted, "And I still treasure the only fan letter I got during the 1914 season. It was from Brother Matthias and it read, 'You're doing fine, George. I'm proud of you.'" (True to form, in his 1928 book Ruth had said the letter came from Brother Gilbert!)

Providence had a storied history of baseball on the major and minor league levels up to 1949. The Grays joined the National League in 1878, two years after its origination, and fared very well in that league (cumulative .612 winning percentage) until the franchise was abandoned in 1885.

Baseball researchers and historians differ over the reason Ruth was sent to the Rhode Island capital by the Red Sox. Some say it was for "seasoning," and others cite the desire of Joe Lannin to win the International League race. Lannin was part owner of the Grays and, as Red Sox owner, he knew that the A's had the American League pennant wrapped up in August. Grays Manager "Wild Bill" Donovan welcomed the powerful pitching arm of Ruth. (Donovan himself had been an active pitcher in the majors from 1898 to 1911 and would pitch sporadically until 1918. He also later managed the Yankees for three years and skippered the Phillies for one season.)

The late-summer contests described by Brother Gilbert were played in Melrose Park before 12,000 spectators, a record Rhode Island throng. Ruth's heroics were not limited to that day's action; for Providence overall, he went 9–2 (some sources say 11–2, 9–3 or 8–2) on the mound, and hit .300, with many extra-base hits, to lead the Grays to their fifth IL pennant. (Winning 95 games, they finished four games ahead of Toronto and Buffalo. Rochester fizzled to a sixth-place finish.) In fact, Babe hit his only minor-league homer with the Grays on September 5, 1914, when he blasted a Toronto pitch over that team's right-field fence as he pitched a one-hit shut-out. Two of Ruth's pitching victories came at the expense of Jack Dunn's then-depleted Orioles by scores of 11–3 and 4–2.

After the Grays' victorious season concluded on September 26, the team was feted and received a loving cup and watch fobs. The following day, an exhibition game with the National League Chicago Cubs took place, and Ruth again rose to the occasion. In addition to hurling the team to an 8–7 win, Babe whacked a ground-rule triple by hitting the ball over a hill and into some water. Several days later, after attending a performance of *Peg o' My Heart* at the Opera House with the Grays, Ruth left to play for the Red Sox during their final season games, appearing in one game, with no decision.

About those weeks in Rhode Island, Ruth later reminisced, "With all of Dunn's stars gone, the Orioles nose-dived into the second division, which gave the Providence team its chance for the pennant. So Lannin sent me over there and I remained for the balance of the season and helped Providence win the pennant.... I was feeling my oats but my hat still fitted me.... I had an odd extra-base record that year — two doubles, ten triples and one homer.

"Though my Providence experience was brief, I shall always remember it because Bill Donovan, one of the finest men of baseball, was my manager ... he was a smart pitcher and a sound baseball man. He taught me a lot about pitching that came in handy later in my Red Sox experience.... Bill convinced me that a real pitcher works as if he knows he has eight men behind him."

* * *

FROM THE MEMOIRS OF BROTHER GILBERT

Babe Goes to the Big League

The eminently sportsmanlike fans of the Hub have always found some satisfaction in the boast that Babe Ruth broke into the big show in Boston. They owe that break to the munificence of Joe Lannin and the perspective of Patsy Donovan of Lawrence, Massachusetts, former scout for the Red Sox. Making micrometric measurements with his critical eyes as he trailed the Orioles in the frolic through the International League, Donovan found that Ernie Shore and Ben Egan also met big league requirements. Accordingly, he advised Lannin that all three were ready for graduate work. "Big league competition," said Patsy, "will hold no terrors for those fellows. We will meet Jack Dunn in Washington to discuss the ransom price."

"But, who is Shore?" asked Lannin.

"A big right hander that Dunn picked up on the recommendation of 'Doc' Adkins at Guilford College, North Carolina. He is ready for fast company right now."

Concluding a swing around the northern loop of the International League, on July 8, the Orioles had the pennant virtually wrapped up in cellophane. The second place Rochester club was struggling far, far astern of them. Playing in Washington on the same day, the Red Sox were housed in the old Ebbett House. Thither went Dunn on the morning of July 9 for a sales talk with Joe Lannin and Patsy Donovan.

The huddle was of brief duration. Emerging from the council chamber, Dunn laconically remarked, "Ring up three sales on the cash register; I'm no longer a retailer."

"Whom did you sell?" a friend inquired.

"Ruth, Shore and Egan."

Later he confided that the selling price of the three players was $22,500.00 for which he brandished a check for $19,500, explaining as he did so, "The other $3,000.00 went to liquidate my indebtedness to Mr. Lannin.

"Let's hustle back to Baltimore," continued Dunn, "I promised that kid Ruth that I would take care of him. He has been loyal." On reaching Oriole Park, the game with Montreal was still in progress. Dunn watched it from the stands. Ensign Cottrell was winning easily. Dunn sent word to the three players to meet him in his office after they had dressed. While waiting, he called the Yankees on the phone and sold Cottrell and Birdee Cree to them.

When the three players reached the office, Dunn informed them of their promotion. Egan and Shore were transparently happy, and expressed their gratitude enthusiastically. Ruth seemed nonplused. Going to Boston meant leaving home, severing association with St. Mary's and all the tender memories that clustered about his life. "You fellows will leave after tomorrow's game. I want you to report at Fenway Park on the morning of the eleventh. Stay here awhile, George, I want to adjust some matters with you," said Dunn as he dismissed Shore and Egan.

As soon as the door was closed behind Egan and Shore, Dunnie took a decidedly paternal attitude.

"Boy, I hate to let you go, but the wolves across the street are gnawing at my vitals. Since I cannot pay you what you are worth, I am going to send you to one who can."

"Mr. Dunn, I am satisfied with what you are paying me; I am very happy here. I do not care to leave Baltimore."

"Gee, you're a great kid. If I did not pay you at all, you'd still pitch your heart out for me."

"Well, why can't I stay?"

"You do not understand, George, that the big leaguers are the ones who get real money. Your promotion entitles you to a 25% increase over your present salary. Your first contract with me called for $125.00 a month.

At Fayetteville, in keeping with my promise, I made it $250.00 a month. On you first pay day here, I raised it to $350.00. Today I am making it $500.00 a month, and that means that you will get $625.00 a month in Boston. Not bad for a kid out of school only four months. When I ran away from home in 1895 to join the Binghamton club, they paid me $65.00 a month.

"When I was your age, I thought that I could play forever. You need security against the years when your legs will warn you that your athletic days are over. In three months, you'll be back here to spend the winter. Don't forget to come to visit me. Sign this contract. I'll mail it to Boston. Tell Dad the news, then go out to the school. I'll go to the train with you tomorrow evening."

"Thank you, Mr. Dunn. I hope that my next manager is as kind as you. Good night!"

With a heavy heart, Babe brought what he felt were sad tidings to St. Mary's School. After visiting the three dining rooms, and all the Brothers, he turned his weary steps homeward, wondering if baseball and money were worth the severe tax that it imposed. His eyes were misty, and his gait had lost its elasticity.

The next evening, Ruth was on his way to Boston and to national fame. Babe was interested in neither.

Restless and lonesome in the Hub, the Babe's early efforts were not impressive. When a ball player goes to the majors, he generally finds someone on the club who played in the same league, or who crossed his path somewhere back in the bush. Egan and Shore found pals. Ruth's contacts were all in Baltimore. For all that the Red Sox knew, Ruth might have been a lighthouse keeper. To such celebrities as Hooper, Speaker, Lewis, Scott, Mays and others, Ruth was a rookie who deserved to be tolerated. Not that they evinced any aversion for him; they simply had no place for him in their day order. Until he met John Igoe, a restaurateur in Roxbury, Ruth existed in Boston; he did not live there. Warming the bench was little comfort to a lad who craved action. Ruth felt that baseball was a game to be played, not to be watched.

On the first Saturday that the Red Sox played at home, his former teacher, Brother Bruno, went over from Somerville to visit Ruth. While all of Babe's teachers had been kind to him, Brother Bruno had been especially so. He was a man who knew no greater impulse than that of charity for the neglected. Each was pleased at finding the other. As the conversation drew out, Ruth stated that he deplored his idleness, in a place where he knew that he could win. Sympathetic Brother Bruno hinted that these big league teams might be too strong for Babe.

"Not the ones that I have seen," said Babe.

"Then, George, you are not afraid of these clubs up here?"

"No, Brother, nothing doing. Our club back in Baltimore could lick any of these teams that I have seen up here." And Babe thought so.

After gathering rust for seven weeks on the bench in Boston, Babe was sent to Providence for seasoning and the improvement of his curve ball. He joined the Providence team on August 20, 1914.

Scarcely had he reached Providence than the echoes from the crack of his bat and the splintering of the fences resounded in International League cities. The entire loop soon learned that his war club was back on their circuit, and that it was reeking with ruin. With the devastation of the Baltimore club, Rochester came with a terrific rush to lead the parade by the scant margin of one game. The second-place Providence club were hosts to Rochester for a Labor Day twin-billing. Ruth was assigned to pitch the first engagement. The day was insufferably warm, and a record turnout jammed the park. As the mob surged the field for the crucial games, ground rules were made limiting to a triple any ball hit into the center field crowd. In the last half of the ninth inning, Providence trailed 5 to 4. With two down, a Providence runner on first, it was Ruth's turn to bat. The Board of Wizardry called a hurried conference to decide on the pinch hitter for Ruth. It took more than courage to face failure before that seething mob. Only a time-worn campaigner dare walk defiantly to that plate with the league leadership hinging on his effort. 'Twas the crucible, no spot for an untried youngster. A lengthy discussion followed. Ruth had already made two hits in that game, and the crowd fairly importuned the manager to "give the kid a chance." Shouts of "Let him win his own game," decided the controversy. Out of the dugout, and up to the plate strode, nonchalantly, the Mauling Mastodon. Little was known of Babe's busting power at that time; more, however, was quickly learned. Much of it on the next pitch. After sizing up the position of Ruth's feet, and his grip on the bat, the pitcher sent the pellet speeding on its way, and so did Ruth. He caught it flush on the label, and sent it sailing deep into the center field crowd, for a ground-rule triple. The blow unstrung the pitcher. Another hit followed, and Providence was in a tie for first place. A noisy recess followed.

By an odd coincidence, almost the same identical conditions obtained in the second game of that double header. In the ninth inning, Providence had a man on first and Rochester was leading, 5 to 4. The only difference being that there was one out. Again it was the pitcher's turn to bat. The frenzied mob once more howled for the Babe. "Trot out the big kid; let's see him hit," came the clamor from field and stands. Ruth had been loaned to Providence as a pitcher, not as a hitter, but the Providence patrons recognized the same gameness that Dunn had seen. Responding to the demands of the cash customers, Ruth once more came out of the dugout, picked up his bludgeon, and the crowd roared its approval. As thoroughly relaxed as any veteran, Babe took a toe-hold, cocked his weapon, and abided the service. It came in the form of a low, inside curve ball. It screamed off his bat, and did not curve again until it passed over the center field crowd. The moment that the ball left his bat, the crowd began one of those long bursts of applause — echoes of which have since been heard in Boston, Chicago, Detroit, New York, and in other arenas on the American League Loop. A few minutes later, Ruth scored the winning run to personally conduct Providence into first place in the race. Police had to protect Ruth from the crowds that rushed to congratulate their new hero.

The chances are that Babe had forgotten his display of hitting power on that Labor Day in 1914, but it is still fresh in the memories of old-time Providence fans — all of whom seem to find more than a tincture of relish in its retrospect. There the batting of Babe Ruth on that eventful day is always an eligible topic of conversation. Over soup, soft drinks, Spanish and soda; in the fanciest of lobbies, in the ritziest of ball rooms, or the swankiest of clubs, Babe Ruth's epic of clout, that made Providence a front runner, can always qualify for intimate and familiar discourse.

To be sure, the wallops have gathered both altitude and momentum with the years. Granted by all. But for the peace of the community that the name of the place suggests, a special jury of eminently honest arbiters have settled for all time the fact that as Ruth left the dugout, his left foot came first; that he picked the bat up on each occasion with his left hand; and that contrary to all orthodox teachings, as he stepped into the batter's box, his cap was tilted at a tantalizing angle on the right side, rather than the left. Having been duly agreed upon, no gentlemanly controversialist of the future will depart from these authoritatively established tenets.

News of his achievements reached the Red Sox office, and at the end of the International League season, September 27, he was recalled to Boston. That was the last time that he saw service in a minor league.

CHAPTER SEVEN

Another Pennant for the Babe

INTRODUCTORY NOTE BY HARRY ROTHGERBER

A modicum of doubt looms over any marriage which matches teenagers, but when one is the soon-to-be irrepressible Sultan of Swat and the other is a sixteen-year-old coffee shop waitress, then that pessimism becomes mountainous. Especially if the groom gives his bride's name as "Woodward" or "Woodring" or other variations at times, instead of the correct "Woodford." Babe said that she "was a waitress at Landers' Coffee Shop when I first met her. She used to wait on me in the mornings, and one day I said to her, 'How about you and me getting married, hon?' Helen thought it over for a few minutes and said yes."

Dorothy Ruth Pirone, Babe's daughter, states, "After a courtship of less than four months, the two eloped, marrying in St. Paul's Catholic Church in Ellicott City, Maryland, on October 17, 1914." In his excellent biography of Ruth, Marshall Smelser computes, "Counting out his days on the road with the major-league club, he may have breakfasted at Landers' as often as twenty times."

Like many of the factual circumstances of Babe's life, specific details about Helen and their marriage vary according to the source. It has been said that Helen was from South Boston; Nova Scotia; El Paso; Galveston, Texas; or Manchester, New Hampshire, and her age has been stated from 15 to 18 years. Their marriage took place in Ellicott City, Providence, or Boston on October 17 or 18, perhaps with two friends in a double wedding. Clear enough? A story in The *Baltimore Sun* of March 4, 1915, states that Ruth "met the daughter of a prominent Texas rancher — a man of wealth and influence in his community. The young lady in the case was attending one of the swell private schools in Boston. She didn't go back last year. She became

Mrs. Babe Ruth and traveled with her husband on every trip the team took." Many of the details in this news account simply do not jibe with other facts of certainty. Working in Landers' Coffee Shop is rather unusual for a purportedly wealthy, refined young lady who certainly did not accompany Babe on his road trips. Also, her mother and siblings were living in South Boston, not Texas, as late as 1929, at the time of her death at age 32.

In the winter after their marriage, they resided in a small apartment over the saloon which Babe's father operated. The ballplayer assisted his father in running the saloon, and a decent relationship was reestablished between the two Ruths, spitting images of each other. On March 4, 1915, Babe left Baltimore on a train bound for St. Louis, where he would go on to spring training at Hot Springs, Arkansas. Helen bid him a tearful farewell before he went off to his first full-season big league campaign.

What different fates awaited these two young people, still "honeymooners" for all intents and purposes! Ruth was headed for fame, fortune, travel, booze, broads, nightlife, infidelity, celebrity and gargantuan appetites. The simple domesticated life which Ruth knew at his father's tavern would disappear quickly. The new lifestyle hurt Helen to an unfathomable degree. She was afflicted with loneliness, Babe's affairs, alcohol, pills, unwanted publicity, depression, "nervous breakdowns," frequent hospitalizations and physical ailments complicated by all of Ruth's jubilant pleasures. To Helen, the man she married was not "Babe," but "George."

Although contradictions and confusion abound about the details and ultimate purposes of Babe's early marriage to a nice, pretty working-class girl, there are no doubts about the goals of Bill Carrigan and Grover Cleveland "Pete" Alexander.

"Rough" Bill Carrigan was a 5'9", 175-pound catcher who played for the Red Sox for ten seasons from 1906 to 1916, including three World Series. Although he was never a league-leader in any category and was a light hitter (lifetime batting average: .257), he commanded respect because of his competitiveness as well as his knowledge and love of baseball. Carrigan held his first managing job with Boston in 1913 at age 29; it lasted through 1916. He then left the game to enter the banking business. His reprise with the Hub team occurred from 1927 to 1929, allowing his lifetime game total as a manager to reach 1,003 (percentage: .494, and two 4–1 World Series triumphs). The manager was born and raised in Lewiston, Maine (dying there at age 85), and was once a "college boy," having attended the College of the Holy Cross, a Catholic institution in Worcester, Massachusetts.

After Ruth's first game, the wise Carrigan immediately identified the rookie's blinding speed, hopping ball and baseball savvy, along with his crudeness and inexperience; but, he branded Babe as a future standout.

Said Ruth in 1948: "Bill was a keen student of the strengths and weaknesses of every hitter in the league; whether he was behind the plate or on the bench he 'called' every pitch thrown. He'd hit the ceiling if any of his pitchers tried to pitch his own game instead of following Bill's game. He could get just about as tough as anybody I ever met." The Babe named Carrigan as the greatest manager he played under, stating, "One reason why I rate Bill on top is the way he kept the Red Sox up front after we lost Tris Speaker, our great centerfielder and best hitter, just before the opening of the 1916 season."

Like the older men before him, Carrigan was a steadying influence who imparted much of his own wealth of baseball knowledge on the young professional. When the intelligent, well-liked manager left the Red Sox to return to Maine and his banking and motion picture deals, Babe worried: "It was a big blow to me. I not only had a great respect for the man himself, but I had a kid's admiration for a great baseball general. I knew how much he had helped me and in my mind began wondering how well I would succeed under another manager."

Brother Gilbert raises "Pete" Alexander's name in comparison to the Red Sox lefty. This alone was heady praise for a 20-year-old rookie fresh out of a boys' training school. For the future Hall of Famer Alexander (inducted in 1938) was in the middle of four astounding seasons with the Phillies in which he won 27, 31, 33 and 30 games. For his career, Alexander ranks third in total games won (373), second in shutouts (90) and tenth in innings pitched. He led the league five times in earned run average, achieving a lifetime total of 2.56; on six occasions, he struck out the most batters for the season. All told, he hurled for 20 seasons with three teams from 1911 to 1930, also earning a 3–2 record in three World Series.

Alexander, like Ruth, had a streak of wildness of spirit which would not be tamed or tempered. He played shortened seasons in 1918 and 1919 when he joined the Army, and he served in France as an artillery sergeant. For the rest of his life, the epilepsy which developed during his World War I service would plague him, as would the excessive drinking that he blamed on his epilepsy. Ruth once said of "Aleck" that "He could go longer and louder than even I could."

"Old Pete" would later face Babe's Yankees in one of the most compelling contests to ever be held, Game 7 of the 1926 World Series. Having won a complete-game victory the day before, followed by an all-night blow-out party, the "ancient" hurler came on in relief with the bases full in the seventh inning with a one-run lead for his Cardinals. Striking out Tony Lazzeri, he held the lead for a dramatic, marvelous win.

In a 1952 film biography entitled *The Winning Team* (Warner Bros.), Alexander would be portrayed by Ronald Reagan. "Old Pete" passed away in St. Paul, Nebraska, in 1950.

While Ruth's fame in this modern era has rested on his slugging feats and records, few pitchers have been able to match or exceed his abilities on the mound. Brother recalls several hurlers of note.

The exact identity of Babe's friend and pitcher "Meadows" is uncertain, but he was quite probably Ford Meadows, a strong southpaw who pitched for Brother Gilbert at Mount St. Joseph's and who had several major league teams interested in him.

Harry "The Cat" Brecheen was a lefty who played in 12 seasons and three World Series with the Cardinals from 1940 to 1953. A league-leading moundsman on several occasions, his fielding was altogether phenomenal. With several errorless seasons to his credit, Brecheen's lifetime fielding average was .983.

It was then and remains to this day an honor to be mentioned in the same breath as "The Big Train," right hander Walter Johnson, an original Hall-of-Fame inductee. In 21 seasons with Washington (1907–1927), he amassed career totals placing him second in wins (417), seventh in ERA (2.17), fifth in complete games (531), first in shutouts (110) and seventh in strikeouts. However, in head-to-head games with Ruth, Johnson fared poorly, losing several 1–0 games and a 13-inning marathon match to the Boston lefty.

Hall of Famer Stan Covaleski was a righty who achieved 205 total triumphs in his 14 seasons in the majors from 1912 to 1928. He was a control pitcher who was allowed to continue using the spitball (with 16 other hurlers) after that pitch was banned in 1920. Covaleski estimated that the spitter comprised 20 percent of his tosses.

The father of a major-league pitcher himself, Jim Bagby was a tall right hander who toiled on the mound in nine seasons and one World Series from 1912 to 1923. In six of those years, he averaged 20 wins, including a 31–12 season in 1920 when he earned the league lead for both complete games and wins in relief.

Wild Bill Donovan, already discussed, was a 5'11", 190-pound righty who won 25 games in both 1901 and 1907 (25–4). Eddie Cicotte, infamous for his role in the "Black Sox" scandal of 1919, won 208 games with Detroit, Boston and the White Sox from 1905 to 1920. Included in these victories are 28- and 29-win seasons in 1917 and 1919.

In only seven seasons in the big leagues, Canadian native Russ

Ford won 98 games, including three seasons in which he won 20 or more games. He retired with a career earned run average of 2.59.

Sherrod "Sherry" Smith lasted 14 seasons with three teams and played in two World Series with Brooklyn (1916 and 1920). He was a 6'1" southpaw who won 114 games in his career.

It is glorious to be likened to pitchers of this stature and to deserve the comparison. Ruth could always slug the ball, especially when he had sufficient daily batting practice, but his five complete seasons as a full-time pitcher were also filled with special, dramatic moments. Even after he was traded to the Yankees, his arm was "alive" enough for him to pitch sporadically, going 5–0 from 1920 all the way up to 1933 when he gave up 12 hits and three walks in a complete-game victory. The record 29⅔ consecutive scoreless innings that he pitched in the 1916 and 1918 World Series would stand until 1961, when Whitey Ford of the Yanks broke that mark. Babe went unde-feated in three Series matches, including a record 14-inning victory in 1916. The Babe recalled in 1948, "I'm still prouder of my achieve-ment of pitching 29 consecutive World Series scoreless innings than I am of my subsequent home-run records with the Yankees. It beat that of the great Mathewson."

As a pitcher, Ruth's physical size dominated most players of his time, but he was not a strikeout artist, averaging less than 100 per season during his primary years on the mound. He fooled batters into grounding out and popping up; he was strong and durable. Opponents described him as having a good fastball, curve and change-up and no "trick" pitches. Ruth was an overhand pitcher who pos-sessed good control and who ended his throwing motion in a stance ready to field the ball. He learned from his managers the importance of studying the habits of his opponents at the plate.

Brother Gilbert includes the box scores for Ruth's titanic duels against Sherry Smith and George "Lefty" Tyler. The latter was a six foot tall southpaw who played for the Boston Braves and Chicago Cubs from 1910 to 1921, appearing in a World Series for each. Tyler won 127 games in his career, with a lifetime ERA of 2.95.

However, the opening game of the 1918 clash, resulting in a rare 1–0 Series score, saw Ruth duel an opponent who rivaled him in size, James "Hippo" Vaughn. This southpaw Texan, who was measured at 6'4" and 215 pounds, earned a career total of 178 victories and a life-time ERA of 2.49, twice leading the league in strikeouts (1918 and 1919). Babe later recalled, "I was cocky enough to believe I could beat Vaughn." This crucial game saw the typical game totals for Ruth: a complete game shutout, only four strikeouts and one walk, surren-dering six hits. Continued Ruth: "He slipped only once, and I worked my way out of two tough spots." (Vaughn did later win the third game of that Series, against Carl Mays, by a 2–1 score.)

The "Merriwell" to whom brother Gilbert refers is, of course, Frank Merriwell, the fictional athlete of heroic proportions whose exploits were popularized in dime-store novels at the turn of the twentieth century. The real-life Ruth would soon displace Merriwell.

*　*　*

From the Memoirs of Brother Gilbert

Babe Pitches for the Red Sox

Back in Boston, Ruth lived in Roxbury across the Fens from Fenway Park. In the restaurant of his friend, John Igoe, he met Miss Helen Woodford, formerly of Meredith, New Hampshire. At the close of the season, they were married in Ellicott City, Maryland, a suburb of Baltimore. Since Babe had employment with his father, and the Fall is so delightful there, the young couple spent the season in Baltimore.

Baseball can be played in Baltimore until Thanksgiving. Each year at the close of the big-league season, exhibition games are played every Saturday and Sunday until about December 1st. Rarely does inclement weather cause a postponement. There are always enough Class AA ball players and major leaguers around to make two clubs. After Ruth's return from the Red Sox, the writer asked him to pitch an exhibition game.

"Sure, I'll be glad to do so," he answered, "if you put Meadows on my club to bat in some runs for me."

Although Meadows was present at the time, Babe did not recognize him.

"What you want, Ruth, is someone to get on base so that you'll have someone to bat in," piped Meadows. The burlesque of the colloquy is that Meadows pitched the game and won it, 4 to 0. Ruth's home run scored Meadows ahead of him, and Meadows' home run scored Ruth.

A big league ball player now, Babe had graduated from motorcycles. Before returning from a shopping trip one day, Babe and the Mrs. indulged in the luxury of a new auto — a culmination devoutly hoped for. Now the Babe could go out to St. Mary's School on the coming Sunday, fill the chariot with his former teachers, roll over the roller coaster roads of Maryland, and whisk along the wind-swept trunk lines of traffic. He did. He filled it with gasoline and water, but made the mistake of substituting éclat for oil. With a capacity load in cassocks rather than street attire, the Babe pointed its nose for Frederick, and the foothills of the Blue Ridge. The inevitable happened. Thirty miles from home, the bearings burnt out. The car was towed to a garage, and the party returned to Baltimore in sections. Babe was not so well known then as he was years later when rolling briskly en route to New York after a game in Philadelphia, he ditched his chariot. Calling a taxi and hurrying to New York, he left the car there to corrode, with the remark, "Let it die of dry rot." At Frederick, he was only Ruth; at Philadelphia he was the Belting Babe Ruth. The overturning of his car called for an Associated Press story. The day after the accident, a baseball enthusiast offered him a new car in exchange for the damaged one. Better still, the fan delivered the new one to him.

The Red Sox trained at Hot Springs, Arkansas, during the spring of '15. Several of them were invited out to a dinner party, the Babe being one of the number. Good athletes habitually arrive early for meals. A young lady of the house was plying a sewing machine very well, but not fast enough for the master stitcher of St. Mary's tailorshop. Gallantly, "May I have the honor of demonstrating my speed and curves on that thing?"

"Don't let him get a hold of that, or he'll throw curves with it," advised Shore. "He's not kidding."

"Huh," said another, "he's looking for the handles now. If he finds a seat on it, he'll ride back and forth to the ball park."

"You fellows have to play ball for a living; I play for fun. This is my trade," laughed Babe.

To the amazement of all, Babe took the asthmatic wheezes out of the instrument and gave it a concert pitch. Zip, zip, zip and the sewing was finished. As he returned to his chair, he held out his hands, saying as he did so, "I haven't got five thumbs on each of those."

The facility of his operation so stunned the athletes that they called a huddle to muster words of approval. Out of the huddle, Shore ventured, "That's the way he sewed up games for Baltimore."

With Baltimore and Providence in the International League Babe had a record of twenty-two wins, and nine losses. From July 11 to August 20 of 1914, he was with the Red Sox, all of which makes his record of thirty-one games the more impressive. Obviously, had he remained in the International League during those forty days, he would have pitched more than forty games during his freshman year in professional ranks.

In 1915, the boy of twenty broke loose. It was the year of the spit ball, the emery ball and the mud ball. No pitches were barred, not even the duster. Great batsmen had the peak of the cap turned around once in every game, or they hit the dirt to escape the drive-him-away-from-the-plate pitch. The last named pitch was known as the duster. As a unit, baseball men of that era subscribe to the dictum that Ruth never used any one of those pitches. Explaining his success, he said, "I merely studied the position of the batter's feet, then looked at his grip on the bat to find out whether he was a choke hitter or a cow-tailer." The cowtailers were blinded with a fast inside pitch, the choke hitters got their shots at outside pitches that shaved the corners. That season, his first of graduate work, he led the American League pitchers, with eighteen wins and six defeats. Grover Alexander, a battled-scarred veteran in the National League, while pitching the Phillies to a pennant, alone surpassed the work of Ruth. The Red Sox also won the pennant that year, and friends of Ruth hoped he would be pitted against Alexander the Great in a Series duel. They were not. Here are their 1915 records:

	Won	Lost	Percent
Ruth (American League)	18	6	.750
Alexander (National League)	31	10	.756

In those years, there was no such thing as the "Rookie of the Year," or Ruth, with a batting average of .315, including four home runs, would have been crowned spontaneously. Nor was there an All-Star game, else he might have been a member of that cast for the entire twenty years of his major league career.

As a pitcher, Ruth threw what is known as a heavy ball. Lithe and loose, his arm was a veritable whip. He was a cross between a side-arm pitcher and an overhand one. At times, he seemed to pull the ball out of his hip pocket. The batter rarely got a look at it until, blazing hot, it was bearing down on him. Ruth never had a great curve ball. What made it effective was the half side-arm motion that helped it slide away from left hand hitters. As fresh in the ninth as he was in the first, Ruth never seemed to tire. His control was always a thing of beauty. It emboldened him in a crisis to shoot for the corners. When he missed, someone walked, which was a rare occasion. It is almost an axiom of baseball that a left hander with control, who fields well, and has a good movement to first base is tough to beat. Ruth was tough to beat.

When Ruth was pitching, his club had five infielders and nine hitters. The catcher wasn't passed to get the pitcher when Babe was in the ninth position. 'Twould have been treacherous strategy — not merely stupid strategy.

While in the box, he cut down many would-be hits. Indeed, it was next to impossible to get a hit through the box when Ruth was in there. If Harry Brecheen's agility at pouncing on bunts has earned for him the complimentary sobriquet "The Cat," then Ruth should have been known as "The Panther." It seemed that he needed only one leap to reach the third base foul line, then with a panther-like speed, he'd wheel and rifle the ball deuce high to Hoblitzel at first. He wasn't only a pitcher; he was also a ball player.

When Ruth was making his bid for pitching honors in 1915 and 1916, the spots were not picked for him. In that first year, he drew a regular turn against such mound celebrities as Johnson, Covaleski, Bagby, Donovan, Cicotte, Ford and other aces. One writer states that Ruth defeated Walter Johnson on six occasions by the score of 1–0!

The Red Sox finished in front in 1916. Once again, one of the best pitchers in the league, Ruth was not to be denied a chance in the World Series. As proof that Bill Carrigan had marked him as a stiff competitor, he matched him against another great left hander, Sherrod Smith, of Wilbert Robinson's Dodgers. Both Ruth and Smith were gamesters. The game was played at Boston on October 9th, 1916.

With two out in the first inning, Chief Meyers hit a home run for Brooklyn. Then Ruth hung up thirteen horse collars for the Dodgers. Boston scored in the third and the 14th to give Ruth a victory in the first World Series game that he pitched. Since Ruth was in the principal role, the game had to be different; it was the longest World Series game ever played.

During his career as a pitcher, Ruth pitched three World Series engagements, and he won them all. The Babe has the distinction of having pitched twenty-nine consecutive innings in World Series without having been scored upon. Oddly Ruthian, in the first inning that he ever pitched in the Series, Brooklyn made one run; and in the last inning that he pitched in Series competition, two years later, Chicago scored twice on him. During his thirty innings of World Series, those are the only runs that he allowed. In his 1918 Series' encounter with the Cubs in Chicago, Ruth drew as his opponent Jim "Lefty" Vaughn, that whom there were few better. From the accompanying box scores at the end of this Chapter, the reader will observe that the three pitchers who went down to defeat before Ruth in World's Series were all left handers, Smith, Vaughn and Tyler. Perhaps the opposition felt the necessity of taking the sting out of the Babe's bat. As a pitcher in three World Series, Ruth made only one hit, a triple.

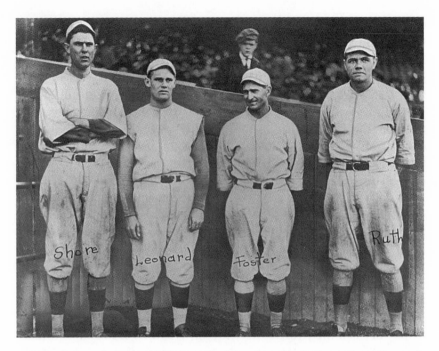

What a fearsome foursome of pitchers for the Red Sox! Ernie Shore, Dutch Leonard, Rube Foster and Babe Ruth led Boston to two consecutive World Series triumphs in 1915 and 1916. Their pitching records those two years were remarkable: Shore, 36–18 with three Series wins; Leonard, 32–18 with two Series victories; Foster, 32–16 with two Series wins; and Ruth, 41–18 with one Series triumph. Even at 6'2", Babe had to "look up" to Shore (courtesy of National Baseball Hall of Fame).

If ever the real Merriwell existed, 'twas here in the person of George "Babe" Ruth. Now regarded as one of the trump pitchers of all time, this lad had sky-rocketed from an obscure, struggling boy in the tailor shop at St. Mary's Industrial School to a national athletic hero. Two years before the experts selected Ruth to defeat "Sherry" Smith in that hectic struggle, Ruth's only claim to athletic fame was that he was the left-hand catcher on St. Mary's team. The fandom of his own city had never heard of him. The lad had literally catapulted himself from oblivion to front page headlines on America's metropolitan dailies. Typewriters and turnstiles beat the melodious new that Babe Ruth was in town "doing his stuff." And his name and prowess were permanently emblazoned across the horizon of our athletic world.

The manager of a World Series contender knows no rest for nights before the impending games. Friends visiting town for the Series are unable to explain the irritability and evasiveness of their pal. Promising to introduce strangers to the manager, the visitor finds that the social side of the boss has suddenly atrophied. And strangely enough, it verily has — for the Series. Very often the manager's attitude is ascribed to conceit. Unfair to organized care! The tragic truth is that the man never knew such humility before. His nerves are tensely stretched to the snapping point and he is at the nadir of depression. Worse still, his melancholic condition reacts on the team. A pitcher can become depressed. The awful anticipation that his club might not garner some runs for him can produce a pair of badly-behaved knees. No sage manager then, will inform even a tried veteran or callused campaigner that he is the pitching selection for the following day. All during the night, the man would pitch ten games and all by himself. On top of which, the spectacle of breakfast would serve as an active emetic. Sorry grooming for so weighty a responsibility! No such fears were apprehended in the case of Babe Ruth; the boy did not have a nerve in his body. The only anxiety that Babe had was one for more work.

And so the front page headlines in bold type, on the eve of the fourteen-inning fray, carried the message: "BABE RUTH GOES TOMORROW." Babe wasn't distressed; he played pool, while groups in downtown lobbies debated the virtue of his left arm. Whatever his mental attitude, he wore the expression "More people die from worry than from hard work, because more people tackle worry." That his team would not score many runs fomented no frets for him. He seemed to sense that his opponents were not going to get many runs for their pitcher. During the thirty innings of Series' games in which Ruth did the gunning, he yielded precisely three runs, while his own mates scored a bare five runs.

In a close game, Babe Ruth was bad news for the opposition. The clubs that beat him had to do it themselves. Ruth would not help them. With a tie score in the eighth or ninth inning, he wouldn't become panicky and throw the bunt into the bleachers — not Ruth. The opposition batted its way to first base; he hit no one, and he walked no one when the "plot was thickening."

World Series, Second Game, at Boston, October 9, 1916
(14 innings)

Boston	AB	R	H	PO	A	Brooklyn	AB	R	H	PO	A
Hooper RF	6	0	1	1	1	Johnston RF	5	0	1	1	0
Janvrin 2B	6	0	1	4	5	Daubert 1B	5	0	0	17	1
Walker CF	3	0	0	3	1	Myers CF	6	1	1	5	1
Walsh CF	3	0	0	1	0	Wheat LF	5	0	0	2	0
Hobl'tzl 1B	2	0	0	21	1	Cutshaw 2B	5	0	0	5	6

Boston	AB	R	H	PO	A		Brooklyn	AB	R	PO	H	A
*McNally	0	1	0	0	0		Mowrey 3B	5	0	1	3	5
Lewis LF	3	0	1	1	0		Olson SS	2	0	1	2	4
Gardner 3B	5	0	0	3	6		Miller C	5	0	1	4	1
**Gainer	1	0	1	0	0		Smith P	5	0	1	1	7
Scott SS	4	1	2	1	8							
Thomas C	4	0	1	5	4							
Ruth P	4	0	0	2	4							
Totals	41	2	7	42	30			43	1	6	40#	25

* Ran for Hoblitzel in 14th.
**Batted for Gardner in 14th.
#One out when inning run was scored.
Errors — Boston 1: Gardner. Brooklyn 2: Cutshaw, Mowrey.

Boston	0	1	0	0	0	0	0	0	0	0	0	0	0	1	2
Brooklyn	1	0	0	0	0	0	0	0	0	0	0	0	0	0	1

Two base hits, Smith, Janvrin.
Three base hits, Scott, Thomas.
Home run, Myers.
Sacrifice hits, Olson 2, Lewis 2, Thomas.
Double plays, Mowrey, Cutshaw to Daubert; Myers to Miller; Scott, Janvrin to Hoblitzel.
Earned runs, Boston 2, Brooklyn 1.
First base errors, Boston 1, Brooklyn 1.
Left on bases, Boston 9, Brooklyn 5.
Base on balls, off Smith 6, off Ruth 3.
Strike-outs, by Ruth 3, by Smith 2.
Time, 2:32.
Umpires, Dineen, Quigley, Connolly, and O'Day.

World Series, First Game, at Chicago, September 5, 1918

Boston	AB	R	H	PO	A		Chicago	AB	R	PO	H	A
Hooper RF	4	0	1	4	0		Flack RF	3	0	1	2	0
Shean 2B	2	1	1	0	3		Hollocker SS	3	0	0	2	1
Strunk CF	3	0	0	2	0		Mann LF	4	0	1	0	0
Whiteman LF	4	0	2	5	0		Paskert CF	4	0	2	2	0
McInnis 1B	2	0	1	10	0		Merkle 1B	3	0	1	9	2
Boston	**AB**	**R**	**H**	**PO**	**A**		**Chicago**	**AB**	**R**	**PO**	**H**	**A**
Scott SS	4	0	0	0	3		Pick 2B	3	0	0	1	1
Thomas 3B	3	0	0	1	1		Deal 3B	4	0	1	1	3
Agnew C	3	0	0	5	0		Killifer C	4	0	0	7	2
Ruth P	3	0	0	0	1		Vaughn P	3	0	0	3	5
							*O'Farrell	1	0	0	0	0
							**McCabe	0	0	0	0	0

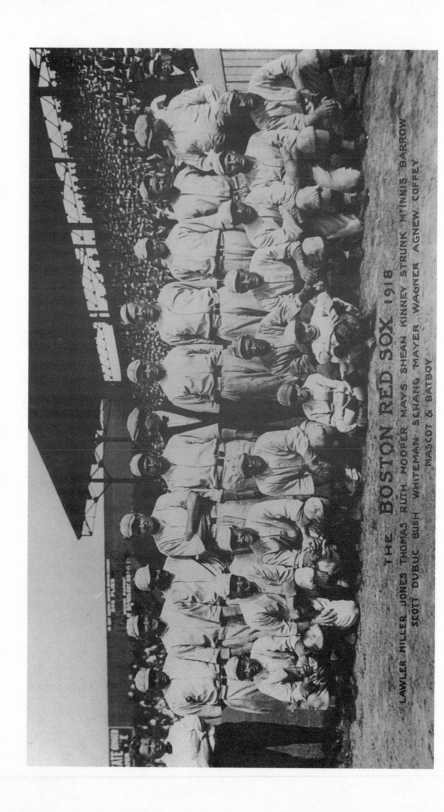

THE BOSTON RED SOX 1918

LAWLER HILLER JONES THOMAS RUTH HOOPER MAYS SHEAN KINNEY STRUNK McINNIS BARROW

SCOTT DUBUC BUSH WHITEMAN SCHANG MAYER WAGNER AGNEW COFFEY

MASCOT & BATBOY

Boston	AB	R	H	PO	A	Chicago	AB	R	PO	H	A
Totals	28	1	5	27	8		32	0	6	27	14

*Batted for Pick in the 9th inning.
**Ran for Deal in the 9th inning.
Errors — NONE.

Boston	0	0	0	1	0	0	0	0	0	1
Chicago	0	0	0	0	0	0	0	0	0	0

Sacrifice hits, McGinnis, Hollocker, Strunk.
Left on bases, Boston 5, Chicago 8.
Base on balls, off Ruth 1, off Vaughn 3.
Strikeouts, by Ruth 4, by Vaughn 6.
Hit batsman, Ruth 1 (Flack).
Time 1:50.
Umpires, O'Day, Hildebrand, Klem, Owens.

World Series, Fourth Game, at Boston, September 10, 1918

Boston	AB	R	H	PO	A	Chicago	AB	R	PO	H	A
Hooper RF	3	0	0	1	0	Flack RF	4	0	1	3	0
Shean 2B	3	0	1	4	4	Hollocker SS	4	0	0	2	0
Strunk CF	4	0	0	0	0	Mann LF	4	0	0	3	0
Whiteman LF	3	1	0	1	0	Paskert C	4	0	0	3	0
Bush P	0	0	0	0	0	Merckle 1B	3	0	1	9	1
McInnis 1B	3	1	1	16	1	Pick 2B	2	0	2	0	2
Ruth P-LF	2	0	1	0	4	Zeider 3B	0	0	0	1	2
Scott SS	3	0	0	3	8	Deal 3B	2	0	1	1	3
Thomas 3B	3	0	0	2	3	Workman 2B	1	0	0	1	0
Agnew C	2	0	0	0	1	Killifer C	2	1	0	1	0
Shang C	1	1	1	0	0	Tyler P	0	0	0	1	4
						Douglas P	0	0	0	0	0
						*O'Farrell	1	0	0	0	0
						**Hendrix	1	0	1	0	0
Boston	AB	R	H	PO	A	Chicago	AB	R	PO	H	A
						#McCabe	0	1	0	0	0
						##Barker	1	0	0	0	0
Totals	27	3	4	27	21		29	2	6	25	12

Opposite: The Red Sox have not tasted a World Series championship since the Babe and his 1918 teammates captured the crown by defeating the Chicago Cubs 4 games to 2. Ruth and Carl Mays each won two games in that Series, with Ruth compiling an amazing 1.06 earned run average. The 23-year-old Babe is flanked by Fred Thomas and future Hall of Famer Harry Hooper (courtesy of National Baseball Hall of Fame).

* Batted for Deal in 7th.
**Batted for Tyler 8th.
#Ran for Hendrix in the 8th.
##Batted for Killifer in 9th.
Errors — Douglas.

Boston	0	0	0	2	0	0	0	1	x	3
Brooklyn	0	0	0	0	0	0	0	2	0	2

Two base hits, Shean.
Three base hit, Ruth.
Stolen base, Shean.
Sacrifice hits, Ruth, Hooper.
Double play, Ruth, Scott to McInnis; Scott, Shean to McInnis.
Left on bases, Chicago 6, Boston 4.
First base errors, Boston 1.
Base on balls, off Tyler 2, off Ruth 6.
Struck-out by Tyler 1.
Hits off Tyler, 3 in 7 innings; off Douglas, 1 in 1; off Ruth 7 in 8; off Bush, none in 1.
Passed balls, Killifer 2.
Time, 1:55.
Umpires, Owens, O'Day, Hildebrand, Klem.

(The above game was Ruth's last performance as a Major League pitcher in the World Series. Babe Ruth had been with the Boston Red Sox five years, during which time they won three world's championships. In 1920, Ruth joined the New York Yankees. Until that time, the Yanks had never figured in a World Series!)

CHAPTER EIGHT

Ruth Becomes a Yankee

Three key events in Babe Ruth's young professional career occurred between July 1919 and January 1920: He was converted from an all-star regular pitcher to a slugging outfielder who appeared in the lineup daily; he was sold by Red Sox owner Harry Frazee to the New York Yankees; and the "Black Sox" scandal surrounding the 1919 World Series between the Chicago White Sox and Cincinnati Reds was uncovered and publicized. Brother Gilbert touches briefly on each milestone in this chapter.

As early as 1916, in the World Series program, the Babe commented on the advantages of being a full-time batter. In the article titled "Why a Pitcher Should Hit — My Ideal of an All 'Round Ball Player," Ruth commented, "At any rate I would like to go through an entire season playing regularly every day, in some position like first base. There is no discounting the fact that a pitcher is handicapped by not taking his regular turn against the opposing twirlers. A man needs that steady training day in and day out to put a finish on his work." Even so, opined Babe, "The pitcher who can't get in there in the pinch and win his own game with a healthy wallop, isn't more than half earning his salary to my way of thinking."

Edward Grant Barrow took full credit for the transformation of the Bambino to an everyday player. Hall-of-Famer Barrow managed the Tigers (1903–1904) and Red Sox (1918–1920), before moving to the Yankees as business manager (equivalent to today's general manager). He achieved greatness by capably blending both the sport and business of baseball from his front-office position with the Yanks for 25 years.

In his 1951 autobiography, written two years before his death,

Barrow recalled, "Many people have said that when I changed Babe Ruth from a left-handed pitcher into a full-time outfielder, I changed the whole course of baseball. In a measure, of course, this is true."

"Cousin Ed" remembered that his mind was "just about made up" after he witnessed a 579-foot Ruth homer in spring training at the Tampa Fair Grounds. He makes no mention of the contribution of Red Sox field captain Harry Hooper to this change. Baseball historian Lee Allen, in *The Sporting News*, recounted an interview with Bill Carrigan, Babe's original Boston manager, who said, "Harry Hooper is the man who made an outfielder out of Ruth." In a later communication with Allen, Hooper described how a "strategy board" composed of Hooper, a coach and another player had to lobby hard to convince Barrow to play Ruth daily, before Barrow reluctantly consented.

In any event, no matter how the ultimate decision was made, Ruth's booming bat, which accounted for a then-amazing record of 29 homers, and the crowds, which were drawn to see another circuit clout, effectively put an end to his appearances on the mound. The business end of the Red Sox appreciated the swollen admissions as much as the fans loved the increased homer output from the Babe.

Much has been written about the Babe's batting style. The Bambino said it best in his 1928 book when he observed, "I'm paid to hit home runs. In a way that's a handicap. To hit home runs, I've got to swing from my heels with all the power in my body. Which isn't good batting style."

While Ruth professed to pay tribute to Ty Cobb's hitting form if one wished to hit for a high average, it is clear that he himself copied much of the stance and manner of the legendary Shoeless Joe Jackson, who was always a difficult out for Ruth the pitcher. Babe described himself as a "swing hitter" rather than a "choke hitter": "I use a golfing swing—loose and easy with a slight upward motion.... I stand with my feet fairly close together, the right foot a little further in than the left, and take a long stride with the swing.... I hit with my entire body coming around on the swing.... Naturally, with my whole body on a pivot I get a longer follow-through...."

Slow-motion and stop-action photos of Babe support his description. He upper-cut the ball deliberately and with great finality to give it a ride. If he missed, he corkscrewed himself into the ground. Thus, fandom was awed by his power even when he didn't connect.

Ruth's war clubs were very much different from the bats used today. His bats in 1919–1920 averaged about 35 inches long and 44 ounces; he owned several which weighed in at 54 ounces. Although thinner in the handle than his predecessors', Ruth's bats were definitely thick-handled compared to the 32–36 ounce sticks enjoyed by today's players.

The Babe's ability to wield these mighty sticks was never questioned. As Ed Barrow recalled, "The Babe Ruth of 1918 was a fine-looking athlete, trim-waisted, strong, fast, a remarkably skillful base runner, and altogether unlike the latter-day remembrances we have of the Babe as a round-waisted fellow of Billiken-like appearance."

Although he amassed many strikeouts in his career, he seldom took a called third strike. Babe was up there to hit the ball, and everyone knew it, especially the opposing pitcher. His very presence at the plate served a challenge to the other team, or answered a challenge, as was the case in 1919 when he hit an astounding four grand-slam homers, all on the road. In his career, he hit a grand total of 16 homers with the bases full. Ruth was thrilling to watch as no previous player had ever been. Humbly portraying himself, the Babe observed, "The balls I hit most squarely and with most power are apt to go high into the air. My home runs, for the most part, are usually high flies that simply carry out of the park. That's because I take a loose swing with a slight upward angle."

After the 1919 regular season play concluded, certain events conspired in October to rob the sport of its innocence and to shake public confidence and support of "organized baseball" to the extreme. The "Black Sox" scandal revolved around the efforts of gamblers to influence several members of the Chicago White Sox to fix certain Series games and to manipulate final scores. Seven players, including standout Shoeless Joe Jackson (.351 in 1919) and pitching aces Eddie Cicotte (29–7) and Lefty Williams (23–11), were implicated in this dishonest corruption of the national game. Also implicated was Buck Weaver, who supposedly knew about the deal to throw the Series but who kept quiet about the matter.

During the past eighty years, this effort to intentionally fail by the White Sox has been the subject of numerous books, movies, plays, articles and learned dissertations. Sportswriters, lawyers, fans, sociologists and others have commented at length on the propriety of the lifetime ban from "organized baseball" of the eight so-called Black Sox. Even the great Boston Red Sox Hall of Famer Ted Williams recently spearheaded efforts to lift the ban on Shoeless Joe Jackson, whose naiveté and unsophistication may have been his downfall.

The Reds won that Series five games to three; however, the revelations of corruption, the investigation, the Grand Jury, and the trial and other court proceedings soon followed. Although some sports followers tried to ignore this ignominious mess, most condemned it as a blow to the purity of the national pastime. Baseball owners reacted by voting to install the rigid Judge Kenesaw Mountain Landis as the game's first commissioner. The repercussions of the scandal were potentially deadly to baseball, especially in the short-term reaction of its loyal and patriotic followers.

However, 25 year old Babe Ruth came to the rescue, as surely as the cavalry in a John Ford western. In her book, *My Dad, The Babe,* Dorothy Ruth Pirone remembers the words that Black Sox scandal historian and author Eliot Asinof spoke to her: "It was Babe Ruth who saved baseball. If it hadn't been for Ruth, no one would have gone to another game. It would have taken years to heal the fans' wounds, and, quite possibly, [baseball] may never have been the same. At the time, there was a feeling that everything from a boxing match to a presidential election might be fixed. Then along comes Ruth and knocks the whole mentality out of the box. Even though everything may have been fixed, you couldn't 'fix' Babe Ruth."

In 1920, the Babe clobbered the astounding total of 54 home runs followed by a colossal 59 homers in 1921. In his own 1948 book, he modestly opined, "It has been said that Landis saved the game from ruin after the Black Sox scandal. Others say that I had a lot to do with the game's salvation. The important thing is that baseball snapped back. If my home-run hitting in 1920 established a new era in baseball, helped the fans of the nation, young and old, forget the past and the terrible fact that they had been sold out, that's all the epitaph I want."

The prior statement was spoken by Ruth as a member of the New York American League club, looking back on the records he set as a Yankee. The trading of the young slugger by Red Sox owner Harry Frazee commenced what writer Dan Shaughnessey aptly called "The Curse of the Bambino" on the Boston team.

Frazee, a New York City theatrical producer, the youngest owner in baseball, with a partner had purchased the Red Sox from Boston real estate magnate Joe Lannin in December 1916 for approximately $1 million. In spite of the Babe's successful conversion to an outfielder in 1919, a year in which he led the league in homers (29) and RBIs (114), the Red Sox finished a disappointing sixth. At the same time, Frazee needed cash money to support his Broadway theatrical productions. He found his source of cash in the pockets of Yankee owners Jacob Ruppert, a millionaire brewery owner, and Colonel "Til" Huston, a millionaire engineer. (In recent years, conjectures that Frazee needed moneys to fund the musical *No! No! Nanette* have been popular but appear not to be grounded in fact. That Broadway production did not even open on Broadway until 1925, having had its debut in Chicago a year earlier.)

On December 26, 1919, the contract by which Ruth was transferred between the two clubs was signed. The price was $125,000 in cash, 20 percent of which was paid on the spot, and a loan of $300,000, which would allow Frazee to continue to operate in Fenway Park which had just opened in April 1912, the same month the S.S. *Titanic* met its doom in the North Atlantic. In their book *The Babe in Red Stockings*, Kerry Keene, Raymond Sinibaldi and David Hickey call this transaction "The Sale of the Century."

Until Ruth was sold, the Red Sox had been one of the dominant American League teams since the club's inception in 1901, becoming World Series champions on five occasions. Since Babe's sale, the Boston club has never won it all, losing four heartbreaking seven-game Series. They have been beset with bad trades, bad breaks and bad luck, all of these events fueling popularity in Shaughnessey's "curse" theory. Frazee's attempts to justify the sale of Ruth were not accepted by skeptical sportswriters or angry fans, all of whom felt jilted over the loss of their young superstar. The sale of other Boston players to New York made it appear as if the Red Sox were a Yankee farm team. The Red Sox thereafter deteriorated until hitting rock bottom (the cellar) in 1922. Boston did not win the American League pennant again until 1946.

The Babe later reminisced, "As for my reaction over coming to the big town, at first I was pleased, largely because it meant more money. Then I got the bad feeling we all have when we pull up our roots. My home, all my connections, affiliations and friends were in Boston. The town had been good to me." The Babe went on, "I knew New York principally as a place where the Red Sox played eleven games a year, where I had hit some home runs, won some shutouts, consumed beer and had a lot of fun ... today it is my home ... and when people think of me as a ballplayer, they think of me as a Yankee."

By most accounts, when he played for Boston, Ruth began living on a farm which he acquired as a retreat and winter residence in Sudbury, Massachusetts. Originally built in 1737, it was located about 20 miles west of Boston. In addition to the old farmhouse (which Babe quickly rid of antiques, describing them as "junk"), the 160-acre piece of property was home to chickens, hunting dogs, a large pond and some woods. No doubt Helen hoped that the time they spent together in idyllic New England surroundings would rescue their rocky relationship.

Home Plate Farm, as it was called, was the scene of intense activity during the Ruths' years there. There was much hunting, fishing and shooting of firearms as Ruth, raised in the teeming big-city waterfront of Baltimore, became a country gentleman for a few months each year.

In her reminiscence, daughter Dorothy recalled, "When he wasn't hunting, fishing or horseback riding, he was remodeling the farmhouse, chopping wood and raising chickens, turkeys and White English pit bulls. I never knew why I was forbidden to go near the barn until one day seventy-five pit bulls escaped from their pen, which was inside, and killed a herd of cows.... Not only did my father have to pay for the cows, he also had to shoot all the dogs."

After a number of years, at times quiet and sometimes stormy, at Sudbury, the Ruths' inevitable official separation in 1925 meant the end of Babe's days as a country squire.

Meanwhile, Brother Gilbert makes reference to a unique cast of baseball characters and personalities who had some interconnection with the Babe.

Ray Morgan, the batter whose walk led to Ernie Shore's perfect fame, played infield for eight years for the Washington Nationals, achieving a lifetime batting average of .254. Pennsylvanian Buck Freeman, who played for three teams in his 11-year career, was a serious offensive threat at the plate. He led the league twice in homers and RBIs and once in triples, occupying fourth place on the lifetime triples list.

The "oafs" Nick Altrock, Dizzy Dean and Rube Waddell were impressive hurlers. Left-hander Altrock's career spanned from 1898 to 1924; his peak seasons, 1904–1906, saw him win 62 games. Hall of Famer Dean won 150 games during his 11 seasons with the Cardinal and Cubs, including a 30–7 year in 1934. He led the National League in strikeouts four years, making frequent use of his "beanballs." Waddell's 192 southpaw wins in 13 seasons from 1897 to 1910 earned him a well-deserved spot in the Hall of Fame. His feats included leading the league in strikeouts an amazing seven times and achieving a lifetime earned run average of 2.16, sixth on the all-time list.

The corps of pitchers who were unable to tame the Babe included: righty Hooks Dauss, 21–9; the first Dutch Leonard (there were two pitchers so named), one of Ruth's Red Sox teammates who was traded to Detroit in 1919 and earned 139 lifetime wins; Frederick "Fritz" Coumbe, 13–7 for the Indians in 1918; the White Sox' Lefty Williams, who excelled on the mound in 1916-1917 and 1919-1920; the Yankees' Hank Thormahlen, whose best year was 1919 when he won 12 games; Dickie Kerr, unfazed by the scandalous air about him, and winner of 53 games for the White Sox during his four-year career; and "Dauntless Dave" Danforth who led the American League in relief wins in 1917 and 1918. The Cleveland Indian manager whose strategy in this chapter was destroyed by Ruth was Lee Fohl, skipper for 1,521 games for three American League teams from 1915 to 1926 (1,516 more than he appeared in as a player).

Brother Gilbert discusses two pairs of battery mates who struggled to solve the problem of how to pitch to Ruth. Catcher Ray Schalk was a master at handling pitchers during his 18-year Hall-of-Fame career. He is credited with being the original catcher to back up first base in the event of an overthrow. As the manager of the White Sox, he later encouraged the famed Princetonian (and future spy) Moe Berg to convert from shortstop to catcher. Pitcher Tommy Thomas won 65 games from 1926 to 1929 for the White Sox during a 12-year major league career.

As the highlight of his 13-year career, Giants' Larry Benton won a league-leading 25 games (with 28 complete games) in 1928. His catcher, James "Shanty" Hogan, hit .333 that same year, his second-best season mark for New York in his career.

In May 1921, Babe again showed the high regard with which he held St. Mary's and Brother Matthias. After smacking a tremendous homer against the Washington Nationals at Griffith Stadium, he returned with Matthias to his "alma mater" to hit some baseballs and talk to the boys. His "batting practice," in which he lost one dozen balls, took place at Mount St. Joseph's Echo Field the next morning. Nonetheless, Babe hit the farthest ball ever batted in the history of Griffith Stadium that Saturday afternoon, May 7, 1921, against none other than the great Walter Johnson.

In fact, throughout the years, the Babe always remembered the Brothers and St. Mary's whether his personal or professional situation was tranquil or turbulent. Some brief examples follow:

In 1915, he consulted the Brothers and received their approval prior to "lending" his father the money to invest in the new saloon at Eutaw and Lombard streets. Four years later, the St. Mary's band received free publicity worth untold dollars during their western swing with the Yankees. The publicity flyers advertising the Grand Musical Concert touted Ruth by stating, "Here is your chance to get a close-up view of the Home Run King." In addition to the pre- and post-game concerts by the band, the Babe arranged a special performance at the Grand Army of the Republic's encampment in Indianapolis and a huge ice cream party in Pittsburgh. (The Yankees played exhibition games against the home team in each of these two cities.) Babe's friend Nick Altrock, the baseball clown, performed as the band's drum major when all returned to the Polo Grounds. Over 400,000 persons saw the band's live performances on this amazing tour.

In 1921, Babe allowed James Cardinal Gibbons of Baltimore to use Babe's name in a national campaign to raise funds to continue the rebuilding of St. Mary's. Any game in Washington, D.C., meant a quick stop at St. Mary's, often with several other Yanks. He also made a gift of a Cadillac to Brother Matthias (on behalf of the Congregation) on two occasions.

At the Polo Grounds in May 1922, a contingent from St. Mary's awarded the Babe with a loving cup filled with dirt from around the school's home plate in the big yard. When Ruth had "the bellyache heard 'round the world," Brother Paul phoned New York every night to check on his condition. Ruth reminisced in his 1928 book: "There were a lot of fine men connected with the school in those days. In addition to Brother Gilbert, there was Brother Matthias. What a friend he was, as I found out during 1924 and 1925 when things were breaking bad and I needed friends as I never had needed them before. Then there were Brother Alban and Brother Paul — men who send me letters of congratulation every time I do something worth while. These men are among the very few people who call me George."

Once when he returned to New York in 1925, among the thousands who greeted his arrival was Father Edward Quinn, a priest who had been assigned previously to St. Mary's. They shared a cab to Ruth's hotel.

In June 1926, during a particularly intense period of Babe's hell-raising, the Yankees requested that Brother Matthias come to Chicago, where, coincidentally, the Catholic Eucharistic Congress was taking place. The Brother did so and surprised Babe one night in the lobby of the Del Prado Hotel. They went to dinner, and Matthias delivered a fine lecture to his former pupil. After that, Babe's antics declined for the remainder of the season.

He picked up a baton in 1928 to lead the St. Mary's band fund-raising performances in Jersey City, New Jersey, and at the Knights of Columbus Hall in New York. As a tribute to the Babe's birthday, the band played and sang "The Batterin' Babe" with gusto after several instrumentals. As late as 1934, the band traveled to Washington and gave a brief concert before a large crowd at Griffith Stadium to bade Babe a warm farewell during his final season in a Yankee uniform.

In Babe's 1948 biography, he mused, " I never got reckless enough to forget St. Mary's Brother Matthias and the kids I left behind in Baltimore. I kept going back."

*   *   *

Sultan of Swat

One of the few, very few, times that Ruth had a rub with umpires eventuated in a banner day for his friend and early teammate on the Baltimore club, Ernie Shore. On June 23, 1917, with the Red Sox, the Babe started in the box against Washington. Ray Morgan, a resident of Baltimore, was the lead-off hitter for Washington. When Brick Owens, the umpire, called "ball four" for Morgan, Ruth resented the decision in language that teemed with sharp aspersions on Owens' vision. Owens promptly erased Ruth from the line up. Ernie Shore replaced him on the mound. Morgan was thrown out stealing, and not another Washington player reached first base. Thus the Babe's brush with Owens gave Shore a chance to place his name on the Honor Roll of those who have pitched a perfect game.

A tradition has made the circuit here in the states that great athletes are men blessed with strong backs and harassed with weak brains. The pseudo dictum has it that they wear a size eighteen collar and a four and one half hat — all of their growth has been by accretion, due south of the Adam's apple. But when the odds pile up on the wrong side — when brains are essential for a trying crisis — the rumor does not hold much more soft water than a sieve. Fellows like Nick Altrock, Dizzy Dean and Rube Waddell gloried in posing as oafs. No one smarter than Nick ever stood on the turtle back. He passed swatsmiths, then picked them off first. As a mimic and comedian, where powers of observation help, Nick is no second-rater. And the Sophoclean irony of Dizzy Dean's reply to the school marms, who resented his mispronunciation of baseball nomenclature, gave those self-appointed paragons a burning lesson in gentleness and charity. Nor did Dean's answer to the prim damsel in Detroit lend luster to her ladyship. In the seventh inning, after 'Ole Diz' with monotonous regularity had silenced the Detroit guns, the queen shrieked with more petulance than prudence: "I hate you. If you were my husband, I'd give you poison." Maintaining his wonted composure, Diz gallantly doffed his cap to reply: "And if you wuz my wife, I'd take it." Even Rube Waddell's meager talents suffered nothing when a dictatorial arbiter missed a third strike that Rube had pitched. Leaving the mound and racing to the plate, Rube scratched a match, held it over the plate and asked innocently: "Can you see it any better now?" Nor was the Rube outgeneraled the year that he tended bar in Baltimore. Illustrative: A duke, meticulously groomed, approached the bar and asked for brandy. When Rube passed the bottle and the glass, the Toff poured a floater, and placed a dime on the bar. Surveying the drink, Rube tested the coin with his teeth. Satisfied that it was not counterfeit, he rang up seven cents, and returned three pennies to His Nibs.

"What," inquired the patron, "don't you charge ten cents for a brandy here?"

"Sure," Rube replied coyly, "but you get it cheaper when you take it wholesale."

And Ruth did not fare too badly in an exchange of banter. The Babe never passed a cemetery without asking, "How many dead are in there?"

On one occasion the writer answered, "I don't know."

"Why, they're all dead."

"Don't be so hasty; there are two digging a grave."

"You know," Ruth came back quickly, "All the dead ones are not buried."

Up the road, we passed a cemetery of a different religious denomination. Without batting an eye, the Babe volunteered, "There are a lot of guys in there who have not had a headache in a long time."

On another occasion, the writer and Babe went to speak at a Sports Night in a small New England town. One who had not been nominated as an official greeter awaited our arrival outside the hall and, recognizing Ruth — everyone knew him — assumed the responsibility. This unofficial greeter had a glow on that a breeze would have fanned to a flame. As he thrust himself on Ruth, the Babe turned to the writer: "It looks as if the Committee on Entertainment drank all the entertainment before the guests arrived." Not bad at all.

In the texture of the so-called dolt's remarks there is not woven one filament of bitterness. Definitely a lesson in charity for that group who, with sedulous devotion to themselves, have acquired that degree of imbecility which makes them always right and oftentimes abusive.

Returning from the Sports Night, the writer asked Babe if any of the athletes badger him with jibes anent his lack of college training.

"Occasionally some piece of tripe, who got into college on a birth certificate and a box score, asks me what college I went to."

"And what do you say, Babe?"

"By the way, Brother, is Daniel Webster a good college?"

"If it were real, it might be. Is that where you tell 'em that you were graduated?"

"Sure, those guys don't know any more about it than I do. Where is a good place to tell them that it is located?"

"Over a fish market up at Billingsgate — a nice place."

"Brother, what are good studies to take up in college?"

"All studies are good, Babe. What do you tell them when they ask you what you took up?"

"Sometimes I don't answer them, but if I hit good that day, I tell 'em Time, Space, the Slack in my belt, and the Chips when I held a good hand."

"Good." Too bad that the foregoing occurred before the advent of Dizzy Dean or he might have told them that "Ole Diz" was Dean.

"Well, Brother, are my answers good?"

"Listen, Big Boy, I've known you a good many years, and your answers have always been all right. You do not put offensive teeth in any of your words. At times, Babe, you have been unfair to yourself; but in your dealings with others, your record is one of lucid simplicity and transparent honesty. There aren't too many with that boast. Stick to the fair play that the kids at St. Mary's practiced."

As we ran through a well-illumined suburb of Boston, the Babe uncorked an ad lib that merited more than a grin. A well-oiled sot was procumbent on the sidewalk right in front of a notorious bootlegger's dispensary. The proprietor, his face a miscellany of grimaces, stood at the door. The Babe slowed up enough to shout: "Hey, Mister, your sign fell down."

As late as 1919, Ruth was still a guileless lad who loved to play ball; but, better still, he loved to hit. That year Ed Barrow, Manager of the Red Sox, gave him a chance to become a regular, and he immediately came into his own. He was told to select his own stance and to hit around the clock. "Hit them where they are pitched, Babe, but hit 'em." Free from restraint, Babe made the Red Sox games festive with circuit punches. He played in 130 games, made 139 hits, 75 of which were for extra bases and 19 of them were home runs. Even so, his pitching percentage of .615 was far ahead of the team's .483.

Ruth broke out in a rash of long clouts in 1919. Buck Freeman's long-standing record of 25 homers during one season was tossed into the dust-laden archives. As the Babe roared around the American League roller coaster, sportswriters bled their brains for monikers that would portray the message of his smiting power and the devastating ruin that his trenchant tomahawk was wielding. The scribes vied with one another in creating appropriate appellations for the boy who had stolen the show. The name Babe Ruth, adaptable to headlines, became over night too brief to convey the havoc that was sweeping down on the home talent. He became the Battering Bambino, the Colossus of the Clout, the Caliph of Crash, the Sultan of Swat, the Behemoth of Bust, the Mauling Mastodon. The picture and the name and the fame, and the extraordinary talents of the poor boy, who five years before was known only to the cheering squads of St. Mary's Industrial School, had now monopolized the headlines and the sports pages of the American press. Stars of the athletic firmament paled into insignificance in the presence of the sun. Cities were athrob and agog with excitement at the news of the coming of Ruth, the adult Babe. The First World War had provided an auto for everyone, and every ribbon of concrete for 200 miles was black with chariots, racing to the ball park where the young Ruth was displaying his formidable wares. Games were not broadcast then, and the parking lots contiguous to Fenway Park, Boston, were a mosaic of cars from Maine, New Hampshire, Vermont, Rhode Island and Connecticut. The same conditions were obtained at every park where Ruth appeared. When Ruth passed the American League record of sixteen home runs for the season, extras rolled off the press with each successive homer, assuring a cheering fandom that the adult Babe was charging high, wide and handsome, with full blown sails on Freeman's record. At each successive belt that parked the pellet, the cheering grew; and when he hit the twenty fifth, it reached a crescendo that smote the empyrean of the athletic universe. Reams of copy, tons of paper informed the waiting nation of each successive home run.

Nor did Ruth ever have a soft pitch to hit. As he stepped into the batter's box that year, the setting was the same as the first time that the writer had ever seen him. Turning his back, the pitcher assured himself that his outfielders were in the best possible defensive positions. Here was a battle of wits. Batters are paid to hit the ball; pitchers are paid to prevent their doing so. The crack of the home run that the batsman cherishes shell-shocks the nerves of the pitcher who threw it. A home run often has such an enervating effect on the pitcher that a 'blow-up" follows, and what had been a hectic duel turns into a random rout. It's been called the psychological moment — the players against whom the hit is made call it the "bad break," and dread its de-energizing and demoralizing influence on the pitcher. The fans start rhythmic hand clapping, interspersed with cries "He's all done," "Lead him to the showers," "Take him away," and other such stock shouts. The players, whose chances of victory are hampered by the hit, rush with words of encouragement to their pitcher: "It was a chance shot — a fluke. Steady boy, we'll get those runs back. We are all behind you." The acclaim that greeted the Babe as he stepped into the batter's box warned the opposition that that ominous moment was imminent. The battle was at hand. Defiance gleamed in the eyes of both batter and pitcher.

Ruth took his peculiar stance, with his motionless gun menacingly cocked on his left shoulder, arms away from his body, his right elbow almost over the plate. The weight of his body was on his left foot, the toe of his right foot barely touched the turf as he awaited the hurler's challenge. Bending his torso back, throwing the weight of his body on right or left leg — depending upon whether he was a right hander or a left hander — the pitcher raised the free leg for a long stride to get the full weight of his body behind the pitch, and sped what he hoped would be a deceptive curve, knee high, over the inside corner of the plate. As the streak of white bore down upon him, Ruth did not swing, — no, he lashed his 54 ounce wagon tongue against the flying agate. The impact was no sooner heard than the crowd recognized the tell-tale thwack, and as a unit they arose uproariously from their seats to watch the mere pill sail over yonder barrier. The Babe had just hit another. Hysteria gripped the horde. Whoever advised the pitcher that a low inside curve was Ruth's weakness was told off, and the search for that blind spot, that every hitter is supposed to have, started anew.

In answer to those who spent years searching for Ruth's weakness at bat, this is the place to dispose of it. Now it can be told: he had none. Ray Schalk, a smart catcher, spent seven years in profound quest of that weakness, and when Tommy Thomas had the Babe two strikes and asked for it, Ray answered: "I started studying this bloke seven years ago, and my guesses the past six years were worse than those of my first year. Don't pitch, just pray." A study of the pitchers from whom Babe made the homers in '19 together with the dates and places bares several truths complimentary to him as a ballplayer's ballplayer.

Certainly the Babe was no morning glory. Baseball players term "Morning Glories" those fellows who hit well in spring, but who fold during the torrid days of July. Boiled down to the bone by mid–July, they can scarcely lift a bat during the August and September stretch drive. There are several reasons conducive to the players' weakening. Minor league teams, as a rule, have one great pitcher. Once he is out of the way, base hits can multiply. In the major league, every pitcher has plenty of stuff. That fast ball, sinker, slider and bender will wear down the chicken-hearted fellow. His Adam's apple will not stay out of his mouth, and he slips into the well-known slump. Fellows who hit in the late days of the race are valuable assets to a ball club. A review of the dates of Ruth's twenty-nine home runs in 1919 uncovers the fact that twenty of them were made after July 4th.

Ruth was a great player on the road. Teams that can win fifty percent of their games away from home rate better than a fair chance to win the bunting. Of Ruth's twenty-nine circuit blows, twenty were made on the road, only nine at Boston. The reader will observe that on four occasions, away from home, when the pond was full of ducks, he hit for the loop. On home runs, alone, that year he drove in fifty-eight runs, and forty-three of those fifty-eight were driven in on the road.

Nor were his homers made from relief hurlers. Dauss led the league that year, while the others were the ace flingers of their various clubs. Moreover, Mogridge, Leonard, Coumbe, Williams, Thormahlen, Kerr, Love, and Danforth were rated among the best left handers of their time. Left hand swatsmiths, such as Ruth, are supposed to be vulnerable to the portsiders or unorthodox hurlers, yet twenty-two of the fifty-eight runs that his homers accounted for were driven in against left hand pitchers. In Cleveland, on July 18, the bases were loaded in the 9th inning as the Babe walked up to the dish. Cleveland was in front, 7–4, two out. Fred Coumbe, a sterling left hander, was summoned by Manager Fohl to halt further traffic on the base paths. One more out and Cleveland would win. Coumbe elected to throw a curve ball at Ruth to break over the plate. Wham! Boston was in the lead 8–7. The ball had cleared the high right field barrier with altitude to spare.

Ruth's Home Run Record with Boston in 1919

Date	Opposing Pitcher	Against	Place	RBI's	Final Score
Apr. 23	Mogridge	New York	New York	2	W — 10-1
May 20	Davenport	St. Louis	St. Louis	4	W — 6-4
May 30	Perry	Philadelphia	Philadelphia	2	L — 3-4
June 7	Dauss	Detroit	Boston	3	L — 5-10
June 17	Morton	Cleveland	Boston	1	L — 2-3
June 24	Robertson	Washington	Boston	1	W — 5-2
June 30	Shawkey	New York	New York	4	L — 4-7
July 5	Johnson	Philadelphia	Boston	2	
	Johnson	Philadelphia	Boston	1	L — 6-8
July 10	Shocker	St. Louis	St Louis	1	L — 3-4
July 12	Danforth	Chicago	Chicago	3	W — 12-4
July 18	Jasper	Cleveland	Cleveland	2	
	Coumbe	Cleveland	Cleveland	4	W — 8-7
July 21	Ehmke	Detroit	Detroit	1	L — 2-6
July 24	Shawkey	New York	Boston	2	W — 4-3
July 29	Leonard	Detroit	Boston	2	L — 8-10
Aug. 14	Kerr	Chicago	Chicago	2	W — 15-6
Aug. 16	Mayer	Chicago	Chicago	2	L — 6-7
Aug. 17	Shocker	St. Louis	St. Louis	2	L — 6-1
Aug. 23	Dauss	Detroit	Detroit	4	L — 4-8

Date	Opposing Pitcher	Against	Place	RBI's	Final Score
Aug. 24	Ayers	Detroit	Detroit	1	
	Love	Detroit	Detroit	2	W — 8-7
Aug. 25	Leonard	Detroit	Detroit	1	W — 5-4
Sept. 1	Shaw	Washington	Boston	2	W — 2-1
Sept. 5	Noyes	Philadelphia	Philadelphia	2	W — 15-7
Sept. 8	Thormahlen	New York	New York	1	W — 3-1
Sept. 20	Williams	Chicago	Boston	1	W — 4-3
Sept. 24	Thormahlen	New York	New York	1	L — 1-2
Sept. 27	Jordan	Washington	Washington	2	L — 5-7
				58	

The packed stadia to which Notre Dame and Princeton football teams had been playing served notice on New York sports promoters that plenty of money would support athletic events, provided the proper material was obtained. Lavished expenditures would pay handsome dividends. Colonel Huston and Jacob Ruppert, two smart businessmen, not allergic to fat profits, decided to buy the New York Yanks, and to stock the club with the best purchasable players. It was a smart decision. They learned that Ruth's attraction was due to the power of his punch. Obviously, the popularity of Jack Dempsey, who sat atop the fistic world, was found in the lethal power of his right. In baseball, too, the knockout was the thing. Fans wanted the fellow who would

> Give them the crash of the circuit smash,
> Not the poke of a well laid bunt;
> But the deafening din, when a guy slides in,
> Shoving his spikes in front.

The trend for the big time operations was toward New York. The people were flush. Colonel Huston and Jacob Ruppert put $100,000.00 on the line, doubled Ruth's salary from $10,000.00 to $20,000.00, and Ruth belonged to the Yanks. Until then that was the highest price ever paid for a ball player. Certainly it was a profitable investment. The sports business was not as big then as it is today, but the upward movement started at that moment. Tex Rickard was not slow to learn. One year later, contiguous to New York, he built Boyle's Thirty Acres for big boxing bouts. Even the colleges got into the rush. In the wake of Ruth's going to New York, Columbia University hired Percy Houghton, Harvard's famous football coach. Fordham University's tempting offer lured to New York the Boston College football mentor, Major Frank Cavanaugh; while New York University's inducements tempted "Chick" Meehan away from Syracuse.

The Babe described Brother Matthias as the greatest man he ever knew. In this picture, "Big Matt" is noticeably larger than Babe's 6'2", 200 pounds. No wonder "The Boss" commanded respect! The car in the rear is a new Cadillac being given to Brother Matthias by Babe, at a cost of $5,000. Notice the cigar in Babe's huge hand (courtesy of Xaverian Brothers Heritage Collection).

In 1919, Ruth's last year with Boston, the Chicago White Sox won the pennant. Cincinnati won in the National League. The White Sox were a powerful organization. They had pitching, hitting, fielding and speed. Tremendous odds were placed on them to overwhelm Cincinnati in the Fall Classic. With such heavy odds in the offing, corrupt men saw a chance for easy money. Some of the White Sox players unfortunately turned a willing ear to the gamblers. Offered huge bribes to "throw" the series, the unprincipled ones sold out. To the kids of the nation, the crime was equivalent to corruption in a holy place. Even adults viewed the scandal as a

Brother Matthias is behind the wheel of his gift from the Babe as (*from left*) Brother Albinus, Yankee outfielder Bob Meusel, Superintendent Brother Benjamin, Babe, his wife, an unidentified man and Adrian Hughes of St. Mary's Board admire the Cadillac, Babe later said, "[Brother Matthias] stalled it on some train tracks near St. Mary's not long after that, and a freight came along and smashed it lopsided. So I gaven him another one. I'd have bought him one every week, if [he] hadn't put a stop to it" (courtesy of Xaverian Brothers Heritage Collection, with special thanks to Mary Smith, niece of Brother Gilbert Cairnes).

menace that might destroy permanently all interest in the pastime. Baseball men dreaded its consequences. At the Major League meeting that year, one magnate counseled several others: "Don't pay your athletes any real money this year; the fellows with passes won't attend your games." And into New York went Ruth, the carefree, harum-scarum adult Babe.

The Yanks were too impoverished to own their own ball park. For their home games, they rented the Polo Grounds from the Giants. Scarcely, however, had Ruth arrived on Manhattan Island, than the Yanks became a great attraction. Ruth proceeded to go on a hitting spree. Ninety of his one hundred and seventy-two hits in 1920 were for extra bases, fifty-four of them being home runs. Game after game, he broke wide open with a long clout. In every game in which he played, Ruth left an impression. Before the season was one half spent, he was clubbing his way to new records. Each home run after his twenty-ninth smashed the all-time record for homers, and he whacked his way through American League pitchers for the grand total of fifty-four circuit blows. Men from all walks of life, from the highest to the humblest, found themselves hurriedly scanning the breakfast table paper to discover whether or not the Babe had hit another. Athletics were given a new impetus, and youngsters wherever he appeared were awed into new determination and new resolutions in the presence of his prowess. Instead of foul stories on street corners and places where the vulgar gather, the home run hitting of Babe Ruth became the predominating topic.

The miracle occurred. Baseball as the national pastime was saved. There was a regeneration of interest in the sport everywhere. What was freely prophesied would be baseball's leanest financial year proved to be the most prosperous. The sports-loving public was really aroused, enthusiasm was at fever heat, and the turnstiles, even in minor leagues, were breaking new clicking records. People wanted to know more about the type of hit that was creating such a furor. During four consecutive days, the very year following the scandal, Ruth played in Chicago—the place where the corruption started—to 136,000 people. Moving on to Detroit for a four-day stand, the Yanks drew 132,000 more, or 268,000 paid admission in eight days. Surely, then, it was the colorful personality of George Ruth, and the potency of his bludgeon that saved professional baseball from precipitation to certain doom. It was the mauling mastodon who batted the game back to popularity and stifled the stench of corruption. Baseball's future was no longer in doubt. Ruth not only held the center of the stage, but through his ability as a hitter, his skill as a fielder, his speed as a base runner, he re-stimulated interest in your national pastime, and he awakened an enthusiasm for the game hitherto unknown. For this alone American fandom owes the adult Babe a debt of lasting gratitude.

No patriotic motives prompted Ruth's hitting home runs. He just reveled in cracking that ball. Even when he struck out, his swing was so distinctly Ruthian, the kids cheered lustily. Life was a whale of a party, and ball parks were playgrounds for the big kid. Long train jumps in up-to-the-minute Pullmans, palatial hotels with swell fodder, and pitchers that were a joy to greet in every metropolis. What could be sweeter! Baseball could have become a game of grab and graft with Ruth. The bloke wouldn't cheat in solitaire. He couldn't. Money could never mean as much to him as hits. Regardless of the consequences, he had to cut viciously at every pitch that the fat of his bat could reach. And it reached plenty. On hearing that a certain player tried to bribe the catcher of another club to signal tip each pitch, Ruth, for a change, became angry and bellowed: "That big punk should be thrown out of baseball."

Unorthodox in everything that he did, he was distinctly different. He had the courage of his convictions—a real American. The English say:

"You've got to do that; it's being done." If it were being done, that was Ruth's best argument against doing the thing. His defiance of ritual got him in the doghouse, but he didn't bark. He ate the raw meat, while his followers clamored for his liberation.

A left-hand catcher, shortstop and third baseman, he started as a misfit. Somehow or other, wherever he played, he qualified. A big, rugged fellow, his minced steps smacked of effeminacy. In sprinting or pouncing on a bunt, his strides were unusually long, decidedly masculine. Defiantly, he glared at a 6'4" pitcher, while his look and stance dared the man to put the ball near the plate. Yet he almost quaked at hearing a child's request. His attitude towards strong men was one of cold indifference; towards children, it was of warm appeasement. His bunts were base hits. When he hit a home run, it did not remain in the bleachers; it cleared them. Connie Mack, in a moment of reminiscence, said: "Ruth's homers are the longest that I have ever seen. Others hit home runs, too, but we must wait for them to drop before we are sure of them. When Ruth's hits leave the bat, there is no doubt of their mileage." In St. Petersburg, Florida, the Yanks and Giants were playing a spring exhibition game. Benton was pitching for the Giants, Hogan was receiving. With two strikes on Ruth, Hogan signaled for a curve. Calling for a time out, Benton beckoned Hogan towards him.

"I am not going to curve him," said Benton. "With a two and one count, he is expecting a hook. Anyhow, I can throw my fast ball once by any batter who ever dared to swing a fifty-four ounce club."

"You're the doctor," agreed Hogan. "Sizzle it up, make it hiss, blind him with it."

Benton let it fly.

"That ball," declared Frank Hogan, "landed on the roof of a hotel within sight of the ball park. Holy Moses," he continued, "I didn't think that a man could hit a golf ball as far as Ruth hit that pitch."

A Return to St. Mary's

The year previous to the Babe's being sold to New York, he purchased a farm in Sudbury, a rural district about ten miles from Fenway Park. Against the coming of those barren years that were sure to follow the fertile ones of baseball, like a tail light, the Swatsmith decided to stock his farm with chickens of the Black Arpington breed. A deep-breasted meaty fowl, the Babe had been told that there was a lot of money in such a business. Each subsequent year, he learned that there was more money in it, more of his own; he had put it there. Tripe! Babe's chicken raising could have been done on the roof of a lighthouse. All of which is merely to state that since he was spending the off-season at Sudbury, he was denied his frequent winter visits to St. Mary's School. During the season he made amends.

Ruth continued, on the occasions that New York played in Washington, to make at least one visit over to the old school. To entertain the boys at school, he always brought along three or four of the much publicized Yankee stars. An off day, due to wet grounds or a postponement for a Saturday or Sunday double header, was the signal to the Babe for an afternoon on the old campus. Though most of this pals were gone, he was not a stranger to those who had come up from the Minims' Yard. He usually brought baseballs or some awards for the teams at the top of their league. Invariably on his arrival, the boys staged a game. To be sure, Ruth had to play on the side that won the toss for his services. The terror of the nation's fastest fire-ball pitchers, he always ignominiously struck out in the kid games. His whiffing the breeze occasioned much glee, and round after round of applause was given to the young hurler who accomplished the feat. Ruth's guests, the New York players, led the cheering. To be sure they knew that the Babe struck out intentionally. When he didn't fan, he bunted. The Brothers and the body of spectators convulsed with laughter one afternoon when, after having struck out three times, Ruth was on his way to the bat for the fourth time. The bases were loaded and the youthful captain sent in a pinch hitter to bat for the Sultan of Swat. In a fit of glee, the Babe patted the captain on the head, as he said: "Boy, you are a smart manager, and a good judge of ball players." The Babe humbly took his seat with the Brothers. He was glad to do bench duty.

"The Yanks," Brother Alban ribbed, "pay you real money to hit, and the boys here are too much for you."

"That's right, Brother. The kid has more than the cover on the ball."

A few minutes later when told by Brother Paul that every one present hoped that he would hit it over the Printing Shop, Ruth explained: "Shucks, Brother, if I had hit the ball back at one of the boys, it would have killed him."

"Terribly true," said Brother Paul.

"Another thing," added Ruth, "the kid will feel pretty good over striking me out three times. They all think that I was doing my best."

"Well, George, do you recall that time when, after you had been released from St. Mary's at your father's request, I sent for you and had you returned? Word had reached me that you were a truant."

"Yes, Brother."

"Do you remember how gloomy you were on reaching the office? If your memory does not fail you, I told you that you would some day thank me for bringing you back."

Ruth arose, took off his hat with his left hand, put out his right, as he apologetically stammered: "That time I couldn't help striking out; I was a foolish kid. Brother, I am glad of this chance to thank you now." His eyes were misty.

CHAPTER NINE

The Babe in Anecdotes and Statistics

INTRODUCTORY NOTE BY HARRY ROTHGERBER

In this chapter, Babe faces a terrific Detroit threesome. "The Georgia Peach," Ty Cobb, was the Babe's unswerving opponent in the battle for the title of most dominant hitter. A 12-time American League batting champion, Cobb's .367 lifetime average ranks first, and his 4,191 hits ranks second (to Pete Rose) on baseball's all-time lists. His fearsome competitiveness and his desire to be unexcelled by any man gave rise to bad feelings (mainly on Cobb's part) between Ruth and him. Cobb would always point to the voting tally for the first Hall of Fame inductees, in which he outpolled Babe, as proof that he was the most respected batsman. But certainly he was not the most beloved, and this surely rankled the Georgian. After their playing days ended, Cobb and Ruth enjoyed a friendlier relationship which even included an occasional round of golf.

"Wahoo Sam" Crawford, also a Hall of Famer, starred in the Tiger outfield with Cobb for many years. With a career batting average of .309, he ranks first on the all time triples list, led the league once in homers (16 in 1901) and three times in runs batted in. The third of these lefty batters, Bobby Veach, although of lesser reputation, was just as dangerous at the plate. A lifetime .310 hitter over 14 seasons, he led the league three times in RBIs and once in hits.

Brother Gilbert's reference to these three Detroit Tiger stars as a "murderer's row" evokes memories of the one-and-only Murderer's Row, of which Ruth was a major part. That team, the 1927 Yankees, won a record 110 games and lost only 44 while winning the AL pennant by 19 games. These Yankees are consistently included on the list of "Greatest Teams of All-Time," and, arguably, should be ranked as the very first on that honor roll. The team's batting average was an amazing .307, with the starting lineup as follows: Earle Combs (.356), Mark Koenig (.285), Ruth (.356 with 60 homers), Lou Gehrig (.373 with 47 homers), Bob Meusel (.337), Tony Lazzeri (.309), Joe Dugan (.269) and Pat Collins (.275). While Ruth and Gehrig led the league in homers, slugging average, RBIs and total bases, Gehrig had the AL's most doubles, Combs was the triples leader, and no one walked more than the Babe. Gehrig and Combs had the most hits in the league and Meusel's 24 stolen bases was second that year. This was a fence-banging outfit which swept the Pirates in the 1927 World Series, on the strength, many say, of a pre–Series batting practice which greatly intimidated and discouraged the Pittsburgh team, no slouch hitters themselves. Only one Murderer's Row has ever really taken its turn at bat, despite Brother Gilbert's kindly sentiments.

In 1948, Babe recollected, "Of the good ones the one that stands out most of all is that of the greatest ball club that ever stepped onto a field, one that I played on and starred for — the 1927 Yankees.... We could do everything bigger and better than any club ever brought together ... we had an individual champ in just about every position."

When he pitched on a regular basis for Boston, Babe seemed to thrive in pressure-packed situations. He seemed to be totally unfamiliar with the concepts of anxiety, tension and "putting on a game-face" — he wore the same one whatever the occasion.

For example, consider his games with "The Big Train," Walter Johnson, by consensus one of the greatest moundsmen ever to play. For the record, they pitched against each other ten times, with the Babe triumphing six times with two defeats. Of his victories, three were by 1–0 scores and two others were one-run low-scoring matches. Twice, Johnson won one-run victories. In his 1928 book, Babe stated: "When I first broke in, baseball was a defensive game. The pitchers and fielders had all the best of the argument, and a two run lead could be cashed in most any time. What an array of pitchers there was in those days! Walter Johnson was in his prime then."

Several of these 1–0 victories over Johnson occurred in Babe's remarkable 1916 season, in which he almost single-handedly willed Boston to repeat as American League champions. Coming off an 18–8 season, Babe went 23–12, including an amazing six in a row in a September in which the Red Sox were mostly on the road. This incredible baseball jaunt, begun when Manager "Rough" Carrigan chose him to pitch on opening day, included the Babe's "handcuffing" of such immortals as Tris Speaker, Ty Cobb and Johnson, as he pitched homerless ball for the entire regular season. His World Series victory that year, of course, was the masterful 13-inning, six-hit, 2–1 win over Brooklyn.

Of his Red Sox of that era, Ruth would later say, "About all our pitchers would ask for would be two or three runs, and very often one would be enough. I don't recall how many low-scoring games we won that season, but we won plenty. Winning those three straight 2 to 1 games in the Series seemed natural."

Meanwhile, the Ruthian legend continually grew and expanded over the years. His persona as baseball's foremost "superstar," with all of his gargantuan appetites and snappy attire, meshed perfectly with the Roaring Twenties' popular culture. Incidents and anecdotes which fueled this "Mythology of Ruth" abound. Some of these stories and anecdotes are actually true!

Sportswriter Paul Gallico, long a fan and admirer of the Babe's, reported in the *New York Daily News* about an incident involving Ruth in 1923, according to original Society for American Baseball Research member Al Kermisch. When a puppy came on to the field in the last inning of a game against the White Sox, Babe started crawling after the dog on his hands and knees. When he threw his fielder's mitt at the wayward animal, the pup ran off with it between its teeth. At the same time, the batter lofted a fly ball which Babe "routinely" snatched barehanded.

The salaries which he commanded from the Yankees were astronomical for their times. In an era which saw the stock market crash of 1929 signal the beginning of the Great Depression, when businessmen were reduced to selling apples on street corners and when tensions flared in bread lines, one of the prime topics of conversation in 1930 was Babe's salary: a whopping $80,000, the highest ever paid to a ball player. To compare Babe's paycheck with other prosperous personages is to discover that the president of the United States made only $75,000 then, and the commissioner of baseball merited $65,000. This is not to say that the public begrudged Babe his big dollars; no, indeed they were fascinated by the hefty sum, which became the stuff of legends.

Ruth had begun those salary discussions seeking $100,000 per year, believing his worth to the club in all respects merited such a pay day. Just prior to his death, he recalled to mind, "Few ball players can point definitely to certain attendance figures and claim them as his own. It so happened I could. Once, in Chicago, I came down sick and when it was announced in the papers two days before the scheduled appearance of the Yankees there on a Sunday, there were more than 15,000 cancellations of ticket orders."

Babe continued, "The Yanks used me in every exhibition game, and scheduled as many of these as they could crowd into the season's open dates. I don't think I had two or three days off during my whole stay with the Yanks.... I think this constant pressure shortened my playing life by a year or two." According to Hadley, Gustafson and Thierry in an article entitled, "Who Would Be the Highest-Paid Baseball Player?" the Babe ranks second (behind Gehrig) on the list of salaries for the great historical hitters, adjusted for the 1990s.

Yankee management, in the form of "Jake" Ruppert and, until 1923, Colonel Til Huston, recognized the golden goose, and as shrewd businessmen, they capitalized on it. On the heels of what many view as Babe's greatest seasons—1920 (.376 with 54 homers) and 1921 (.378 with 59 homers)—plans were made to end the agreement to share the Polo Grounds with the Giants in favor of a new edifice. This new stadium would be immortalized as "The House That Ruth Built," a name by which Yankee Stadium is still recognized. The stadium was christened by a game-winning three-run homer by Babe on April 18, 1923, in front of an announced crowd (probably exaggerated) of 74,217 fans. No other player would have his name so connected to a stadium. "In writing his story of the opening game of the 1923 season, Fred Lieb referred to Yankee Stadium as 'the House that Ruth Built' in the *New York Evening Telegram*. Other writers liked the phrase ... and I always feel proud when I see it," recalled Babe.

Additional Ruthian mythology has been created by the never-ending debate over whether Babe actually "called his shot" in the fifth inning of the third game of the 1932 World Series against the Cubs (and pitcher Charlie Root) at Wrigley Field. It appears that bad blood existed between the two teams because of the Cubs' perceived sleight against Mark Koenig, a popular shortstop just acquired from the Yanks. The National Leaguers had voted to award Koenig only a one-half Series share, despite his fine play. This action riled the Yankees, and the Series became a torrent of verbal abuse and taunts between the clubs.

The dispute culminated in the "called shot," in which Ruth allegedly pointed to the centerfield bleachers and proceeded to hit Root's next pitch over the flagpole in center, the farthest part of the field. Questions remain to this day regarding the circumstances of this incident. Did Babe point to the bleachers, the fans, the opposing dugout or to Root? If so, why? What was the count: 0-and-2, 2-and-2, or 3-and-2?

As usual, the Babe is no help in sorting out what actually happened on October 1, 1932, describing several differing versions of those events over the years. His account in the 1945 book My Greatest Day in Baseball, told to John D. Carmichael, states: "But right now I want to settle all arguments: I didn't exactly point to any spot like the flagpole. Anyway, I didn't mean to. I just sorta waved at the whole fence, but that was foolish enough. All I wanted to do was give that thing a ride ... outta the park ... anywhere." But, in his 1948 auto-biography, he recalled, "I pointed to the bleachers which rise out of deep center field ... the ball just went on and on and hit far up in the center-field bleachers in exactly the spot I had pointed to."

Numerous other eyewitness accounts dispute the theory of the called shot, and even the recently-discovered home movie of the event ("the Kandle film") has been picked apart and debated endlessly by viewers. The only sure thing which we know occurred that day (other than the homer) was the creation of another Ruthian legend.

Another article recently published by Frank Ardolino discussed the Chinese banyan tree planted in Hawaii by the Babe on October 29, 1933. It has grown to huge size, dense and umbrella-like, and stands in front of the Hilo Hawaiian Hotel. This tree has become a testament to the continued growth and size of the Ruthian myth.

In 1921, the Curtiss Candy Company of Chicago began market-ing its "Baby Ruth" candy bars, which remain popular today. This occurred over the reported objection of the Babe, who never shared in the sweet profits that were generated. To this day, the Curtiss Candy Company denies any correlation between the fame of the slugger and the development of its candy bar, stating that the candy was named after President Cleveland's daughter, Baby Ruth Cleveland, who vis-ited the candy plant prior to her death (at age 11 in 1904, 17 years prior).

Even in losing, Ruth set legendary standards. Seldom has a player made the final out to end two World Series as did Ruth. In 1921, laboring with an infected elbow, as a ninth-inning pinch hitter, he tapped a ball weakly to first base for the final out in a 1–0 loss to the Giants that ended the Series. Then, in 1926, Ruth made one of his rare blunders when he was thrown out attempting to steal second base with hard-hitting Bob Meusel at bat with two out in the bottom of the ninth and the Yanks down to the Cardinals 3–2. It was a hard way to lose in the seventh game of a Series, but none of his team-mates blamed him for the loss. They knew his value, his ability and the nature and extent of his competitiveness.

How did Ruth become such an athletic achiever? The answer which beckons, that he possessed innate and natural ability, also fuels the "superman" mythology around him. In 1921, Ruth agreed to take certain tests involving his motor responses, coordination and reflexes. Interpreted by Columbia Professor B. Pitkin in 1930 in his work titled, *The Psychology of Achievement*, the results were flabbergasting. After examining the Babe's general coordination, nervous stability, eyes, ears and basic physical metabolism, it was concluded that "Babe Ruth, far from being 'one man in a million,' is at least one man in 50 or 60 million."

Already mentioned have been the "epic" stories of "the stomach ache heard round the world," and Babe's "heroic" sized baseball bat. Dorothy Ruth Pirone tells of her father sitting in St. Alban's golf course clubhouse taking target practice with a .22 rifle by shooting at the door knob for a dollar a shot. "Without warning," she recounted, "a man opened the door, and Dad missed hitting him by six inches. The near victim was scared to death, while Dad remained totally unfazed. His tongue-in-cheek reaction: 'He should've knocked.'"

From the accounts of teammates, friends and family, Babe did not consider rules to be meant for him. If so, he broke them with childlike impunity.

On certain occasions, Babe thought he had excellent cause to bend rules. Sportswriter Dan Daniel told the story of a day in 1921 when the Yankees played the Dodgers in Macon, Georgia, in an exhibition game. Prior to the New York team's departure at 8 o'clock, Babe couldn't be found. Daniel related, "Half an hour later Ruth showed up. He had gone out to an orphanage in the country and played another nine-inning game with a lot of delighted youngsters for whom it was the day of their lives.

"The Bam was red and hot and covered with Georgia clay. And he had missed his dinner. But he had got a great kick out of that experience. For a day he was back at Baltimore, back at St. Mary's."

Since Brother Gilbert wrote his memoirs in 1947, a number of the Babe's records have been surrendered, mostly to later New York Yankees. At one time Ruth held the record for appearances in the most World Series with 10 (now held by Yogi Berra with 14 and Mickey Mantle with 12), most Series games with 41 (surpassed by Berra's 75, Mantle's 65, and Elston Howard's 54, and six others) and Series homers with 15 (now held by Mantle with 18). Even Babe's Series slugging average of .744 is only good for second place to Reggie Jackson's .755. As a pitcher, Babe's superlative 0.87 ERA was surpassed eventually by Jack Billingham (0.36) and Harry Brecheen (0.83).

Brother's observation about Ruth being the only Yankee to lead the league in hitting (.378 in 1924) was unfortunately in error. Other Yankees who led the AL in batting were Lou Gehrig (1934), Joe DiMaggio (1939, 1940), and Snuffy Stirnweiss (1945). In later years, Mickey Mantle (1956), Don Mattingly (1985) and Paul O'Neill (1994) would also earn league trophies for batting average.

John Benson summarized it best in his and Tony Blengino's

Baseball's Top 100 when he observed, "Babe Ruth is so far above the rest of the player population, by any objective measure, it can be downright amusing to debate with anyone who believes otherwise."

*   *   *

FROM THE MEMOIRS OF BROTHER GILBERT

Some Closing Observations About "The Babe"

Apparently George Herman Ruth had reserve for every crisis — that little something that gets one over the hump. In the fever of conflict the fellow actually improved. When there was disaster on every thrown ball of that fourteen-inning World Series classic, he did not become obsessed with fear. Wrathy because he himself hadn't a hit off Sherrod Smith, he vented his spleen on the Dodger batsmen. Fans who saw him on the mound that day for the first time, as he hung up those thirteen horse collars, thought that he grew there. To Ruth, the games in the Senior League at St. Mary's had been more important.

Great pitchers are not necessarily the titans who can unfold an assortment of benders. Great pitchers are fellows who have resistance when they are being crowded. As the baseball men put it, "Great pitchers are the ones who can take the ammunition away from the opposition when the 'ducks are on the pond.'" And "ducks on the pond" are men on the bases.

In the heat of one Red Sox campaign, Ruth was pitching a game in Detroit. The ducks were on the pond — three of them. Cobb had no sooner left the "on deck" circle, wielding his three magic willows, as a tuning up process, than he was replaced by Wah-Hoo Sam Crawford. To aggravate the terrifying effect on Ruth, the kid pitcher, was Bobby Veach, standing on the top step of the dugout and serving notice that the same raw meat diet was to follow. There they were in the full view of the young Ruth — a concatenation of human dynamos, enjoying the privilege of legalized mayhem, three legitimately popular homicides — the original murderer's row. Cobb discarded two bats, and stepped in the batter's box brandishing the third. On fourteen pitched balls, the murderer's row went down swinging. The ducks left the pond unmolested. The feat was flashed across the country; it merited headlines on all sports pages the next day. All fans, save one, read an account of it, gloated over it, then commented at length on it. The one who did not bother to gloat over it was the hero. The Babe never swelled with pride at another's misfortune — not Ruth.

Perhaps young athletes of the present day do not realize what mean war willows those men wielded. They had spent many long summers away from mamma, the family hob irons, and the bird dog, Rex. They remained away to get hits and checks, and both were numerically large. An anecdote of Al Schact reveals the awe in which they were held by twirlers. Al had been purchased from Buffalo by Washington. He was ordered to join the Washington club in Detroit, where the two clubs were playing. Just as Al ordered a sandwich, Detroit broke loose with a fusillade of hits. Scarcely had he taken one bite when the manager shouted: "Hey, Al, run out there and stop that barrage."

"Who are the next hitters?" queried Al.

"Cobb, Crawford and Veach," came the quick response.

"Here, Bill, hold this sandwich for a minute; I'll be right back." And Al was right back.

Babe Ruth knew the tricks of the pitching trade. He preferred a tough competitor with an awesome reputation to an untried youngster. His reasons are logical: "When the manager chooses me to oppose Dauss, Coveleski or Johnson, he just about tells me that I am a good pitcher. Experience, too, has taught me that my club will play faster and tighter baseball when they realize that the margin of victory will be narrow. In a duel with one of these fellows, I am assured of good support. It's up to me to use my wits and bear down. If I win, I have done something; if I am licked, I am not ashamed." No quarrel there.

It was mentioned that Johnson, Dauss and Coveleski could make a lot of trouble for his batters.

"They do," added Ruth, "but don't forget that during the winter months over the apples, the pecans and the fruit cake when chin music is chanted, players love to recall a hit that they made to beat such pitchers. If there is one thing that a hitter likes better than one hit, it's another hit. After that, what he like is still more hits."

"Yah, Babe, but when a fellow makes 150 or 160 hits a season, can he recall where he made them?"

"Two thirds of 'em were made off crooked arms — guys who had to wait for the wind to blow before they could get 'em up to the plate. Fellows don't want to remember those knocks; but they do not allow themselves to forget the ones that they made off Johnson. They are saved for home-town sports gatherings."

Odd it was that Babe should refer to home-town sports gatherings. He existed in sheer dread of them. And there was wisdom in the attitude that he took towards them. In his public remarks he never referred to his pitching or hitting. And while his audiences were gratified at his cordial mannerisms, they were invariably disappointed that he did not dwell on some of the games that his playing featured. Asked why he did not, he brusquely replied: "Why should I? Only swelled heads talk about themselves."

His talks on such occasions had a ludicrous delivery. In strong terms, the Babe counseled boys to piously avoid cigarettes. His perorations amounted to: "Now, I've never smoked a cigarette in my life. Cigarettes affect a person's appetite and rest. I need my appetite to be strong and my rest to be fresh for the game. If the game goes extra innings, I'll need the energy to carry me through it."

Nor had he ever smoked a cigarette. That is magnificently true. The travesty of the situation was that concurrently the daily papers carried an ad telling the kind that best suited his tastes — the very brand that would promptly restore him to normalcy after the fatigue of a hard game had Babe's endorsement. And during those days, Babe's only objection to strong tobacco was that it was too weak. [*Editor's note:* For a more realistic view of Babe's use of tobacco, see page 53.]

Even so, Babe could pitch smartly and courageously. Here's the proof: seven pennants. Indeed, among ball players — and the public for that matter — the slogan obtained, "As Ruth goes, so go the Yanks." In the 1932 World Series, it wasn't those other stars that the Cubs heckled; it was the forgotten fellow named Ruth.

In vindication, his record as a member of the Yanks is given below. His World Series record, too, is appended, since he is the only player in either league who ever took part in ten of the fall classics:

	Games	AB	R	H	2BH	3BH	HR	RBI	Bat. Avg	F. Avg
1920	142	458	158	172	36	9	54	137	.376	.936
1921	152	540	177	204	44	16	59	171	.378	.967
1922	110	406	94	128	24	8	35	99	.315	.964
1923	152	522	151	205	45	13	41	131	.393	.973
1924	153	529	143	200	39	7	46	121	.378	.962
1925	98	359	61	104	12	2	25	66	.290	.974
1926	152	495	139	184	30	5	47	145	.372	.979
1927	151	540	158	192	29	8	60	164	.356	.963
1928	154	536	163	173	29	8	54	142	.323	.975
1929	135	499	121	172	26	6	46	154	.345	.984

	Games	AB	R	H	2BH	3BH	HR	RBI	Bat. Avg	F. Avg
1930	145	518	150	186	28	9	49	153	.359	.966
1931	145	534	149	199	31	3	46	163	.373	.972
1932	133	457	120	156	13	5	41	137	.341	.961
1933	137	459	97	138	21	3	34	103	.301	.967
1934	125	365	78	105	17	4	22	84	.288	.962
Totals	2084	7217	1959	2518	424	106	659	1970	0.349	0.967

In 1925, Ruth was hospitalized for two months. He hit only .290 that year and the Yanks finished seventh in the race, the lowest during his stay on the club. His final year and the year of his illness are the ones that he batted lower than .300. He exploded in '26 and '27. Babe Ruth is the only New York batsman ever to lead the American League in hitting. He accomplished the feat in 1924.

World Series Record

Year	Club	G	AB	R	H	2B	3B	HR	RBI	Bat. Avg.	Winner	Loser	Games
1915	Boston	1	1	0	0	0	0	0	0	0.000	Boston	Phil.	5
1916	Boston	1	5	0	0	0	0	0	1	.000	Boston	Brooklyn	5
1918	Boston	3	5	0	1	0	1	0	2	.200	Boston	Chicago	6
1921	N.Y.	6	16	3	5	0	0	1	4	.313	Giants	Yanks	8
1922	N.Y.	5	17	1	2	1	0	0	1	.118	Giants	Yanks	5
1923	N.Y.	6	19	8	7	1	1	3	3	.368	Yanks	Giants	6
1926	N.Y.	7	20	6	6	0	0	4	5	.300	St. Louis	Yanks	7
1927	N.Y.	4	15	4	6	0	0	2	7	.400	Yanks	Pitts.	4
1928	N.Y.	4	16	9	10	3	0	3	4	.625	Yanks	St. Louis	4
1932	N.Y.	4	15	6	5	0	0	2	6	.333	Yanks	Chicago	4
Total		41	129	37	42	5	2	15	33	0.326			54

Ruth played in seven winners of the World Series, his team making a clean sweep of the series on three occasions.

Babe Ruth's Pitching Record

Year	Club/League	G	IP	W	L	Pct.	H	BB	SO	ERA
1914	Boston — American	4	23	2	1	.667	21	7	3	3.91
1915	Boston — American	32	217.2	18	8	.692	166	85	112	2.44
1916	Boston — American	44	323.2	23	12	.657	230	118	170	1.75
1917	Boston — American	41	326.1	24	13	.649	244	108	128	2.01
1918	Boston — American	20	166.1	13	7	.650	125	49	40	2.22
1919	Boston — American	17	133.1	9	5	.643	148	58	30	2.97
1920	New York — American	1	4	1	0	1.000	3	2	0	4.50

Year	Club/League	G	IP	W	L	Pct.	H	BB	SO	ERA
1921	New York — American	2	9	2	0	1.000	14	9	2	9.00
1930	New York — American	1	9	1	0	1.000	11	2	3	3.00
1933	New York — American	1	9	1	0	1.000	12	3	0	5.00
Total		163	1221.1	94	46	.671	974	441	488	2.28

In 1916, Ruth pitched in 44 games, but an inspection of his record for that year reveals that he played in 67 games. In 1918, he pitched in 20 games, but he played in 95 games; and in 1919, he pitched in 17 games, but played in 130. His conversion to an outfielder was already in process. Playing the outfield takes a severe tax of a pitcher's arm. Certainly it robs him of control.

*   *   *

Thus will I cease this reminiscence of the young Babe and leave it to wiser authors and scholars to document his twilight years. In the writer's opinion, the most important story concerns how this mastadonic mauler was lifted from the obscurity of a school yard to the pinnacle of national fame; how he passed from the St. Mary's Industrial School big yard to become the idol of millions — the immortal "King of Swat" — in just a few short years.

Babe had many obstacles to overcome during his trip to manhood. He was a poor boy with handicaps that might have discouraged others. He was impetuous and inclined to lose his temper. He had other human weaknesses which cropped out even at the height of his career. But the gifted, zealous and conscientious Xaverian Brothers who became his family at St. Mary's surely abided by the gentle philosophy that "the surest way to make a boy bad is to tell him he's a bad boy."

The Babe followed his guiding lights to achieve his astounding success as a professional player excelled by none in America's national pastime. Along the way, he became the idol of baseball fans all over the world, not only because he could hit more home runs than any other man but also because he had a big, kind, charitable heart — one that understood and went out to the kids of America.

The Babe's Yankee Years and Thereafter

by Harry Rothgerber

The Babe's progression and maturity as a professional ball player coincided with the first "Golden Age" of baseball — the 1920s — an era when baseball alone owned the world of sports in America and claimed the exalted title of "the National Pastime." Hometown heroes still caught the imagination of the fans, the ball was becoming more lively, women would not dare attend a game unescorted, and the standard attire for gentlemen was suit and tie with a fresh-collared shirt. The flamboyant Babe not only dominated this era — he *owned* it. And, aided by a print media which romanticized his wild side while not revealing the brutish and boorish aspects of his character, the Babe carried all of "organized baseball" to a new level of fan support. He was truly ubiquitous in the 1920s.

Ruth's Yankee years saw him lead that club to the pinnacle of dynastic success. However, his personal and professional relationships could too often be described as "turbulent."

Prior to the disintegration of his marriage and his eventual permanent separation from Helen in 1926, the Babe's daughter Dorothy had mysteriously appeared as first announced by the press in September 1922. The headline from the *New York American* screamed, "Ruth a Daddy for Sixteen Months and Has Hidden Facts from World," while the *New York Daily News* later followed up with "Babe Ruth and Mrs. Babe All Mixed Up on Baby's Birthday." The facts of Dorothy's birth were shrouded in rumor, innuendo and speculation, which especially strained the mental health of Helen Ruth.

In her book *My Dad, The Babe*, Dorothy wrote of her discovery that she was actually the child of an affair her father had in 1920 with Juanita

Jennings, an attractive woman whose grandfather had been president of Mexico from 1911 to 1913. Babe eventually decided to raise Dorothy himself, thereby giving Helen the child she had always wanted. "My father made Juanita swear on her life and mine that she would never tell the truth," recalled Dorothy.

For years, talk of a formal divorce circulated, but that never occurred, whether due to Babe's Catholicity or disagreements over the property settlement. One writer reported that Brother Matthias went to New York at one time to talk the Babe out of a divorce. However, the marriage came to an official end with the death of Helen Woodford Ruth in a fire on January 13, 1929. It became known to a shocked country and to a disbelieving Babe that Helen had been living since 1927 with Dr. Edward Kinder, a Watertown, Massachusetts, dentist. One night when Dr. Kinder was away, his house burned, killing Helen. Although the Woodford family suggested foul play, such was never proven in any way. (Again, though, sensational headlines blared from the *New York Daily News*: "Babe Ruth's Wife Dies in Fire at Secret Love-Life Bungalow.") In the course of time, defective wiring was found to be the culprit.

Within months of Helen's death, Babe married Claire Hodgson, whom he first met in 1923. Claire had an adolescent daughter, Julia, by her first husband. The intrafamily relationships described by Dorothy in her 1988 memoir depict a family embroiled in bitter and dysfunctional relationships, with Claire attempting to assume control over every aspect of the Babe's life. Babe's former flame Juanita even became best friends with Claire in order to be closer to Dorothy, who later stated, "Claire died in 1976 without ever learning the truth."

While Dorothy's unhappiness with her new family would continue for many years, the Babe settled into life with Claire very comfortably. In 1930, Babe's biographer Daniel M. Daniel described Claire in this way: "And then there is Mrs. Ruth, the real boss of the Babe's menage. She's petite; she has a winning smile and a way of handling the Babe. And she is a keen financial manager, too."

Babe's baseball life also yielded many tensions over the years. While with the Red Sox, he clashed with manager Ed Barrow over the issue of late night carryings-on. Angry words and challenges to a fistfight led to the boss' suspension of the Babe. In Barrow's 1951 autobiography, he wrote, "If there ever was a big shame-faced kid with a guilty conscience trying to get off the hook, that was the Babe ... he told me all about his boyhood and the tough going he had had as a kid. My heart went out to this big, overgrown boy, and I understood him better." From then on, Babe was to leave a note in Barrow's box telling the manager exactly when he got in that night.

Babe was suspended by Baseball Commissioner Landis at the start of the 1922 season for defying Landis' order not to go on a barnstorming tour. That season witnessed numerous run-ins with umpires by a thin-skinned Babe, followed by a suspension by American League President Ban Johnson. Ruth was clearly out of control. Playing only 110 games that year, his production dropped in every offensive category. However, to the Babe's credit, after an off-season public chiding by James J. Walker (later mayor of New York City), who asked, "Babe, are you going to once again let down those dirty-faced kids in the streets of America?" the Babe righted himself admirably.

That's certainly not to say that Babe ever came close to sainthood. He clashed with Yankee manager Miller Huggins on a multitude of occasions, culminating in a suspension and $5,000 fine for another curfew violation. That was the same year as Babe's "bellyache heard 'round the world," and it was also his poorest year at the plate, earning only a .290 batting average. Unquestionably, his erratic behavior and challenges to authority figures affected his on-field play.

In spite of being the sport's highest-paid player, the contract negotiations between Babe and owner Ruppert were always times of tension and anxiety, spurred on by the offers and counteroffers of negotiation. (Ruppert usually prevailed.) Ruppert angered Ruth when, after Huggins' untimely and early death in 1929, the Yankee owner passed over the Babe for that post, saying, "How can you manage the Yankees, when you can't even manage yourself?"

When the new manager, Bob Shawkey, was fired after one year, Ruth again was overlooked in favor of Joseph Vincent McCarthy, who went on to become a Hall of Famer and one of the two most successful men ever to manage a professional ball club. Still, the Babe did not like him and complained about his handling of the Yankees on a regular basis. The only order which McCarthy ever gave to Ruth was to always be on time (and Ruth complied).

Even his relationships with fellow stars on the Yankees were tumultuous at times. Although friendly with Lou Gehrig for years, they fell out in 1934 over a remark allegedly made by Gehrig's mother that the Babe and Claire dressed Claire's daughter Julia in good clothes while keeping Dorothy in "rags." The two slugging teammates did not reconcile until July 4, 1939, at the famous "Lou Gehrig Day" speech when Lou was in the throes of his terminal illness.

But beyond these stormy relations off the field, the Babe was a celebration of life itself at game time. By the time he retired, he owned dozens of individual season, career and World Series records, not to mention his pitching marks. His record 60 homers in 1927 only begins his list of achievements. In their classic *The Hidden Game of Baseball*, baseball statisticians John Thorn and Pete Palmer introduced the Linear Weights System (*LWTS*) to measure proficiency in batting. Their review of all players up to 1985 concludes with the Babe emerging as the best player, and his pitching performance was not even factored in the calculations. Ruth placed high in the following *LWTS* categories: lifetime batting runs (first), lifetime on base average (second), lifetime slugging (first), lifetime isolated power (first), lifetime relative batting average (thirteenth) and lifetime overall player wins (first). As recently as 1993, another baseball statistician, Gabriel B. Costa, proposed a measure for slugging called the Total Power Quotient — the Babe ranked first. And in a 1986 ranking of baseball's most complete sluggers by measuring players' 80-extra-base-hit-seasons (EBH), the Babe amassed the best season EBH totals, and hit for 80 EBH nine times, second only to Gehrig's ten.

Whether one uses "newer" statistical methods such as Tom Boswell's Total Average, Bill James' Runs Created, or Thorn and Palmer's Batting Runs, Ruth consistently ranks at or near the top. If not, then that particular statistical analysis is void on its face. Even the small corps of contentious baseball historians who wish to revise history to dim Babe's luster must surrender in the face of this numbers game. Conventional wisdom has it that it was more exciting to see Babe Ruth strike out than to see any other player hit a homer!

In a collection of All-Star Team lists published in 1990 by Al Davis and Elliott Horne, Ruth is found on the following:

American League All-Time All-Star Team,
All-Time All-Star All-Star Team,
Remarkable Record All-Star Team,
RBI's (Season) All-Star Team,
Home Run Hitter (Season) All-Star Team,
Home Run Hitter (Career) All-Star Team,
Lefty Batting All-Star Team,
and
Alcoholic All-Star Team,
Lover All-Star Team, *and*
Umpire Baiter All-Star Team.

In a recent book by famed baseball researcher Bill James, the Babe finishes a close third overall (to Willie Mays and Christy Mathewson) in a measure of standards met by players selected for enshrinement in the National Baseball Hall of Fame in Cooperstown, New York. Ruth finishes second to Hank Aaron in a rank of hitters, using James' formula of hits times batting average, plus home runs.

He constantly traveled over the years: in Cuba and Japan he assumed the status of a demigod. His barnstorming team, the "Busting Babes," visited scores of non–major league cities all over the country during the off-season playing Lou Gehrig's "Larrupin' Lous." These trips earned him a fortune in money, fame and adulation.

As his stellar career as a player faded, the Babe desperately longed for a managerial position, but the call never came. Convinced that the Yankees would never elevate him, and refusing to go to the minor leagues for seasoning as a team skipper, Ruth was traded to owner Emil Fuchs' Boston Braves for the 1935 season. The Babe had high expectations that this move would lead to a field manager position, but he soon saw the truth: He was being used as a drawing card to bolster attendance for a weak, last-place team. His playing career ended about a week after a remarkable game he played in Pittsburgh on May 25, 1935. At Forbes Field that day, he hit three homers — including one over the roof — and a single, earning six RBIs.

In June of 1938, Babe joined the Brooklyn Dodgers as a coach, again with hopes of replacing Burleigh Grimes as manager. This move put him in direct conflict with Leo Durocher, who was the shortstop and captain of that team. When owner Lee MacPhail named Durocher the new Dodger manager in October, Babe's career in organized baseball was over.

Until his sickness felled him in 1946, the Babe waited for a call from organized baseball which never came. He felt betrayed and was sometimes depressed, but he continued to travel, golf, fish, hunt, play in charity and exhibition games and devote more time to Claire and his family. Consistently throughout his career and subsequent retirement, he loved to visit children who were sick or less fortunate, in schools and hospitals.

The only shame in Babe's later years belonged to organized baseball, which all but ignored him. Instead of utilizing his fame and celebrity to advance the game, most major league executives seemed to shun him.

The Passing of Brother Gilbert

The fact that Brother Gilbert's reminiscences finish somewhat hurriedly should not reflect negatively on his writing powers and abilities. For years he labored on, but never finalized his Ruthian remembrances. This was due, no doubt, to the real-world intrusions on his time and talent. Actual people needed his counsel more than the pages before him needed ink. Gilbert had a keen understanding of young people and a sincere interest in their activities and problems. In and out of class, his attitude toward his charges was always one of helpfulness. His remarkable ability to make friends and his splendid ability as a conversationalist and speaker contributed to his "busy-ness." Brother Gilbert's tale of the young Babe's early days would not be published in the Xaverian's lifetime.

Friday evening, October 17, 1947, saw Brother Gilbert walking the sidelines and enjoying every play of the Keith Academy–St. John's football game, according to Brother Alexius Joseph Lally, C.F.X. The next day he traveled to attend the wedding mass of a relative in West Medford. While dining, he entertained those near him with stories and witticisms. After the meal, he accepted an invitation to accompany several Boston Braves officials, including his brother Joseph (later president of the Braves), to Pawtucket, Rhode Island.

The following day, Sunday, he did not complain of being ill, and he attended all the exercises of that day of retreat. But that afternoon, October 19, 1947, at 2:45, Brother Gilbert died suddenly of a cerebral hemorrhage while participating in the closing exercises of his monthly community retreat. He was at prayer with his fellow Brothers in the Keith Academy Chapel in Lowell, Massachusetts, when the end came, in the presence of his colleagues who knelt by his side reciting the prayers for the dying. His unexpected death brought to a close a faithful and extraordinary service of 46 years to the teaching congregation which he had joined as a young man in 1901.

The news of Brother Gilbert's passing quickly caught nationwide attention, and his friends in many parts of the country mourned his death. Much of the resultant publicity about his death stemmed from the fact that he played a leading role in launching the Babe on his baseball career. Indeed, upon receiving the news, Babe Ruth, himself ailing with the disease which was terminal, sent a telegram saying, "It was a great shock to me to hear that my good friend Brother Gilbert passed away as young as he did because he was a true friend to all boys and everyone who knew him. He will be missed by millions. Deepest sympathy from the Ruth family." Gilbert and Babe had kept in touch over the years, and the Brother's death hurt him deeply. Even the great Connie Mack telegraphed, "Regret to hear of Brother Gilbert's death. Please accept my deepest sympathy in your great loss. Admired him greatly and will miss him on my visits to Boston."

Many Happy Returns!

The Centennial Celebration of the Xaverian Brothers in America was cause for many newspapers to remember the Congregation's accomplishments. Gus Bell, in the "Baseball" portion of the list, played at Flaget High School in Louisville, Kentucky. He is the father of Buddy Bell and grandfather of David Bell, both major leaguers. Bernie Crimmins, listed in "Football," played at St. Xavier in Louisville, starred at Notre Dame and was head coach at Indiana University (courtesy of Xaverian Brothers Heritage Collection).

Brother Gilbert's part in helping baseball's mightiest slugger receive his start was well known and appreciated. However, his bona fide stature as a religious teacher, a sincere friend of the young, and a good Xaverian Brother could truly be appreciated only by his colleagues, family and those of his friends who knew him well. He was a great person because he was kindly and decent, not because he had opened the door of opportunity to a potential major or minor league baseball player. He desired to serve the less fortunate around him, and he did so with enthusiasm and distinction. Just as his life was an inspiration, so too was his death. When God called him to judgment, He found him on his knees praying in the solemn stillness of the chapel at Keith Academy.

Frank Sargent wrote in the *Lowell Sun*, "The end came suddenly for one of the greatest ecclesiastical orators of all time, and the good Brother,

THE SPORTS
WORLD MOURNS

REV. BROTHER

GILBERT c.f.x

THE DISCOVERER OF
BABE RUTH!

LEO
WHITE

A BRILLIANT ORATOR.
HE UNCEASINGLY PREACHED
CLEAN SPORT AND IDEALS
TO THOUSANDS OF BOYS
IN 20 STATES!

RUTH

THE GOOD BROTHER
FIRST SAW RUTH WHEN
THE BABE WAS IN AN
INDUSTRIAL SCHOOL
IN BALTIMORE.

Veber Evens
Old Score

Beats Joey Angelo
in Return Meeting

BOSTON, Oct. 21 (AP)—
kie Weber, the New England
itweight boxing champion
n Pawtucket, R. I., today had
son to gloat over

Keith Squad Idle
After Teacher's Death

LOWELL—Keith academy
gridders will not practice today. The squad will remain
idle out of respect to the
memory of Rev. Bro. Gilbert,

The death of Brother Gilbert in 1947 was remembered in newspapers throughout the country. At the Brother's funeral, 11-year old Frankie Haggerty acted as substitute for the Babe, who himself would be dead in less than a year (courtesy of *The Lowell Sun* from the *Boston Post* of March 26, 1954).

who so often eulogized athletic heroes who 'died with their boots on,' went out the same way — the way he'd want it." In New York, John Griffin of United Press interviewed the Babe and reported, "You could tell that the great, human heart of Babe Ruth was stirred deeply as the greatest baseball hero of them all spoke of the death of the man who got him his first job in baseball — Brother Gilbert. Speaking of his old friend, the Babe's hoarse, strained voice, showing the effects of his recent prolonged illness, was tense and cracked as he said, 'Young boys have sure lost a great pal.'"

Another testament to Brother Gilbert's oratory came from Dover, New Hampshire, and Bill Stearns, who wrote in *Foster's Daily Democrat*: "The world of sports lost an inspiring figure, and many of us in Dover lost a warm friend.... He was one of the greatest after-dinner speakers we ever heard. There was always a message in his words, a message delivered with fire and eloquence, but tempered by a sparkling sense of humor."

In the *Lowell Sun*, columnist John Kenney observed, "If American baseballdom loses much with the death of Brother Gilbert, be assured the American youth has lost more in the passing of one more gifted, zealous, conscientious Xaverian Brother."

These comments in the days that followed his death were typical of the stories that were reported across the country on front pages, editorial columns and sports pages.

True to his vows, and despite the plaudits which he received from friends, Brother Gilbert died as he had lived — in religious poverty. The wallet removed from his clothing contained only a prayer card for boys in the service of their country, a paper bearing the autograph of the "Little Flower" (St. Therese), and a train ticket for a ride from Salem to Boston.

A Brother in the Congo wrote, "Yesterday we received the news of the death of our dear Brother Gilbert. God rest his soul. Shall we ever see his like again? For those of us who have known him in life, he will always stand out as the ideal Xaverian, the true religious and the idol of his boys."

The Babe was too ill to attend the funeral of his friend. Choked up, he said, "I sure wish I could go. He was always a great fellow for helping the young boys, both in school and afterwards. They are going to miss him now. Young fellows were everything to him." Instead, Babe sent a replacement in the form of 11-year-old Frankie Haggerty, a second baseman in the local Catholic Youth Organization league.

Haggerty knew Brother Gilbert and often talked to him about the Babe. When Gilbert died, Frankie, at the urging of the child's mother, wrote to Babe, saying, "I am very sorry your friend Brother Gilbert died.

If you wish and I can get permission from the other Brothers, I will go for you as I live in Danvers. I will behave."

The Babe wired Frankie back, giving him permission to "pinch-hit" for him, by the following words: "I will be most grateful to you if you will represent me at Brother Gilbert's funeral. I am unable to go but I will feel I am there in spirit through your gracious gesture to go in my place."

Sports and civic leaders joined in giving Brother Gilbert an emotional farewell at his funeral mass at St. Peter's Church on October 22, 1947. Joe Cronin, Eddie Collins, Lou Perini, Tom Yawkey, John Quinn and other dignitaries crowded the church to overflowing. Afterwards, Brother was buried in the cemetery at St. John's Prep, a Xaverian School in Danvers, having been taken there by six pallbearers, all fellow Xaverians. Among the mourners were his brother, Brother Samuel, C.F.X. of St. Joseph's Juniorate in Peabody, Massachusetts, and his nephew, Brother Omer, C.F.X. of St. Michael's in Brooklyn.

When Brother Samuel visited his brother's room, he found the desk as Gilbert had left it: a small hand Bible was there, two sets of rosary beads, a photograph of his mother, and the poem "Others."

If the only achievement of Brother Gilbert had been his timely friendship to Babe Ruth, it would have been noteworthy. But it was through Brother's assistance to countless other young men through the medium of Catholic education, his loyalty to his Congregation and his persevering service of his God that Gilbert accomplished much more.

The End of a Baseball Era

"The summer of 1946 drifted by, and, as I said, in the fall of that year my friends began to notice what had long been noticeable to me — my failing physical condition." So said the Babe in his 1948 autobiography, written with Bob Considine. Although the word "cancer" was carefully avoided by the Babe, the cause of the excruciatingly painful headaches was a malignant undiagnosed tumor in the left side of his throat and neck. Tests conducted in November of that year confirmed that deadly diagnosis; nonetheless, Babe continued to blame the hoarseness of his voice on the ill-advised treatment with silver nitrate which the Red Sox trainer had applied to his throat so many years before. Notwithstanding Brother Gilbert's observation in Chapter Nine that the Babe did not indulge in cigarette smoking, the slugger enjoyed nicotine-bearing products in all forms, especially cigars, so potent in inducing mouth and throat tumors.

In spite of the extraction of three bothersome teeth and continuing doses of penicillin and aspirin, his condition worsened to the point that his physicians advised surgery. In January 1947, Babe underwent a major surgical procedure that proved to the doctors the cause of his pain. Radiation therapy ensued; his weight fell from 278 pounds to 150 pounds in a matter of weeks. His physical appearance became ghostly.

Ruth did rally and was released home in February. He gained weight and his spirits were buoyed from the tens of thousands of get-well cards he received. He was delighted at the card he received "from Brother Gilbert, who had helped me get my first break in baseball. Brother Gilbert, who was to die so soon after that, led his class of boys in prayer for my recovery." Flying to Florida, he attempted golfing and deep-sea fishing, both of which left him exhausted. Dying of throat cancer, Babe was still photographed with his ever-present lighted cigar as late as April 28, 1948.

In March, Baseball Commissioner A.B. "Happy" Chandler, a former governor and United States senator from Kentucky, released the news that a national "Babe Ruth Day" would be held in all ball parks in organized baseball on Sunday, April 27. The ceremonies would be broadcast nationwide through a special system. Dorothy Ruth Pirone later recollected that "At a time when most of baseball had forgotten about my father, Happy Chandler reunited him with the game."

Babe was not a pretty sight on the day he was feted. Gaunt and skeleton-like in his camel-hair coat, he doffed his cap and addressed the nation (including the boys of St. Mary's, who were attending the Orioles' game in Baltimore) with the words:

> Thank you very much, ladies and gentlemen. You know how bad my voice sounds. Well, it feels just as bad. You know, this baseball game of ours comes up from the youth. That means the boys. And after you're a boy, and grow up and know how to play ball, then you come to the boys you see representing themselves today in your national pastime.
>
> The only real game, I think, in the world is baseball. As a rule, some people think if you give them a football or baseball, or something like that, naturally they're athletes right away. But you can't do that in baseball. You've gotta start from way down the bottom, when you're six or seven years of age. You can't wait until you're fifteen or sixteen. You've gotta let it grow up with you, and if you're successful and you try hard enough, you're bound to come out on top, just like these boys have come to the top now. There's been so many lovely things said about me, I'm glad I had the opportunity to thank everybody. Thank you.

However unfocused, rambling and inarticulate, Babe's sentiments were straight from the heart, and they touched many people.

The pain returned to him in June, and he began to receive an experimental folic acid treatment. Despite its good intentions, it had no effect in arresting the cancer which had spread through his body.

One of Ruth's last thoughts in his 1948 autobiography was recorded in these words: "The important thing in my life at this point is to shake off the pain around my head and fully regain my health. I honestly don't know anybody who wants to live more than I do. It is a driving wish that is always with me these days, a wish that only a person who has been close to death can know and understand."

On June 13, 1948, to celebrate the 25th anniversary of Yankee Stadium, the Babe was persuaded to make an appearance at an old-timers' game in his famous uniform, Number 3, which would be retired. Borrowing Cleveland player Bob Feller's bat on which to lean, Babe spoke to his adoring crowds for the last time, saying, "I just want to say one thing. I am proud I hit the first home run here in 1923. It was marvelous to see thirteen or fourteen players who were my teammates going back twenty-five years. I'm telling you it makes me proud and happy to be here. Thank you."

Despite occasional rallies, the Babe's overall physical condition continued to decline. He made an ill-advised trip to see *The Babe Ruth Story* on July 26, 1948, and he and Claire walked out halfway through the movie. (Earlier in July, he flew to Baltimore and talked with his sister Mamie and a number of Xaverian Brothers. His Fayetteville roommate from 1914, Rodger Pippen the sportswriter and editor, also met with him to recall old times.) Returning to Memorial Hospital Center for Cancer and Allied Diseases in New York City, Ruth went into his final decline. His spiritual efforts in the hospital were aided by Father Thomas Hilary Kaufman, a Dominican priest who once had been a student at St. Mary's.

On August 16, 1948, at 8:01 P.M., 53 year-old George Herman "Babe" Ruth died in his sleep. Daughter Dorothy later said, "I took the loss of my father very hard, as did the entire nation. My grief was shared by the American people, because in many ways Babe belonged to the public. Many people did not want to believe he had actually died; it was as if they had lost someone in their own family."

In Waite Hoyt's remembrance of his former teammate entitled : *Babe Ruth as I Knew Him*, Hoyt recalls hearing the news of Babe's passing: "It was as if someone had chipped part of my life away. The lives of baseball players are so interwoven; the successes of some are vital to the successes of others."

The extent of the nation's outpouring of grief for the Babe's passing proved that he touched lives from the largest city to the smallest hamlet.

Brother Hilarion *(foreground)* joins the boys of St. Mary's in prayer for the Babe after Ruth's initial surgery on his throat and neck. The Brothers never forgot the Babe, nor did they permit the newest wards of that residence to forget their most successful alumnus (courtesy of Xaverian Brothers Heritage Collection).

His body was taken to Yankee Stadium for viewing by the public. For the next two days, mourners lined up for many blocks to pass by his coffin, situated near the main entrance. The numbers have been estimated at from 75 to 200,000 people, many with their young children. Ruth biographer Tom Meany concluded his 1947 story of the Babe with the insightful words, "After all, this bond between Ruth and the kids is not so terribly strange that it passeth all understanding. For the big fellow, you see, was never anything but a kid himself."

On August 19, 1948, the funeral mass was held at St. Patrick's Cathedral. Once again, hundreds of thousands of New Yorkers lined the rainy streets to pay their final respects to the Babe as his hearse passed in the funeral procession to the Cathedral and then to the Gate of Heaven Cemetery in Hawthorne, New York, 25 miles away. When the funeral cortege reached St. Patrick's, a crowd of approximately 75,000 people awaited, only 6,000 of whom were allowed to enter for the mass, conducted by Francis Cardinal Spellman. Babe's daughter Dorothy recalled that day in her book *My Dad the Babe*: "A tremendous crowd stood silently in the rain ... You could hear a pin drop in Manhattan. I'll never forget looking out the window of the car and seeing a blind man with his dog. When the hearse went by, the dog went down on his front feet, crouching down with his head bowed between his front legs, as if he somehow knew."

At St. Mary's, the Brothers gathered the boys in the chapel to say their prayers for the repose of Babe's soul in the same manner in which they had prayed for him during his final days of life on earth. In her remembrance, Dorothy Ruth Pirone quoted Brother Albert, who began his teaching career at St. Mary's in 1910. Brother remembered what the Babe said when he last visited that school: "We're all in life to do good, and I hope that when I die I will have lived so I can help the boys of America lead cleaner and straighter lives."

Thus was Babe laid to rest, with the prayers of a mournful nation accompanying him.

The marble monument that stands over the Babe's final resting place was inscribed with these words spoken by Francis Cardinal Spellman: "May the Divine Spirit which animated Babe Ruth to win the crucial game of Life inspire the youth of America."

Death Takes Other Xaverians Influential to the Babe

"Big Matt," the Xaverian prefect of discipline at St. Mary's for 38 years, passed away suddenly in Peabody, Massachusetts, at St. Joseph's Juniorate on October 16, 1944. He was found dead in his room by the Superior, Brother Godfrey, after Matthias' absence from his customary place in the chapel had been noted. Brother Matthias had been in poor health for some years. He outlived his sibling, Brother Amandus, by six years. Matthias was buried in the Brother's Cemetery at St. John's Preparatory School, Danvers, Massachusetts. He had been stationed at that school from 1932 to 1942, prior to his last assignment at the Juniorate.

Some months before his death, Matthias had celebrated his Golden Jubilee as a Brother. A Xaverian reporter noted that there were 51 Xaverians present at the grand jubilee dinner — "one for each year and one for good measure, for Brother Matthias is a man of generous measure, as well as heart, himself."

After his death, Matthias' role in the development of the Babe came before the public eye with the release of the motion picture *The Babe Ruth Story*, starring William Bendix and Claire Trevor. Although this 1948 film has generally been panned over the years by movie critics and baseball fans alike, it did place considerable emphasis on the part played in the great slugger's life by Brother Matthias. Undoubtedly it was the first time that the movie industry took cognizance of the work of the Xaverian Brothers.

Played by Charles Bickford on the screen, Brother Matthias' contribution to the molding of young Babe Ruth's character was dramatized for worldwide attention. It was very fitting that "Big Matt" in the story became symbolic of the Babe's early training. After viewing the movie, one Xaverian commented, "Though many ... failed to benefit from the care of the Brothers at St. Mary's, a countless number have gone forth to live better Catholic lives. None made such a spectacular showing before the public as Babe Ruth ... there has been only one Babe Ruth and one Brother Matthias; but the good work of a religious teacher emphasized in the story has been performed over and over again."

Claire Ruth, in *The Babe and I*, relates an interesting conversation the Babe had with a friend: "The friend said, 'Babe, you were what Brother Matthias had been looking for all his life. He was a frustrated ball player and saw in you everything he wanted to be.'

"The Babe was outraged. He roared, 'The hell he was frustrated. He was doing what he wanted to do. And Brother Matthias liked me before he ever saw me hit or throw a baseball."

The 1954 juvenile book *Babe Ruth — Baseball Boy*, by Guernsey Van Riper, Jr., was unique in that it was dedicated to "the Brothers of the Xaverian order," and the author acknowledged a special indebtedness to Brother Herman, among others, for his many courtesies in providing background information. Four Brothers were mentioned by name in this story: Dominic, Paul, Matthias and Herman. The latter two are by far the most directly connected with the narrative.

Of those four, only Brother Herman was still alive at the time of the book's publication. At age 75, he was retired at Mount St. Joseph's College in Baltimore after working for years at both St. Mary's and St. James Home in addition to his positions in Massachusetts, Michigan, Virginia and West Virginia. Badly handicapped by arthritis, he still maintained a friendly smile and a lively twinkle in his eye. Brother Herman always freely gave Brother Matthias the credit for developing Ruth's skills, although Herman's contemporaries unanimously testified that he was an outstanding ball player and mentor in his own right.

Brother Herman died in Baltimore on Christmas Eve, 1956, a few weeks after he celebrated his Diamond Jubilee as a Xaverian.

Another mentor close to Ruth was Brother Alban, stationed at St. Mary's from 1911 to 1938. This former star player devoted himself to the cause of the orphaned and unfortunate boy. He was long remembered for his work with the Babe. His transfer from St. Mary's occurred about the same time as the combination of diabetes and gangrene which struck him necessitated the amputation of both legs. However, he continued to work, helping to teach and train young Brothers of the Order.

Alban never lost his spirit and remained to the end deeply committed to the work of the Xaverian Brothers, with whom he spent 51 years in the service of God. Brother Alban died in Peabody, Massachusetts, on September 18, 1954, at the age of 68, ending his years of patient cross bearing. He was buried in the Brothers' cemetery at St. John's Prep in Danvers, Massachusetts, as was Brother Gilbert earlier.

When Brother Paul Scanlon died at Old Point Comfort, Virginia, at age 86 on June 18, 1950, he was within three weeks of having completed 65 years in the Congregation. The Baltimore *Evening Sun* eulogized him:

> A long life of such great usefulness as that of Brother Paul, of the Xaverian Brothers, is granted to only a few men. For even fewer is that great usefulness dramatized for all to understand as was Brother Paul's.
>
> George Herman Ruth ... was only one of the many, many boys who had, and have, so many profound reasons for being grateful that there was a Brother Paul and others like him. His would indeed have been a splendid memorable work even if there had never been a Babe Ruth. But as it happened, the career of Babe Ruth, which cannot now be imagined without the early, patient and admirable influence of Brother Paul, not only gave America a sports hero of huge stature; it also served to demonstrate in a manner which none can fail to see the importance of the Brother Pauls of the world...
>
> Babe Ruth was the example almost without peer. Had there been no Brother Paul at St. Mary's Industrial School in the years that the young George Herman was there, a man who re-inspired the whole national game at a time it was at a low ebb might have become just another wayward tough boy.

Brother Paul spent most of his Xaverian years serving in positions of authority and supervision, including the 18 years he spent as superintendent of St. Mary's. In 1925, he was elected provincial (chief) of the American Province of Xaverian Brothers, and three years later in Belgium he was chosen superior general of the entire order, the first American to hold that position. He served in that capacity for nine years and established the

Brother Herman had aged quite a bit in this photo, taken at St. Joseph's Home in Detroit, but he could still wield a mean bat! Brother Quentin umpires. In 1920, the Babe Ruth Boys Band stayed at this Xaverian home when they traveled with the Yankees. While in Cleveland, they quartered at the Euclid Hotel, and they lodged at the Christian Brothers' Protective when in New York City (courtesy of Xaverian Brothers Heritage Collection).

first Xaverian mission schools in Africa. He was a member of the order's General Council after that until his health failed.

After his death, Brother Paul's body was taken to Baltimore for burial from the chapel at St. Mary's, where he had served so many years. The fact that over a hundred Brothers, many former students, and the boys of St. Mary's attended the funeral gave testament to his character.

Another key figure from St. Mary's, Brother Simon, the natural musician and "maestro" of the famous Babe Ruth Boys Band, remained active with the band boys at Mount St. Joseph's High School until shortly before his death in St. Agnes Hospital in 1960 at the age of 76. He had spent 56 years in the Congregation and served at St. Mary's Industrial School from 1919 to 1935 and 1941 to 1950. From the ranks of his students came many famous musicians of their times, as well as professional men, priests and Brothers.

The Last Years of St. Mary's

At St. Mary's, young Babe was provided with a program which tried to create a degree of religious faith, discipline, sense of security, growth opportunity and integration into the adult world which his birth family could not furnish for him.

In the years after the fire, St. Mary's Industrial School continued to prosper and succeed in its guidance of troubled boys . Brother Paul Scanlon was succeeded in 1925 by another capable organizer, Brother Benjamin. This Xaverian administrator, along with his staff of 30 Brothers, effectively directed the activities of St. Mary's in spite of the hand-to-mouth financial existence it led, having no endowment and depending upon some governmental aid and "charity."

One of Babe's brief placements, St. James Home, long associated with St. Mary's, continued to operate as a boarding home for boys for many years. Founded in 1878 and operated under the same management as St. Mary's, St. James Home began accepting fewer St. Mary's boys in the 1920s. No city or state aid was received because no government wards were accepted. The main income came from the working boys who boarded there and from collections from charitable organizations. Brother Gaudentius took the leadership of this home in 1925.

As America settled into the depression and the 1930s, the nature of the resident population at St. Mary's slowly changed. More delinquent boys were accepted than ever before from juvenile courts in Baltimore and throughout Maryland. By 1937, boys of "sub-normal mentality" were not accepted, nor were boys under 10 years old. The admission of orphans was discouraged unless there was absolutely no other placement available. Delinquent boys usually stayed for two or three years before returning home; the few orphans stayed until age 18. The Brothers emphasized their work with children who were wayward or incorrigible at home.

(In an amusing side trip, Dizzy Dean once visited St. Mary's during Ruth's waning playing years and told the assembled boys that he, not Babe, was the best baseball player alive!)

The trade school aspect of St. Mary's flourished and led to many boys achieving a high level of success, in spite of the fact that they were labeled "slow" mentally. Classes in printing, tailoring, mechanics, shoe repair, chauffeuring, maintenance, electrical engineering, small motor repair, plumbing, carpentry, band and barbering were offered by 1938.

Loving and loyal alumni remained connected in spirit to St. Mary's, as did the Babe. School officials said he once turned down twenty-five invitations so he could attend a simple alumni banquet at the school.

By 1940, St. Mary's admission requirements directed the acceptance of delinquent boys, 10 years of age and older, committed by the courts of Maryland. Delinquents from other states were accepted if that jurisdiction's social service agency agreed to pay $30 a month in advance. Medical care was included; clothing was extra. No private placements, such as the Babe had been, were accepted. The superintendent, Brother Liguori, insisted upon the receipt of numerous reports upon admission, including: family and case history, psychiatric evaluation (showing I.Q.), school or work report, report of current behavior and a medical report. Such detail was quite a change from Ruth's day.

The school was governed by a Board of Trustees which had numerous lay persons, in addition to Brothers and priests. Trustees representing state and city government were also appointed. The facility was still operated under the Brothers' tight discipline and structure. Boys had to request parole from Brother Liguori, and the Parole Board was required to approve any release.

By the early 1940s, the Board of State Aid and Charities recommended renovations to improve the living quarters and indoor recreation space. Although these two suggestions were deemed to be beyond the school's financial means, a new library with 12,000 volumes was installed. St. Mary's continued to take pride in the progress of its trade shops, and the Brothers closely cooperated with social services personnel for the betterment of the residents.

The average daily population in 1940 was 331, down 66 from the year before. This gradual decrease was following a trend which the Brothers had predicted due to "the progress of case work service in all child-caring agencies." However, the Xaverians remained strongly committed to the concept of St. Mary's as a training school, rather than a penal institution or a facility giving only shelter care. They did not desire to accept boys exhibiting the most serious delinquent behavior. Brother Liguori emphasized, "It should be our earnest endeavor to be completely dissociated in the public mind from penal and punishment ... the atmosphere of St. Mary's is one of easy and friendly comradeship. There is order and discipline but a freedom from petty restrictions and repression which is delightful. No averted eyes or furtive expressions are evident. There is a warmth of human response to the children by the adults and demonstration of it. This undoubtedly fills a need in the emotionally-starved lives of many of these boys."

By this time, the athletic program, still vital to the daily life of this boy-centered school, featured five large athletic fields, two gymnasia and one swimming pool.

Regarding religious instruction, Brother Liguori stated, "Briefly, religion is the foundation of our moral educational program. There is no boy at St. Mary's who isn't made aware of the fact that religion is a matter between the individual and God. No outside pressure nor undue persuasion would be tolerated. Formal religious worship at the school is limited to approximately one-half hour in chapel each morning, and formal religious instruction to one-half hour in school. For the other twenty-three hours, however, religion is a vital thing with the Brothers. In short, we make every effort ... to teach by example."

On the subject of the relationship with women by the residents, Brother set forth, "It is accepted as psychologically necessary to normal development that both boys and girls have contact with men and women ... it seems that this need for contact with women as mother persons can best be had through capitalizing visiting possibilities."

St. James Home remained a placement option for boys who were ready to be released, but where insufficient conditions did not allow them to return home.

In 1940, spurred on by the war in Europe, the school even began an armament program in order to serve the country patriotically by training young men to work in war trades in case of the outbreak of such a conflict involving the United States.

Brother Clarence, the school psychologist, reported that 300 Catholic boys were tested at random during the year and that the median I.Q. was 84.6. (Six had I.Q.s less than 60, and 12 had I.Q.s over 110.) The average court contact per boy was 2.49, and 44.3 percent were from "broken homes."

However, not even the most glowing reports by all who visited St. Mary's could reverse the emerging trend regarding facilities of its type. Student population continued to decline. The Xaverian Brothers eventually closed St. Mary's in June 1950, stating that "Due to the gradual failure of state appropriations necessary to help maintain the institution, the Board of Trustees had at last come to the decision that closing its doors was inevitable." It was observed that in the late 1940s, when all orphans were withdrawn and only committed cases were placed at St. Mary's, its numbers declined sharply, and "opportunities for good were necessarily restricted."

Nevertheless, the Xaverian Brothers under Brother Charles who were assigned to the school in its final days made the best of existing conditions and continued to work faithfully. Although it was never the property of the Brothers who managed it, but rather of the Archdiocese of Baltimore, St. Mary's Industrial School had its roots deep in the history of the Xaverians in America. One Xaverian observed, "The passing of St. Mary's has left a gap — at least so it seems to our human prudence; perhaps God will see fit to give us another St. Mary's to fill that vacancy."

Brother Charles, the school's final superintendent, was transferred to Kentucky and became headmaster at St. Joseph's Prep School in Bardstown. Cardinal Gibbons High School now occupies the remaining St. Mary's buildings and surrounding property.

The Xaverian and Ruthian Legacies

The legend of the Babe is very much alive today. The person who was the Bambino engendered more books, articles, stories, monuments, memorabilia and collectibles than any other baseballer who ever lived. His story is retold, sooner or later, to new generations by such men as *Washington Post* columnist Shirley Povich. Prior to his death in 1998, the 92-year-old Povich's final column included an argumentative comparison of Ruth with the modern longballer Mark McGwire in the latter's chase for the single-season homer record.

Indeed, every appearance of a new long-ball hitter evokes memories of Ruth from sportswriters who weren't born till long after his death. Each pursuit of Ruth's season home record stirs frenzied excitement in the hearts and minds of fans. Thirteen years after the Babe died, Roger Maris chased not only his sixty-first homer, but the ghost of Ruth. Maris repeatedly said, "There's only one Babe Ruth, and there's only one Mickey Mantle. I'm really not trying to be either one of them. All I want to be is Roger Maris. I'm not trying to break [Ruth's] record. I'm not trying to run him down or take his place." But the American public would not believe or accept this statement, and they never forgave Maris for intruding on the Babe's immortality. In similar fashion, Hank Aaron, a magnificent representative for baseball, was constantly vexed by the specter of Ruth during Hammerin' Hank's quest for homer number 715 in 1973–74.

In spite of his legendary slugging prowess, Babe Ruth, the prototype baseball superstar, may well have never succeeded in this modern era. The media would have simultaneous adored and scolded him for his outrageousness. His loutish side may have been emphasized to a baseball public which loves to hate an Albert Belle chasing Halloween revelers in his truck and a Roberto Alomar spitting in an umpire's face. Few media moguls would have seen newspaper sales-potential in playing up the side of Ruth which is more like a Cal Ripken in his knowledge and love of the *game* of baseball. In today's talk-show era, the Babe may have become media-molded, brash and hateful. Can you imagine modern newshounds trailing a man who was described by baseball writer Robert Smith as follows: "Babe, in a public place, had learned to feel as much at home as if he were in the back room of his own apartment. He asked for what he wanted in an unmodulated tone, told his stories without regard for their color, and took hold of whatever interested him — be it drink, a doughnut, or a passing waitress — with the uninhibited egoism of a man whose heart was pure."

The Babe's gross excesses and oftentimes inexcusable conduct can better be placed into context if the following unassailable psychological fact is kept foremost in mind: His behavior was that of a boy who never grew out of his adolescence emotionally. His words and deeds were sincere and from the heart. There was no pretense about him. If he didn't like you, you knew it, and it didn't really matter because in an hour he forgot his beef with you and he became your pal. If he liked you, well, it didn't make any difference because he couldn't remember your name anyhow.

In his excellent memoir, *Baseball as I Have Known It*, sportswriter Fred Lieb observed, "Ruth loved young boys, especially those who reminded him of himself at St. Mary's." It is generally acknowledged that Babe spent an inordinate amount of time with less fortunate children — those sick, hospitalized, orphaned and "at-risk." His lifelong debt to the Brothers was repaid by these visits and by the myriad of child-serving missions he accomplished.

Ruth knew how to be a hero who cared about more than himself; he became larger than life, and grew to be worshipped by baseball fans, kids and common folk all over the globe. In spite of the low points in his life — his relationship with Helen, his early umpire-baiting, his drunken, gluttonous and boorish behavior, among other things — he was genuine, and "average" people sensed that. He was never a phony whose reactions were based on the electronic and print media; indeed, modern baseball professionals could learn much from that side of the Babe. The real Ruth was revealed in his role of charity similar to the precept passed on by Jesus Christ to His followers: "As long as you did it to one of these, My least brethren, you did it to me."

In Christy Walsh's book *Baseball's Greatest Lineup*, sportswriter Joe

Williams states, "I never knew a great man — and Ruth was truly great — who was more completely himself every minute he lived." The Babe celebrated life each and every minute he lived, from chucking apples at Baltimore teamsters who drove their horses through the waterfront, to thumping out homers by the dozens, to quaffing brews by the score. His boundless energy was harnessed and channeled into baseball activity by the clear and compelling charisma of the Xaverian Brothers.

In writing the historical commentary to Brother Gilbert's memoirs, the author was reminded of a warning from the late English author and poet G.K. Chesterton, who observed, "It is quite easy to see why a legend is treated, and ought to be treated, more respectfully than a book of history. The legend is generally made by the majority of the people in the village, who are sane. The book is generally written by the one man in the village who is mad."

Fortunately, the Xaverian Brothers got their chance with Ruth in 1902 and, through discipline, understanding and love, facilitated the development of his baseball talents and, more importantly, his big, kind, charitable heart.

Founded in 1839 by Theodore James Ryken, the Dutch shoemaker, the Xaverian Brothers became a missionary Congregation which has traditionally ministered in the area of education. The Xaverian Brothers presently minister in the United States, Belgium, England, Bolivia, Haiti, Kenya, the Congo and Lithuania. The Congregation sponsors educational institutions in the United States, Belgium, England, Bolivia, and the Congo. While many Brothers are still involved in the Congregation's sponsored institutions, Brothers also work in other areas of education and in health care, prison ministry and aid to immigrants. Their worldwide headquarters is currently located on Frederick Avenue in Baltimore.

When the Xaverian Brothers first came to the United States in 1854, this country was still considered mission territory. From that uncertain foundation, the American Xaverians presently sponsor 12 secondary schools and one junior high school. Over 10,000 young men and women are enrolled in Xaverian-sponsored schools in the United States. Over 2,000 are enrolled in Xaverian schools in other countries. In keeping with the missionary character of the Congregation, the Brothers established missions in the Belgian Congo in 1931, and it is presently the Congolese branch of the Congregation that is growing in numbers. In the last 20 years many African young men have entered the Congregation, and the Congolese Brothers presently sponsor five schools (a high school and four elementary schools) for the very poor in the Congo.

In 1961 the Brothers from the United States went to Bolivia and established a mission, and there are presently American Xaverians working in various ministries in that country. In 1989 American Xaverians went to Haiti, in 1997 American Brothers also went to Lithuania — in both instances to work in the field of education.

Wherever they find themselves in ministry, Xaverian Brothers, true to their founder's charge, are men who have "fallen in love with the service of God" and who "participate in the Church's mission of evangelization through a life of Gospel service, living in solidarity and availability among the people."

From the days of their beloved ward Babe Ruth, the Brothers increased their rolls until a zenith was reached in the mid–1960s. By that time, the Congregation — 800 strong — fully staffed dozens of schools, primarily in the United States and England. A firm outpost had been established in the Congo and a foothold in Bolivia had been made.

Then, adversity struck in the form of the countercultural revolution of the late 1960s and early 1970s in America. The number of religious vocations to Catholic religious orders such as the Brothers drastically diminished, and many persons already enrolled in religious orders chose to "drop out." Although the Xaverians' numbers have stabilized since those dark days, age and declining vocations are taking their toll on the American Province. Worldwide, approximately 50 Xaverian communities, composed of less than 300 Brothers, are maintained in eight countries and twelve states.

Since Ryken brought his first small band of religious men to the shores of America, the children of this country have been well-served by the Xaverian Brothers. "In the final analysis, it is the spirit of the personnel which gives the institution a 'soul'," according to the Child Welfare League in 1937, commenting on the operation of St. Mary's. But the League's words could be applicable to any child-serving institution staffed or operated by the Xaverians. These religious men dedicate themselves to a life of service to others, and they bring to their charges a loyalty and devotion difficult to find among adults today. Their lives, consecrated to obedience and service, serve as models for children who need such beacons during difficult adolescent years. On many occasions, the young men who are most affected by the guidance and direction of the Brothers are those who are economically poor or academically troubled. The moral influence of the Brothers on their wards is unmeasurable. Their consistent goal over the years has been to mold the character of the boys in their charge so that they will prove to be an honor and credit to their school, their church, their communities and themselves. To say that the Brothers' discipline "never took" with Babe is not accurate. Babe's life was far too complex for such a simple summation, and to set forth such an opinion trivializes the efforts of Babe and the men who raised him. What they did for him, the Brothers did for a million other young souls. And in repaying them, the generous, affectionate and selfless Babe uplifted the spirits of children throughout America, young people who yearned to model his upward struggle against an impoverished background. Babe and the Brothers were American originals then, and now. Their names, each and every one, deserve to be written in the Book of Legends.

Sources Consulted

Aldridge, Gwen, and Bret Wills. *Baseball Archaeology*. San Francisco: Chronicle Books, 1993.

Alexander, Charles C. *Our Game: An American Baseball History*. New York: Henry Holt 1991.

Allen, Lee. *Cooperstown Corner: Columns from The Sporting News*. Cleveland: SABR, 1989.

Alvarez, Mark. "Ruth's First Rival." *The Ol' Ball Game*. New York: Barnes and Noble, 1990.

_____, Mark Rucker and Tom Shieber. *Baseball for the Fun of It*. Birmingham, AL: SABR, 1997.

Anderson, Dave, Murray Chass, Robert Creamer and Harold Rosenthal. *The Yankees*. New York: Random House, 1979.

Ardolino, Frank. "Babe's Banyan Tree Grows in Hawaii." *The National Pastime*. Cleveland: SABR, 1998.

Babe Ruth — The Home Run. New York: Sportscope Company of America, 1931.

Barber, Red. *1947 — When All Hell Broke Loose in Baseball*. Garden City, NY: Doubleday, 1982.

Barrow, Edward Grant, with James M. Kahn. *My Fifty Years in Baseball*. New York: Coward — McCann, 1951.

Beim, George, with Julia Ruth Stevens. *Babe Ruth — A Daughter's Portrait*. Dallas: Taylor, 1998.

Blenko, Jim. "Nick Altrock." *The National Pastime*. Cleveland: SABR, 1998.

Bucek, Jeanine, ed. dir. *The Baseball Encyclopedia*. 10th edition. New York: Macmillan, 1996.

Carmichael, John P., ed. *My Greatest Day in Baseball*. New York: Grosset and Dunlap, 1945; Tempo Books Edition, 1968.

Carroll, Bob. *Baseball Between the Lines*. New York: Perigee Books, 1993.

Cohen, Richard M., David S. Neft and Jordan A. Deutsch. *The World Series*. New York: The Dial Press, 1979.

Connor, Anthony J. *Voices from Cooperstown*. New York: Macmillan, 1982.

Creamer, Robert W. *Babe: The Legend Comes to Life*. New York: Simon and Schuster, 1974.

Daniel, Dan, with H.G. Salsinger. *The Real Babe Ruth*. New York: C.C. Spink and Son, 1948.

Daniel, Daniel M. "Babe Ruth: Greatest Player, Golden Figure in Golden Era." *Baseball Magazine*, October 1948.

_____. *Babe Ruth — The Idol of the American Boy*. Racine, WI: Whitman Publishing Company, 1930.

Devadder, Brother Jan, C.F.X. *Rooted in History — The Life and Times of T.J. Ryken, Founder of the Xaverian Brothers.* Bruges, Belgium: self-published, 1986.

Dewey, Donald, and Nicholas Acocella. *The Ball Clubs.* New York: HarperCollins, 1996.

Doyle, Edward "Dutch." "Sandlot Babe." *The Ol' Ball Game.* New York: Barnes and Noble, 1990.

Edelman, Rob. *Great Baseball Films.* New York: Citadel Press, 1994.

Einstein, Charles, ed. *The Baseball Reader.* New York: McGraw-Hill paperback edition, 1983.

Gallico, Paul. *The Golden People.* New York: Doubleday, 1965.

"George Herman 'Babe' Ruth and His Providence Connection." *SABR 14th Annual Convention Booklet* Cooperstown, NY: SABR; 1984.

Brother Gerald Edward, C.F.X. "My First Xaverian." *The Xaverian.* Silver Spring, MD: The Xaverian Brothers Auxiliary, June 1958.

Grimm, Charlie, with Ed Prell. *Jolly Cholly's Story.* Chicago: Henry Regnery Company, 1968.

Grossinger, Richard, and Kevin Kerrane, eds. *Into the Temple of Baseball.* Berkeley, CA: Celestial Arts, 1990.

Hadley, Lawrence, Elizabeth Gustafson and Mary Jo Thierry. "Who Would Be the Highest-Paid Baseball Player?" *Baseball Research Journal.* Cleveland: SABR, 1992.

Harris, Paul F. Sr. *Babe Ruth: The Dark Side.* Self published booklet, 1995.

Heath, Steven H. "Babe and Big Train." *Baseball Research Journal.* Kansas City: SABR, 1988.

Holland, Gerald. "The Babe Ruth Papers." *Sports Illustrated,* December 21, 1959.

Honig, Donald. *Baseball America.* New York: Galahad, 1985.

Hoyt, Waite. *Babe Ruth as I Knew Him.* New York: Dell, 1948.

Izenberg, Jerry. *The Rivals.* New York: Holt, Rinehart and Winston, 1968.

Jenkinson, Bill. "Somewhere the Babe Is Smiling." Program for The First Opening Day at Camden Yards. April 6, 1992.

Brother Jogues, C.F.X. "Who's Got 'Em All?" *The Xaverian.* Silver Spring, MD: The Xaverian Brother Auxiliary, March 1951.

Brother Julian, C.F.X. *Men and Deeds — The Xaverian Brothers in America.* New York: Macmillan, 1930.

Kandle, Kirk. "We Begot You, Babe." *Louisville Magazine,* April, 1995.

Keene, Kerry, Raymond Sinibaldi and David Hickey. *The Babe in Red Stockings.* Champaign, Illinois: Sagamore Publishing, 1997.

Kelley, Brent. *In The Shadow of the Babe.* Jefferson, NC: McFarland, 1995.

Kermisch, Al. "Eye Injury Handicapped Young Babe." *Baseball Research Journal.* SABR: Garrett Park, MD, 1989.

Kermisch, Al. "Forgotten Facts Fill Researcher's Notebook." *Baseball Research Journal.* Cooperstown, NY: SABR, 1985.

Koppett, Leonard. *The Man in the Dugout.* New York: Crown Publishers, 1993.

Lally, Brother Alexius Joseph C.F.X.. "Cyrenian No. 13, Brother Gilbert C.F.X." *Cyrenians.* Baltimore, MD: Xaverian Brothers, 1980.

Leisman, Lou. *I Was with Babe Ruth at St. Mary's.* Aberdeen, MD: self-published pamphlet, 1956.

Lieb, Fred. *Baseball as I Have Known It.* NY: Coward, McCann and Geohegan, 1977.

Macht, Norman L. *Babe Ruth.* New York: Chelsea, 1991.

_____. "Woody English Insists — The Babe Didn't Point!" *Baseball Research Journal.* Cleveland: SABR, 1991.

Meany, Tom. *Babe Ruth: The Big Moments of the Big Fellow.* New York: A.S. Barnes, 1947.

Neft, David S., and Richard M. Cohen. *The Sports Encyclopedia: Baseball.* 16th ed. New York: St. Martin's Griffin, 1996.

O'Dea, Marie. "They Reared Babe Ruth." *St. Anthony Messenger*, August 1938, and *Catholic Digest*, September 1938 (condensed).

Okkonen, Marc. *The Federal League of 1914-1915: Baseball's Third Major League.* Garrett Park, MD: SABR, 1989.

O'Neal, Bill. *The American Association: A Baseball History, 1902–1991.* Austin, TX: Eakin Press, 1991.

_____. *The International League: A Baseball History, 1884–1991.* Austin, TX: Eakin Press, 1992.

Page, Brother Thomas More C.F.X.. "Brother Matthias Boutelier: The Most Influential Brother in Babe Ruth Life and Career." *Concordia*, November 1995.

_____. "Remembering St. Mary's." *Concordia*, November 1995.

Pirone, Dorothy Ruth, and Chris Martens. *My Dad, The Babe.* Boston: Quinlan Press, 1988.

Ritter, Lawrence S. *The Glory of Their Times.* New York: Macmillan, 1966.

_____, and Mark Rucker. *The Babe: A Life in Pictures.* New York: Ticknor and Fields, 1988.

_____, and Mark Rucker. *The Babe: The Game That Ruth Built.* New York: Total Sports, 1997.

Rogers, Nolan H. "From B & O Railroad to Ballpark." Article, circa 1992.

Rothwell, C. Brooke. "The Never-Before-Collected Works of Babe Ruth." *The Best of Spitball (Magazine).* New York: Pocket Books, 1988.

Ruiz, Yuyo. *The Bambino Visits Cuba, 1920.* Unedited Notes. Puerto Rico: Self-published, 1996.

Ruth, Babe. *Babe Ruth's Own Book of Baseball.* New York: G.P. Putnam's Sons, 1928.

_____. "Why A Pitcher Should Hit." World's Series Program, 1916.

_____, and Bob Consodine. *The Babe Ruth Story.* New York: Dutton, 1948.

Ruth, Mrs. Babe, and Bill Slocum. *The Babe and I.* New York: Avon Books, 1959.

St. Mary's Industrial School for Boys. *Fiftieth Annual Report.* Baltimore: Xaverian Brothers, 1918.

_____. *Seventy-Second Annual Report.* Baltimore: St. Mary's Industrial School Press, 1940.

Shaughnessey, Dan. *The Curse of The Bambino.* St. Paul, MN: Penguin, 1991.

Shehan, Tom Jr. "Xaverian Brothers Influenced Babe Ruth's Early Life." *The Church World.* April 4, 1996.

Skipper, James K. Jr. "Baseball's 'Babes'— Ruth and Others." *Baseball Research Journal.* Cooperstown, NY: SABR, 1984.

Smelser, Marshall. *The Life That Ruth Built.* Lincoln: University of Nebraska Press, 1975.

Smith, Robert. *Babe Ruth's America.* New York: Thomas Y. Crowell Co., 1974.

_____. *Baseball.* New York: Simon & Schuster, 1947.

Sobol, Ken. *Babe Ruth and the American Dream.* New York: Random House, 1974.

Spitball-The Literary Baseball Magazine. No. 50, 1996.

Sterne, Brother John Joseph C.F.X. *Child of Two Worlds.* Self-published book, 1992.

Sullivan, Neil J. *The Minors.* New York: St. Martin's Press, 1990.

Thorn, John and Pete Palmer. *The Hidden Game of Baseball.* New York: Doubleday and Co., 1984.

_____, Michael Gershman and David Pietrusza. *Total Baseball,* 5th ed. New York: Viking Penguin, 1997

Tourangeau, Richard. "The Babe Saves Boston's Season." *The National Pastime.* Cleveland: SABR, 1992.

Van Riper, Guernsey Jr. *Babe Ruth: Baseball Boy*. New York: Bobbs-Merrill, 1954.

Vass, George. "Pre-Season Mishaps Often Dash Team's Pennant Hopes." *Baseball Digest*, July 1997.

Wagenheim, Kal. *Babe Ruth: His Legend and His Life*. New York: Praeger, 1974.

Walsh, Christy. *Baseball's Greatest Lineup*. New York: A.S. Barnes, 1952.

Williams, Pete. "Did the Babe Call His Shot? Sportswriters and the Creation of Myth." *Baseball Research Journal*. Kansas City: SABR, 1987.

Xaverian Brothers. *The Xaverian Menology*.

"Xaverian Brothers Celebrate George 'Babe' Ruth 1895–1995 Hundredth Birthday Anniversary." *Concordia*, November 1995.

Xaveriana. Pamphlet. Xaverian Brothers, 1997.

Index

Numbers in *italics* refer to photographs or illustrations.

DATE DUE
